MANAGEMENT POLICIES
FOR
COMMERCIAL BANKS

SECOND EDITION

MANAGEMENT POLICIES FOR COMMERCIAL BANKS

HOWARD D. CROSSE

Franklin National Bank

GEORGE H. HEMPEL

Washington University

PRENTICE-HALL, INC., ENGLEWOOD CLIFFS, N. J.

Library of Congress Cataloging in Publication Data

CROSSE, HOWARD D
  Management policies for commercial banks.

  Includes bibliographical references.
  1. Banks and banking.   2. Bank management.
I. Hempel, George H., joint author.   II. Title.
HG1601. C774 1973   658'.91'33212   72–8946
ISBN   0–13–549014–6

10   9   8   7   6   5   4   3   2

Printed in the United States of America

PRENTICE-HALL INTERNATIONAL, INC., *London*
PRENTICE-HALL OF AUSTRALIA, PTY. LTD., *Sydney*
PRENTICE-HALL OF CANADA, LTD., *Toronto*
PRENTICE-HALL OF INDIA PRIVATE LIMITED, *New Delhi*
PRENTICE-HALL OF JAPAN, INC., *Tokyo*

CONTENTS

PART II

BASIC CONSIDERATIONS IN BANKING

PART III

BALANCE SHEET MANAGEMENT

PART IV

OTHER BANK POLICY AREAS

PREFACE

This book is written for both bank practitioners and students of banking. It covers the policies made by the Boards of Directors and senior managements of commercial banks. Our prime objective is to assist the reader in understanding each of the major policy areas and the interrelationships between these policy areas in a commercial bank.

The field of banking has undergone many significant changes in recent years. Strong inflationary pressures pushed interest rates to unprecedented heights. The holding company has emerged as a very significant banking institution. Bank management, which used to assume that inflows of funds were given, now stress attracting funds as much as profitably using these funds. Many new forms of bank liabilities and capital are now viable management alternatives. Bankers can now meet at least part of their liquidity needs by liability management. These and similar changes have, to a large extent, dictated the revisions made in this second edition of *Management Policies for Commercial Banks*.

Some of the more significant alterations from the first edition are: material on the banking structure has been thoroughly updated; major experiences and policies with liability management as well as asset management are presented; the chapters on lending policies and practices have been substantially expanded; the material on commercial bank personnel and marketing policies has been substantially revised and updated;

and new chapters have been added on attracting deposits, portfolio management, and management of the bank's own capital structure.

Much of the specific content of the book is the distillation of Mr. Crosse's thirty years experience as a central banker and bank supervisor and seven years experience as a senior bank executive plus Dr. Hempel's experience as a bank director and consultant as well as a Professor of Finance at Washington University.

The book is organized into four major sections. The environment in which commercial banks must operate is described in the first section. The basic commercial banking functions, including earning an adequate return for owners, are reviewed in Chapter 1. The present banking structure, including recent material on branching and holding companies as well as the structure of supervision, are presented in Chapter 2. Chapter 3 introduces the reader to characteristics affecting the structure (for example, size, location, competition, organization) of a commercial bank.

The second section covers the basic ingredients affecting bank management's objective of maximizing earnings consistent with acceptable risk levels. The nature of the principal risks that bank managements typically face are analyzed in Chapter 4. Chapter 5 covers the functions of bank capital, the need for having adequate bank capital, and some of the various methods that have been used to attempt to measure bank capital adequacy. The trend and composition of bank revenues and expenses and approaches that bank management can use to achieve highest bank earnings consistent with risk and capital considerations are discussed in Chapter 6.

The acquisition and management of banking funds is the topic of the third section. Potential sources of bank deposits and possible methods of attracting such deposits are discussed in Chapter 7. Chapter 8 describes the basic instruments of liquidity that commercial banks can use and discusses the need to have sufficient funds on hand to meet the demands for money that may be made on bank management. The basic policies and procedures that bank managers can use to estimate and meet a commercial bank's liquidity needs are discussed in Chapter 9. The objectives of Chapter 10 are to examine the importance of lending to bank management's total objectives and to identify the different nature of the various types of bank loans. Policies and procedures relating to lending authority, credit review, collection policies, lending charges, compensating balances, and loan development are examined in Chapter 11. Chapter 12 covers the objectives of an investment portfolio, the types of instruments that may be used in attempting to achieve this objective, and the basic considerations affecting portfolio decisions. In Chapter 13, basic policies and procedures that the individual commercial bank may use in implementing the investment portfolio objectives are examined.

The fourth and final section includes several other bank management policy areas that seem worthy of additional attention. Chapter 14 provides some information on the need for achieving adequate bank control; Chapter 15 provides some information on the way banks can correctly use their most important resource, that is, the human resource. The importance of modern marketing policies and techniques is covered in Chapter 16. Finally, Chapter 17 discusses policies for the bank's own capital management, including ideas for evaluating the alternative methods of raising bank capital.

We are indebted to several bankers and professors—William Baughn of the University of Colorado and the Stonier Graduate School of Banking, William Chapman of the First National Bank in St. Louis, George Coleman of the American Bankers Association, and Richard Johnson of Southern Methodist University and the Southwestern School of Banking—for their suggestions for improving the preliminary manuscript. In addition, William Emory of Washington University and Tim Andre of Franklin National Bank offered helpful suggestions for the chapter on bank marketing, and Walter Klostermier of First National Bank offered useful suggestions for the chapter on bank personnel policies. Jane Warren and Patrice Sobin offered helpful editorial assistance. William Baughn then carefully reviewed the final manuscript. In spite of the help received, deficiencies undoubtedly remain. For these, we take full responsibility and urge readers to call them to our attention.

HOWARD D. CROSSE

Vice Chairman of the Board
Franklin National Bank

GEORGE H. HEMPEL

Professor of Finance
Washington University

PART I

THE
BANKING ENVIRONMENT

I

COMMERCIAL

BANKING FUNCTIONS

INTRODUCTION

A clear understanding of the role of commercial banks in the economy is obviously a prime prerequisite for the formulation of bank policy. Often the banker's concept of that role shapes the nature and character of his bank. The deposit-minded banker may stress conservatism and liquidity; the loan-minded banker may underemphasize safety. Their attitudes often reflect the nature of the locality in which their banks operate; conservatism is frequently the mark of the stable, long-settled community, and more aggressive banking is found where growth is rapid and the need for credit is greatest.

Actually, commercial banks perform a number of interrelated functions, many of which are necessary parts of our private, free-enterprise system. Commercial banks bring into being the most important ingredient of the money supply—demand deposits—through the creation of credit in the form of loans and investments. Banks are the custodians of the community's money as well as the suppliers of its liquidity. For those bank customers who seldom borrow, the depository function may be the most important. Commercial banks also provide flexibility and mobility to the money supply by maintaining the interchangeability of currency and bank deposits and by providing the mechanism through which money payments can be most speedily and efficiently made. Commercial banks participate with other institutions in the process of accumulating and investing savings and perform a number of other services.

CREDIT CREATION

It is the ability of the commercial banks to create money in the form of demand deposits by making loans and investments that distinguishes them from all other financial institutions. The banking system can build up deposits by increasing loans and investments so long as banks keep enough currency and reserves to meet the requirement imposed on them by regulation and to redeem whatever amounts the holders of deposits want to convert to currency. This is a unique attribute that is often difficult for the layman to understand and that occasionally even baffles bankers. As contrasted with the banking system as a whole, however, an individual bank cannot expect that the deposits it creates will remain with it. The money it can lend and invest, at any moment, is its excess of cash and bank balances over required reserves and minimum cash requirements. The individual bank must stand ready to pay out the deposits it creates when it makes new loans and to pay for the securities it buys upon delivery.[1]

In practice, out of the vast aggregate of financial transactions, the individual bank gains and loses funds in the course of each day's business. From its net gains the bank can increase its loans and investments. If the bank has net losses it must collect loans or sell investments. As one of the theoretical aggregate of all banks, it competes for its share of the deposits that the banking system as a whole may create when additional reserves are supplied by the Federal Reserve System.

A bank does not create credit in a vacuum; it creates credit in order to supply the funds that are needed by the community it serves and the nation of which it is a part. Bank loans and investments may finance production, distribution, investment, consumption, and the needs of government. Credit enables goods to move through the channels of trade, people to acquire homes, factories to be built, workers to buy automobiles, the nation to finance its defense, and many other useful or profitable purposes to be fulfilled. Without credit, business as we know it would be almost impossibly impeded, and our standard of living would never have been attained.

Bank credit supplies money where and when it is needed, and the

---

[1]For a complete explanation of deposit creation, see *The Federal System: Its Purposes and Functions,* Board of Governors of the Federal Reserve System (Washington, D. C., 1972), or *Modern Money Mechanics,* Research Department of the Federal Reserve Bank of Chicago (Chicago, 1971).

repayment of bank credit removes money from circulation when the specific need for it has passed. When the economist speaks of a "balanced" economy he envisions an overall balance between production and consumption. With respect to both the businessman and the individual, however, such a balance usually involves a time lag. The farmer invests seed, fertilizer, and six months' effort into a crop before he can harvest and sell it. The manufacturer must assemble, pay for, and put to use plant, materials, and labor before he can produce a salable product. The individual who wants to buy a car or must meet unexpected medical expenses may not have the money on hand but is able to make his purchase or pay his bills out of future income. In supplying credit to farmers, manufacturers, and individuals, the commercial bank bridges the time lag between production and consumption and thus helps to bring the financial affairs of the economy into balance.

This is another way of saying that commercial banks supply liquidity to the economy. Through their ability to lend and invest, they can provide money immediately in consideration of assets or efforts that have a future money value. Commercial banks use many different means and organizational forms to supply this liquidity. Seasonal self-liquidating business loans, consumer home-mortgage loans, tax anticipation notes, business term loans, bank credit cards, and many other forms are used. In larger banks, separate departments are generally established to specialize in certain forms of lending. The foreign departments of some large banks, for example, are almost separate institutions in themselves. In smaller banks, one or a small number of bank officers is generally responsible for bank loans and investments; however, farm lending or consumer credit is frequently departmentalized. The important aspect is not the particular means or organizational form but the bank's active effort to supply the funds that are needed in the community that it serves.

THE DEPOSITORY FUNCTION

It is easy to say, as the layman does, that a commercial bank "is a place to keep your money." So it is, but to put it thus is an oversimplification. Commercial banks hold different kinds of deposits and hold them in a variety of forms. There are also other places to keep your money, ranging from the cookie jar to a mutual investment fund.

The most useful way to examine the depository function of the commercial banking system is to look at the purposes for which money is deposited. Again the layman's concept is likely to be misleading—"For convenience," he says, "or for safety." These are partial truths that shed little light on the functional role of banks as depositories.

Demand deposits in commercial banks constitute the major portion of the money supply.[2] A primary function of money is its use as a means of payment. Consequently, one of the most important reasons for becoming a bank depositor is to use the payment facilities of the commercial banking system. Demand deposits also frequently consist of funds kept with a bank to support credit requirements or to compensate the bank for a wide variety of banking services. All such funds can be collectively designated *working balances*. Whether held by individuals or corporations, working balances are funds needed in the transaction of daily business and cannot be invested even temporarily. They are funds that must be kept in the most liquid of all forms—money.

Money has another primary function—that of providing a reservoir of purchasing power for the future. It shares this attribute with a number of other assets that can normally be exchanged for money on short notice and with minimum risk of loss. Such assets include short-term government securities, commercial paper, bankers' acceptances, and, for individuals, funds held in depository forms, such as bank savings deposits or savings and loan share accounts. These assets are held for reasons of liquidity (known or anticipated future expenditures) and, in contrast with working balances and longer-term savings, may be designated *investment funds* or *liquidity reserves*. Such funds generally seek the highest available interest return consistent with ready or specific availability at minimum risk.

Finally, funds may be deposited in commercial banks for accumulated savings purposes. Such funds are usually accumulated by individuals over relatively long periods of time for nonspecific purposes, such as the proverbial rainy day, retirement, or unknown personal emergencies. These funds have greater stability than investment funds, and the latter, in turn, are less volatile than working balances. Accumulated savings are more likely to be deposited in banks for the sake of convenience than for the sake of interest return and are, therefore, less sensitive to interest rate differentials between different savings media and savings institutions.

It is important to recognize that form does not necessarily follow function in bank deposits. A considerable number of depositors still keep their liquidity reserves—and, in the case of individuals, even their savings —in the form of idle demand deposits. The past reluctance of some banks to aggressively seek time deposits stemmed from their appraisal of the

---

[2]The *money supply* is usually defined as currency outside commercial banks plus demand deposits held by the public. The amount of demand deposits outstanding is not, however, an accurate measure of their importance as money, because of their relatively rapid turnover.

degree to which depositors kept a portion of their liquidity reserves in noninterest-bearing demand deposits. Conversely, some individuals may try to keep their working balances in savings accounts, although commercial banks discourage this practice because of the resulting abnormally high, costly account activity.

Essentially, demand deposits are likely to represent working balances; time deposits (other than savings deposits)[3] usually consist of the liquidity reserves of corporations, including municipalities and foreign banks, and of individuals when banks offer higher rates on longer-term certificates of deposit. Savings deposits are likely to represent a combination of accumulated savings and investment funds or liquidity reserves of individuals.

Because commercial banks are the primary source of commercial and industrial loans and because they operate the payments or check collection system, they have little competition for the deposits that represent purely working balances. This is the bread-and-butter business of the commercial banking system. For investment funds and savings deposits, the competition is very keen and has grown keener with the postwar rise in interest rates.[4] This fact has vital implications for bank policy and practice. When banks could pay interest on demand deposits,[5] it was customary for corporations and individuals to keep their liquidity reserves as well as their working balances in the form of demand deposits (though in 1928 and 1929, when market rates reached high levels, large amounts of such funds were placed, through the banks, in the "call loan" market). During the long depression of the 1930s and through the Second World War, interest rates were kept so low that it did not pay depositors to transfer their liquidity reserves from demand deposits to other short-term investment media. This was a period of very high bank liquidity. When short-term interest rates began to rise after 1947, the cost of keeping money idle rose commensurately. As a result, both individuals and corporations tended to convert that portion of their demand deposits that they did not need for working balance purposes into earning assets.

---

[3]*Regulation Q of the Board of Governors of the Federal Reserve System* distinguishes between "time certificate of deposit" with fixed maturity and "time deposits open account" subject to stated notice of withdrawal. It provides further that "savings deposits" may be held only for individuals and certain nonprofit organizations engaged in charitable, educational, and similar activities.

[4]George K. Kardonche, *The Competition for Savings,* Studies in Business Economics No. 107 (New York: The Conference Board, 1969), and Jules I. Bogen, *The Competitive Position of Commercial Banks,* New York University, Banking Research Study.

[5]The payment of interest on demand deposits was prohibited by the Banking Act of 1933.

The holding of such assets has risen steadily since that time, imposing an increasing squeeze on the growth of demand deposits. The slower growth of demand deposits has forced commercial banks to turn more and more to time and savings deposits and other sources of funds in order to perform their credit functions. The impact of this dramatic shift will be discussed in later chapters.

PAYMENTS AND COLLECTIONS

The commercial banking system not only creates the principal means of payment (demand deposits) and serves as the custodian of this supply of money but also provides the means by which payments can be simply and expeditiously made. This is the collection system through which checks, primarily, but also notes, drafts, coupons, and money transfers by letter and telegraph are made each day in tremendous and ever-increasing volume. As we move toward a "checkless" society, payments will still be made through electronic debits and credits to bank accounts maintained in bank computer memories.

Checks serve as money, although they are not legal tender, because they can be collected quickly and cheaply through the banking system. The collection of checks and other forms of payment orders is largely a routine banking function. The law with respect to negotiable instruments has been well standardized, and the procedures of collection, almost as uniformly followed, are set forth in detail in the regulations of the Federal Reserve System. Nevertheless, if one includes the payment and receipt of funds through the teller's window, more man-days are spent by banks in the performance of the collection function than in any other. Available figures indicate that close to one-third of bank operating costs, exclusive of interest paid, are the direct costs of their teller, transit, and bookkeeping operations. The growth in use of bank credit cards as a means of payment may shift these costs but will probably not reduce them.

From the viewpoint of bank policy, the operation of the collection system is primarily a service function. Although banks may not pay interest on demand deposits, the Board of Governors of the Federal Reserve System, in administering the law, has usually taken the position that the failure to levy service charges is not an interest payment. As a result, banks have often competed for demand deposits on the basis of services that they are willing to render the depositor, mostly in the handling of his collection problems. When the deposit is not large enough to support the related collection activity, banks generally impose service charges. If these charges exceed the cost of the services, the operation of the collection function can be a source of additional income to the bank.

SAVINGS ACCUMULATION AND INVESTMENT

A function that the commercial bank shares with a number of other financial institutions is that of accumulating and investing savings funds. The savings process takes place when a holder of money elects to defer spending it for current consumption until some future date. The saver exchanges his money for a claim on money subject to varying but specific conditions. These claims on money range in liquidity from savings deposits and savings and loan share accounts, which are normally payable virtually on demand, through securities of various maturities, to equities with no fixed payment date, the liquidity of which depends upon their marketability.

Through the savings process, purchasing power is diverted from current consumption into the market for capital goods. As savings are invested in plant and equipment, in homes, or, through government, in schools, roads, and exploration of space, the productive capacity and therefore the real wealth of the economy are increased. In this vital process, commercial banks play two roles: they themselves help to channel savings into productive uses and, through their short-term lending, they supplement or provide liquidity to other savings institutions and investment media.

Although it might be possible to operate commercial banks without time and savings deposits—in the past some banks did operate without such deposits—it would be impossible to serve the credit needs of a growing community without the availability of savings funds at the present time. In recent years, time and savings deposits have accounted for roughly 55 percent of the total deposits of commercial banks.

TRUST SERVICES

The fiduciary field is a specialized function not directly related to ordinary commercial banking operations. Commercial bank trust departments, nevertheless, are by far the most important group of corporate fiduciaries in the country. Trust business is generally handled by a specialized and separate staff (except in the smaller banks), and the operations of the trust department are subject to a separate body of law and tradition.

Trust business is nevertheless an important adjunct to the activities of many of the country's commercial banks. A recent report on trust activities of commercial banks indicated that the aggregate trust assets of the 3,406 reporting institutions were valued at $288 billion at the start of 1971. Of this amount, $91 billion (32 percent) was in employee benefit accounts, $135 billion (47 percent) was in private trust accounts, and $62 billion (22 percent) was in investment agency accounts. Almost two-thirds of the assets were in stocks, and slightly over 27 percent were in bonds. Approximately 82 percent of the reporting banks had trust assets of less than $25 million, 9 percent had trust assets ranging from $25 million to $100 million, 7 percent from $100 million to $1 billion, and 2 percent had trust assets in excess of $1 billion.[6] Because of widely differing accounting practices, however, book value figures are not a good measure of the relative importance of trust business. A more accurate measure is the income from trust business. An earlier report indicated that income from trust activities amounted to about 5 percent of the gross operating income of all commercial banks that were members of the Federal Reserve System (including those not exercising trust powers). For the large banks in New York City, where the nation's trust business is concentrated, income from trust departments represents more than 10 percent of gross income.[7]

For some small banks, however, the operation of a trust department is not profitable by itself; these banks run their trust departments primarily in order to be able to offer a complete package of banking services.

OTHER SERVICES

Commercial banks render many additional, miscellaneous services to the public. Most of these are profitable; however, a few are loss-leaders intended to draw business to other more profitable areas of the bank. Most banks operate safe deposit facilities and hold securities and other valuables in safekeeping for their customers. Many banks are either involved in direct bill-paying or act as agents for the collection of bills. More and more banks have been offering consumer credit cards. Nearly all banks provide credit information to their business customers.

In recent years, many larger banks have entered the field of computer

---

[6]*Trust Assets of Insured Commercial Banks—1970* (Washington, D. C.: Federal Deposit Insurance Corporation, 1971), pp. 5–13. The 3,406 reporting banks included all larger commercial banks offering trust services and most smaller commercial banks offering trust services.

[7]Joseph H. Wolfe, "Report of National Survey of Personal Trust Accounts," *The Trust Bulletin,* Vol. 39, No. 1, September 1959, p. 2, and Cecil P. Bronston, "The Patman Report on Trust Activities of Commercial Banks," *The Trust Bulletin,* Vol. 48, No. 2, October 1968, pp. 62–67.

services. These banks use electronic data processing equipment to perform services for their customers, which may include other banks, as well as for themselves. Banks provide such services as bookkeeping, billing, and inventory-control accounting for their business customers. Often there is little difference between the kind of records that banks keep and the kind of bookkeeping that their customers do.

A very important aspect of banking service is the form in which traditional bank credit and depository facilities are offered to the public. Whatever the virtues or deficiencies of check credit and charge-account plans, they represent an effort on the part of banks to tailor their traditional credit-granting and depository functions to the needs or desires of their customers. Christmas clubs, special checking accounts, and bank money orders similarly are new forms for old functions—adaptations to the changing economic and social scene.

A prominent banker has called the miscellaneous services that banks render to their customers "the greatest give-away program in history." They do not need to be. Under the pressure of competition, banks have provided services of all kinds in lieu of interest payments to attract and hold deposits. Well-run banks are beginning to examine the cost of these services more closely and to develop a market for them at fair prices.

All too often, one hears the public relations officer of a bank make the statement that "all we have to sell is service." Actually, the most important thing banks have to sell is credit, which is another name for liquidity or purchasing power. Service is not a product but a price—the cost of a bank's deposits, which are, in turn, the raw material of its credit-creating business. Where services are truly sold, they are an adjunct to the true banking function.

EARNING A RETURN FOR OWNERS

Commercial banks, thus, perform many useful roles in the economic life of the nation. They are not, however, charitable institutions. Bank management is responsible for earning enough to provide an adequate reward to present and prospective suppliers of ownership funds. In the authors' opinion, bank management should use the same basic framework for decision making as any other private business corporation. That is, the basic evaluation of bank management policies should be in terms of maximizing the value of the owners' investment in the bank. Achieving this maximization involves earning a high return on the owners' investment and avoiding excessive risks.

The sources of earnings for a bank are slightly different from those for other private businesses, but the same idea of selling a good or service above what it costs applies to banks. Banking risks are slightly different—the liquidity needed to meet deposit outflows and loan demands is difficult to estimate and, because of a bank's monetary responsibility, its liquidity and solvency may be subject to greater public scrutiny. Nevertheless, banks are similar to most other businesses in that they need to have both liquidity available to meet their obligations and reasonable long-term solvency.

Questions naturally arise about possible conflicts between banks' responsibilities in simultaneously performing the necessary commercial banking functions and maximizing earnings without excessive risks. In a competitive environment, there are strong reasons to believe that these two broad responsibilities are compatible. Adequate earnings will be forthcoming only if the bank is performing the necessary commercial banking functions efficiently.

In summary, the task of competent bank management is to perform the economic functions inherent in the banking business in such a way as to maximize the return on the owners' investment over time without taking excessive risks. It is the authors' conviction that the return on the stockholders' investment will indeed be maximized only if a bank serves the economic needs of its community effectively. The management policies discussed in subsequent chapters are those that experience has shown will best serve both the stockholder and the public.[8]

---

[8]In the limited number of situations in which there is conflict between the responsibilities of performing banking functions and earning an adequate return for owners, the authors' believe the remedy should be statutory and administrative regulation rather than the altruism of bank management.

2

THE BANKING STRUCTURE

The concept of structure is often used in a static and formal sense, such as that of building blocks placed one upon the other. More recently, physicists have used the word *structure* to describe the dynamic relationship that exists between forces held together in some meaningful way, as one speaks of the structure of matter.[1]

In much the same manner, the banking structure is more than the aggregate of banking institutions. The banking structure encompasses the forces of law and tradition that constitute the dynamic framework within which banking institutions function to provide the banking services required by their communities. The banking structure includes the legal and historical development of both state and Federally chartered banks. It encompasses the system of correspondent banking relationships that have enabled banks to work together in ways in which the thousands of small local banks can serve their communities to a degree far beyond their individual powers. And finally, involved in the banking structure are the diverse ways in which banks themselves are organized as unit banks, branch banks, or members of banking organizations. These institutional forms and legal relationships have developed over the years

---

[1]"Scientists today picture the basic building block of the universe, the proton, as a mere bundle of forces." Robert Hofstadter, Report to the Tenth International High Energy Physics Conference, University of Rochester, August 29, 1960. (Reported in the *New York Herald Tribune,* August 30, 1960).

in response to changing needs of the economy, both national and regional, and in response to public attitudes reflected in political views, which have sometimes been more emotional than logical.

In the broadest sense, the banking structure encompasses the whole complex of financial intermediaries through which the liquid funds and savings of the public are channeled into the loans and investments that supply the credit base to the economy. This discussion, however, will be confined to a narrower concept—the structure of the commercial banking system. This structure is constantly in transition. In recent years, important new Federal legislation regarding the structure and activities of bank holding companies has been enacted. Several states (for example, Virginia, New Jersey, and New York) have recently enacted laws liberalizing their policies related to branch banking, mergers, and/or bank holding companies. Constant pressure is being exercised to bring about similar changes in other states.

CORRESPONDENT BANKING

Before the existence of the Federal Reserve System, many of its functions were performed for the smaller banks by the larger banks in the principal financial centers. This earliest form of banking organization still vigorously survives in the system of correspondent banking. Without such a form of organization, the thousands of unit banks could not have served the credit needs of a rapidly expanding economy.

The correspondent banking system is an entirely informal arrangement whereby the small banks in towns and villages maintain deposit balances with larger banks in nearby cities and look to them for a wide variety of services and assistance. The city banks, in turn, keep correspondent balances with still larger banks in the principal money centers. Before the establishment of the Federal Reserve System, checks were collected entirely through this network of correspondent banks (often by roundabout routing), and, most importantly, the correspondent system served as a means of mobilizing the supply of credit and channeling it to areas where and when it was needed. Thus, correspondent banks provided liquidity and credit fluidity to a diverse economy. Country banks could deposit their idle funds with their correspondents, who invested them in money-market loans (theoretically, at least); and then, at times of peak demand for seasonal agricultural credit, the country banks could not only draw down their balances but borrow from their correspondents as well. The inadequacies of these arrangements, which did not include a central bank, were evident in recurring panics and finally led to the establishment of the Federal Reserve System. Nevertheless, without correspondent relationships, the credit needs of the country could hardly have been met at all.

Correspondent banks are still active in the collection of checks and still supply credit to the smaller banks in consideration of the balances that the latter maintain. In addition, correspondent banks perform many services that would otherwise be unobtainable to the smaller banks and their customers. They give investment advice, hold customers' securities in safekeeping, arrange for the purchase and sale of securities, arrange international financial transactions, trade in Federal funds, participate in loans too large for the small banks, sell participations in large loans to small banks with surplus funds, and provide a wide range of other services.

The larger correspondent banks, nearly all of which are members of the Federal Reserve System, indirectly channel the benefits of that system to those banks that are not members and at the same time provide some services even to member banks (such as giving investment advice) that would be inappropriate for the central bank to perform. The correspondent banking system tends to extend economies of scale to smaller banks. Smaller banks experience infrequent demands for some services, such as international financial transactions, but must generally be prepared to offer such services to customers. Returns would rarely compensate the initial investment required for small-scale production of these services. Larger banks, however, encounter sufficient demand from the public and from other commercial banks to provide these services profitably and at a lower unit cost to their customers. Aside from direct expenses incurred in providing these services or the fees required for data processing, correspondents rarely charge customer banks. The deposit balances a bank holds with its correspondent is expected to compensate for the services.[2]

The volume of interbank demand deposits provides some indication of the usage of correspondent services. In 1896, correspondent balances represented 10 percent of total demand deposits in commercial banks. These balances climbed to 13 percent in 1913, just before the organization of the Federal Reserve System, and then fell gradually to 7 percent in 1928. They reached roughly 12 percent of total demand deposits in the late 1940s, declined to 9 percent by the early 1960s, and then rose back to approximately 11 percent by early 1972. The rather sharp increase in the late 1960s appears to have been caused by the increasing

---

[2]By far the largest share of these compensating correspondent balances is held as demand deposits. A recent survey found fewer than 6 percent of the banks favored a fee arrangement. Part of the reason for the general preference for demand deposits as compensation for correspondent services may be that nonmember banks can normally count correspondent balances toward reserve requirements.

need for correspondent services and the substantial increase in loan participation among correspondent banks.[3]

A recent survey of over 2,100 commercial banks provides further insight into the use of correspondent banking services. Over 90 percent of all banks surveyed preferred to send checks drawn on nonlocal banks to correspondents rather than to the Federal Reserve. Only banks with deposits in excess of $100 million had a decided preference for clearing checks directly with the Federal Reserve. Approximately 60 percent of the banks surveyed had loans in which correspondents were participating. A majority of the banks surveyed reported that they had received investment advice from correspondents, had regularly sold Federal funds through correspondents, and had regularly bought, sold, or exchanged holdings of U.S. government securities with correspondents. Nearly all the banks reported using correspondents for security safekeeping, and about 90 percent indicated that their correspondents offered assistance with international transactions, bankwire, credit information, and electronic data processing.[4]

Correspondent banking enjoys a measure of emotional as well as logical support. Correspondent relationships are frequently justified on the grounds of loyalty or appreciation for past services rather than their present-day economics. Many large banks, seeking to maintain or enlarge their correspondent balances, have aggressively sought account activity, sometimes without careful cost studies.

In order to be economically sound, all correspondent balances should be justified by careful evaluation of the service-cost relationships. The services provided should be at a lower cost than the recipient bank can perform them, yet contribute to the profits of the correspondent bank. It is probable that some correspondent relationships are unprofitable to one or both of the participants.

BRANCH BANKING

Most banks in the United States have traditionally been and still are unit banks—single-office institutions serving primarily their local communities. At the start of 1972, there were 13,759 commercial banks in the United States, of which 9,375 were unit banks. The tide toward

---

[3]*All Bank Statistics, 1896–1955* (U.S. Board of Governors of the Federal Reserve System, 1959); Federal Reserve Bulletins, 1956–1971; and Robert E. Knight, "Correspondent Banking," *Monthly Review* (Federal Reserve Bank of Kansas City), November 1970, pp. 3–14 and December 1970, pp. 12–24.

[4]More detailed information on these and other correspondent services in this survey is contained in Knight, *op. cit.*

multiple-office banking, however, is running strong. The number of branch banking offices increased from 4,613 in 1948 to 10,605 in 1960 to 23,362 at the start of 1972.[5] This increase has resulted both from the establishment of new branches in growing communities and the absorption of previously independent banks by merger. The pros and cons of bank mergers and multiple-office banking are in the forefront of bank policy considerations today.

Historically, branch banking has been a controversial subject since the earliest days of the Republic. As early as 1790, Secretary of the Treasury Alexander Hamilton had grave doubts about it.[6] Nevertheless, both the First and Second Bank of the United States were branch banking institutions.[7] In many instances, the early state banks also had branches. The 406 state banks in 1834 operated 100 branches. On the eve of the Civil War, there were 170 state bank branches in eleven states. However, the existence of over 1,500 banks by that time indicated a clear trend toward unit banking.

Opposition to branch banking arose from two directions. First, the remoteness of some branches (as well as of some unit banks) tended to facilitate some of the worst abuses of the note-issue privilege in the days of wildcat banking, so that banking reform and early attempts at bank supervision often led to the abolition of the branch banking privilege.[8] Second, the Jacksonian campaign against The Second Bank of the United States and the subsequent Populist campaigns for cheap money were in a real sense directed against the concentration of monetary power in large eastern banks, some of which were branch institutions. The resultant political furor helped to establish the emotional tone that is still evident in much of the popular and political opposition to branch banking.[9]

---

[5]*Annual Report of the Federal Deposit Insurance Corporation, 1971* (Washington: Federal Deposit Insurance Corp., 1972) pp. 176, 180.

[6]"Report on a National Bank," December 13, 1790, in *Papers on Public Credit, Commerce and Finance,* ed. Samuel McKee, Jr. (New York: Columbia University Press, 1934).

[7]The Second Bank, organized in 1816, had established nineteen offices in fourteen states by October 1817.

[8]By the early 1840s, Massachusetts, New York, and Rhode Island had passed legislation providing that no one should conduct the business of banking except at his place of residence.

[9]In a recent court case, Old Kent Bank and Trust Company *vs.* William McC. Martin *et al.,* Judge Washington, dissenting, said "...There has long been public hostility to the extension, by means of branches, of a bank's geographic area of operation. At one time branch banking was almost uniformly forbidden in the United States. Many persons feared, and still fear that, among other things, unrestrained bank operations would enable a few wealthy urban banks to extend their operations to a point where the independence and prosperity of the poorer banks...would be seriously jeopardized."

When the National Bank Act was passed in 1863, the question of branches was not even discussed. The Federal Reserve Act of 1913 extended the privilege of membership to state banks without prohibiting them from operating existing branches but did not accord to national banks, for which membership was compulsory, the right to establish new branches. Gradually, limited branch powers were granted to national banks and subsequently extended until, in 1952, national banks were, in effect, empowered to establish branches as freely as banks chartered by the respective states.

The history of banking in the United States, therefore, starts with branch banking, veers in the direction of unit banks, and is now quite rapidly swinging back again. Opposition to branch banking is still strong in some areas, however, and state laws concerning the establishment of branches vary from one part of the country to another. State-wide branching is permitted in seventeen states (all of the western states and a few of the eastern states). Branching is prohibited or permitted in an extensively limited manner in fifteen midwestern states and Florida. The remaining seventeen eastern states allow limited branching.[10]

Against this background of diversity in law and tradition, those who are responsible for managing banks must attempt a logical assessment of the virtues and deficiencies of unit banking. The issues are obviously not clear-cut or they would have been resolved long ago. Nor is the available evidence entirely conclusive, even when weighed objectively. It is, nevertheless, incumbent on bank management and legislative bodies regulating bankers to carefully appraise the banking structure, actual and prospective, in the light of economic reality and the expanding needs of a complex and dynamic economy.

Studies Evaluating Branch Banking

In recent years, numerous studies have attempted to evaluate branch banking as objectively as possible. The New York State Banking Department published a study dealing with the effects of branch banking in New York State during the postwar period. This study sought to determine whether the public had benefited from the branching and merging of commercial banks in New York State from 1950 to 1961. According to this study, the beneficial effects of branching included:

1. Lower loan rates
2. Higher rates paid on savings deposits
3. More liberal maturities and loan/value ratios
4. Greater availability of services and banking facilities

---

[10]*Annual Report of the Federal Deposit Insurance Corporation, 1971, op. cit.*

5. Larger lending authority

The detrimental effects included:

1. A lower volume of unsecured lending
2. Higher service charges on special and regular checking accounts of individuals[11]

Several studies support the idea that the number of banking facilities and the convenience and accessibility of these facilities are higher in states that permit branch banking. For example, it was shown that (after adjustment for population and income growth) the increase in offices during the period 1946 to 1965 was significantly greater in states allowing branch banking. This phenomenon was found especially in metropolitan areas—there was an average of 10,400 persons per banking office in larger cities in states that permitted branch banking compared with an average of 18,900 per banking office in large cities in sates that allowed only unit banking.[12]

In a study emphasizing the convenience and accessibility of a banking office, Jack Woods compared the number of banking offices per square mile in unit- and branch-banking states and concluded that unit-banking states could significantly improve the adequacy of their banking facilities by adopting some form of branch banking.[13]

It should be emphasized that these advantages of the branch banking systems are potentials that may not be fully realized in all cases. The successful operation of a branch banking system requires a high degree of management competence, good intrabank communications, and intelligent cost control, all of which will be considered in later chapters. Suffice it to say here that, in the absence of sound management, branch banking can be self-defeating and subject to the criticisms so frequently heard. Among these criticisms are charges that:

1. Branch officers lack flexibility and initiative. They operate solely "by the book."

---

[11]*Branch Banking, Bank Mergers and the Public Interest* (New York: New York State Banking Department, 1964), pp. 8–34.

[12]Donald Jacobs, "The Interaction Effects of Restrictions on Branching and Other Bank Regulations," *Journal of Finance*, Vol. 19, No. 2, May 1965, p. 351. Other studies on the number of banking facilities, all of which reached similar conclusions, include Paul M. Horvitz and Bernard Shull, "The Impact of Branch Banking on Bank Performance," *National Banking Review*, Vol. 2, No. 2, December 1964, pp. 143–89, and Jack M. Guttentag and Edward S. Herman, *Banking Structure and Performance* (New York: Institute of Finance of New York University, 1967).

[13]Jack Woods, "The Convenience and Accessibility of Banking Offices in Unit and Branch Banking States," An unpublished study at Continental Illinois National Bank, Chicago, 1971.

2. Branches lose close personal contact with the community. Rotation of branch officers, which may be a sound personnel policy for the bank as a whole, results in the branch community doing business with "strangers."

3. Branch officers fail to rely on character and reputation in granting credit. Many local businesses resent filing elaborate credit information. Although any well-run bank should have this information, small unit banks frequently dispense with it.[14]

The authors' conclusion from the combined results of these studies is that, in spite of the benefits of branch banking, well-run local banks do not find it excessively difficult to compete effectively for local business with the branches of larger banks. The touchstone of success in banking, as in other endeavors, is not form or structure but capable management. Any bank, small or large, where this is found can be outstandingly successful. The larger a bank becomes and the more far-flung its branch operations, the more difficult its management problems. On the other hand, the larger banks have the resources to attract and train a higher caliber of general management and specially trained staff specialists and therefore are able to provide a wider range of highly specilized banking services to the public.

GROUP BANKING

Group banking is a generic term used to describe the ownership or substantial control of two or more banks by the same interests. The term *chain banking* is generally used to designate such organizations when the controlling interest is vested in an individual or group of individuals. The term *bank holding company* refers to a corporation that owns or controls one or more banks. Both chain banking systems and bank holding companies originally came into being partly to circumvent branch banking prohibitions and partly to extend the banking interests of aggressive groups over wide areas, particularly in farm communities and the rapidly expanding states of the Far West.[15]

Chain banking may refer to ownership of several banks by a single individual or by a group of individuals, or the Boards of Directors of several banks may be composed of many of the same members. Such organizations are often built around one of the larger banks in an area

---

[14]Unpublished study made under Howard Crosse's supervision in the Bank Examination Department of the Federal Reserve Bank of New York.

[15]Gerald C. Fischer, *American Banking Structure* (New York: Columbia University Press, 1968). It is interesting to note that bank holding companies are no stronger in states that prohibit branch banking than in those that permit it.

or state. The principal bank is generally referred to as the "key bank" because it sets the pattern for banking operations for the chain group. Chain banking is self-limiting, because the large amounts of capital required are today only rarely available to individuals. Because of the advantages of the corporate form of control, many original chains were converted into branch banking or holding companies. Under the 1970 amendments to the Bank Holding Company Act of 1956, most remaining banking chains have been brought under the supervision of the Board of Governors of the Federal Reserve System as *de facto* holding companies.

Different sectors of the public have held widely divergent opinions about bank holding companies. Various restrictions were placed on such companies by Federal laws, principally the Banking Act of 1933 (Glass-Steagall Act) and the Bank Holding Company Act of 1956. These two acts defined bank holding companies differently, and some types of bank holding companies were not affected by the provisions of either act. Amendments to the 1956 act were passed in 1966 and 1970 to eliminate most of the inconsistencies. Restrictions on bank holding companies in some states also reflect wide differences of opinions about bank holding companies.[16]

There are two general types of bank holding companies, the one-bank and the multi-bank. Prior to the 1970 amendments, one-bank holding companies did not fall within the 1956 act's definition of a bank holding company and therefore were not subject to the specific control of the Board of Governors of the Federal Reserve System. One-bank holding companies can be subdivided into nonbank-originated and bank-originated. The nonbank-originated bank holding company, or conglomerate form, is a company that owns a substantial interest in a single bank, although the company's major activities are in nonbanking areas of business. In early 1971, there were approximately seventy such companies.[17]

The bank-originated one-bank holding company is created when an existing bank organizes a holding company of which the bank becomes a subsidiary. Large banks that have converted their structure to the one-bank holding company form are often called "financial congenerics," because their intent has often seemed to be to form or acquire additional

---

[16]In early 1972, twenty-nine states placed no limitation on the acquisition of bank stocks by bank holding companies; state approval of acquisitions were required in five states; three states had moderate restrictions on the acquisitions of bank stocks by bank holding companies; and bank holding companies were prohibited or severely limited in thirteen states.

[17]*Wall Street Journal* (New York), March 11, 1971, p. 26.

subsidiaries in financially related activities, such as leasing, insurance, data processing, and so on.

The growth of one-bank holding companies is traced in Table 1. The rationale behind the exclusion of one-bank holding companies from

TABLE 1

NUMBER AND DEPOSITS OF ONE-BANK HOLDING COMPANIES
(AT THE END OF SELECTED YEARS)

	1955	1965	1967	1969	1971
Number of one-bank holding companies	117	550	810	894	1,414
Deposits (in billions of dollars)	11	15	108	181	207
Deposits as a percentage of all bank deposits (%)	6	5	27	42	38

Source: "The Growth of Unregistered Bank Holding Companies: Problems and Products," Staff Report for the Committee of Banking and Currency, House of Representatives, 1969. The most recent figures are based on data from the Association of Registered Bank Holding Companies and the Federal Reserve Board.

the 1956 act and the 1966 amendments to that act was that one-bank holding companies were not a particularly significant part of the total banking system. However, in the two or three years following the passage of the 1966 amendments, many of the largest banks converted their corporate structure to the one-bank holding company form. As Table 1 shows, by the start of 1972 the one-bank holding companies' share of all bank deposits had risen to 38 percent, up from 5 percent only six years earlier.

Multi-bank holding companies own or control, either directly or indirectly, 25 percent or more of the voting shares of two or more banks. The 1966 amendments defined bank holding companies in this manner. The growth of multi-bank holding companies, shown in Table 2, was slow from 1956 through 1965; however, after the passage of the 1966 amendments, the number of multi-bank holding companies began increasing at a more rapid pace.[18] By the end of 1971, the 153 registered bank holding companies held nearly one-fourth of the total deposits of all commercial banks in the country.

18Federal Reserve approval to form a registered holding company seemed to become easier to obtain in 1966. From 1956 through 1965, seventeen of the twenty-five requests for multi-bank holding companies were approved; from 1966 through 1969, forty-six of the fifty requests for multi-bank holding companies were approved.

TABLE 2

OFFICES AND DEPOSITS OF BANKS
AFFILIATED WITH MULTI-BANK HOLDING COMPANIES
(AT THE END OF SELECTED YEARS)

	1956	*1960*	*1962*	*1965*	*1967*	*1969*	*1970*	*1971*
Number of multi-bank holding companies	53	47	49	53	74	97	121	153
Number of banks	428	426	442	468	603	723	895	1,112
Number of branches	783	1,037	1,215	1,486	2,085	2,674	3,260	4,633
Total number of offices	1,211	1,463	1,657	1,954	2,688	3,397	4,155	5,745
Offices as a percentage of all bank offices (%)	5.8	6.2	6.5	6.7	8.6	10.1	11.8	15.6
Deposits (in billions of dollars)	14.8	18.2	21.2	27.5	49.8	62.5	78.0	134.0
Deposits as a percentage of all bank deposits (%)	7.5	7.9	8.1	8.3	12.6	14.3	16.2	24.9

Sources: *Bank Holding Company Facts* (Spring 1972), by the Association of Registered Bank Holding Companies.

By early 1972, the total combined deposits of one-bank and registered bank holding companies represented about 63 percent of the total deposits of all commercial banks in the United States; therefore, it was not surprising that legislators, bank organizations, and bank regulatory agencies devoted considerable attention to the question of bank holding companies. The 1970 amendments to the Bank Holding Company Act of 1956 brought the one-bank holding companies under the same restrictions as multiple-bank holding companies and essentially forbade such companies to engage in activities unrelated to banking. The definition of unrelated activities is left to the Board of Governors of the Federal Reserve. Apparently it will be many years before decisions and interpretations are made on some activities.[19]

It will also be many years before the final effects of these amend-

---

[19]By mid–1971, the Federal Reserve System had permitted bank holding companies to retain or acquire interest in companies that engaged in one or more of the following activities: (1) making or acquiring loans; (2) operating as an industrial bank, Morris Plan Bank, or industrial loan company; (3) servicing loans; (4) performing trust company activities; (5) acting as an investment or financial counselor; (6) leasing personal property or equipment; and (7) making equity and debt investments in corporations or projects designed primarily to promote community welfare. Many more activities are to be studied by the Federal Reserve during the 1970s.

ments are known. It appears that the majority of the nonbank-originated bank holding companies will divest themselves of their banking interests.[20] Most larger, bank-orientated, one-bank holding companies appear likely to become registered multi-bank holding companies. Since one-bank holding companies have lost their advantage of being able to expand into non-banking activities, they may find it advantageous to acquire other banks.

Under the current legislative structure, the distinctive feature of any form of bank holding company lies in its ability to realize many of the benefits and render most of the services of wide-spread branch banking organizations while retaining the decentralization of management that can preserve the "local touch." Typically, each banking unit of a holding company system is managed by a Board of Directors comprised of local citizens, who retain a substantial measure of autonomy in forming lending policies and dealing with local management problems. Without a substantial grant of local autonomy, the outstanding citizens and business leaders of the various communities could hardly be induced to serve as directors, because in most cases they hold only a nominal stock interest in the bank or the holding company. Given enough local authority, they will look upon their directorships as a form of public service.

The relationship of the holding company to its subsidiary banks is largely that of an informed and helpful stockholder. This role combines many of the functions often rendered to country banks by their city correspondents with provision for effective group action in such fields as accounting, purchase of supplies, or investment analysis. The holding companies have, in short, developed as staff organizations for their constituent banks.[21]

The holding company form of organization also tends to encourage a certain amount of healthy rivalry among its units. Such competition provides stimulus for experimentation and can lead to a diversity of approach that is less likely to be found in a branch organization, where final management authority stems from one top-management team and a single Board of Directors.

---

[20]Some of the companies controlling larger banks—for example, CIT and World Airways—may remain in banking, because their banking activities fall under a grandfather clause allowing companies to remain in activities they continually operated since June 30, 1968. If they choose to remain in banking, these companies are not permitted to enter any non-banking activities in which they were not already engaged as of June 30, 1968. Any new venture must be related to banking and approved by the Board of Governors.

[21]Fisher, *American Banking Structure, op. cit.,* pp. 92–120.

BANK MERGERS AND ACQUISITIONS

Much of the rapid growth in branch banking and bank holding companies in recent years has taken place through the merger and acquisition process. In the 1960s, a yearly average of approximately 150 commercial banks were absorbed through mergers or were holding company acquisitions. The acquiring banks or holding companies were generally larger than the acquired banks; however, in many cases the differences in bank size were not as great as might have been expected. In addition, a surprisingly large number of relatively small banks were involved in mergers.[22] Partially responsible for this phenomenon are the present Federal laws and court cases regarding bank mergers and acquisitions that will be discussed in a succeeding section of this chapter.

There is no single reason for the large number of mergers. Small banks willing to sell out or be merged into other banks typically cite such reasons as:

1. Advancing age of management and failure to provide successor management
2. Attractive terms (price), well above limited local markets
3. Desire to provide more effective competition to larger neighboring banks
4. Failure to keep up with aggressive competition
5. Inability of small banks to meet borrowing needs of their customers
6. Loss of business through acquisition of local concerns by national industries
7. Greater fringe benefits and compensation paid to employees by larger banks

Banks seeking to acquire other banks may be doing so for one or several of the following reasons:

1. Need to increase volume of retail business
2. Need or desire to better service existing business

---

[22]A study of merger activity in the Fourth Federal Reserve District from 1960 through 1967 demonstrates that relatively small banks were often involved in mergers. Approximately three-fourths of the 139 acquired banks had less than $10 million in assets, and only 6 acquired banks had assets of more than $25 million. Nearly 60 percent of the acquiring banks had assets of less than $50 million, while acquiring banks with more than $250 million in total assets participated in only one-eighth of the acquisitions. Source: "Bank Merger Activity in the Fourth Federal Reserve District," *Economic Review* (Cleveland: Federal Reserve Bank of Cleveland), March 1969, pp. 3–6.

3. Need or desire to follow customers to the suburbs
4. Desire to expand lending limits
5. Normal urge to accelerate growth
6. Desire to improve earnings

The analysis of 139 mergers in the Fourth Federal Reserve District provides some additional insights. Significant differences were found in the asset structures and loan portfolios of the banks involved in merger activity. The typical acquired bank had invested a lower proportion of its assets in loans and other securities and a higher proportion in U.S. government securities than the typical acquiring bank. Acquired banks generally tended to concentrate more on real estate loans, while acquiring banks made more business loans. Data on revenues and expenses in these mergers suggest that the acquired banks tended to charge slightly higher prices for loans and depositor accounts and to incur slightly higher expenses in interest on savings and time deposits than did acquiring banks. The interest expenses were higher because time and savings deposits represented, on the average, a larger proportion of total deposits at the acquired banks. In spite of these asset and earnings differences, which in general reflect less aggressive management in the acquired banks, there was virtually no difference in overall profitability between the acquired and acquiring banks.[23]

Many of the costs that bring about bank mergers are not revealed in such statistics, because they are prospective costs—those that the small bank faces but has not actually met. They include the salary cost of a suitable replacement for top management, the cost of fringe benefits that have never actually been provided for the employees, the cost of meeting widespread competition in rates of interest on savings, and the cost of mechanization and modernization that have never been undertaken. These are costs that a successful bank must pay in a competitive situation if it is to provide the services offered by other banks, but they are costs that dismay the stockholders and directors of many small banks who have not faced up to the obsolescence of their management practices and their physical plant.

Another important facilitating factor is the failure of bank management, in many cases, to provide for successor ownership by developing a local market for the bank's stock at a fair price. Many small banks do not publish their earnings figures or in any way indicate to their shareholders the true value of their stock. Too often, the older directors are reluctant to relinquish their positions and bring in some of the younger businessmen of the community as directors and stockholders. These

23*Ibid.*, pp. 6–15.

aspects of bank management will be discussed at greater length in later chapters, but they also contribute to the merger trend.

In addition, many recent mergers have been initiated by aggressive and expansion-minded bank management. Expansion through merger is, in itself, a competitive practice. Some bankers feel that external growth may be easier, faster, or more profitable than internal growth. In states where entry or branching is severly restricted, bank acquisitions may be the primary avenue available for aggressive bank management. In some states, the competition for acquisitions has become so intense that the acquiring banks have had to offer substantial premiums to acquire additional banks.[24]

The most important factor behind the large number of bank mergers and acquisitions, however, lies deeper than the facilitating factors usually cited and goes beyond the aggressiveness of expansion-minded management. The merger trend in banking is part and parcel of the economic development of the nation. It is a response to the changing character of the communities served by banks. Improved transportation, great improvements in communication, increased mobility of the population, and the merger trend in industry generally have had more to do with bank mergers than most of the banking factors discussed above. After looking at the changes on Main Street in most American communities in the last twenty years—from local merchant to chain store, from small local manufacturer to the branch of a nationally known company—one has to realize that supermarket banking, like supermarket retailing, is often necessary if the public is to receive the banking services it desires.[25]

DESIRABLE EXTENT OF BRANCH
AND HOLDING COMPANY BANKING

Bank management and government officials need not debate the potential advantage of multiple-office banking so much as its appropriate extent. The problem is, in fact, twofold. Over what areas should multiple-office banking be permitted? And to what extent should the traditional

---

[24]Some of these premiums may be illusory. Potential pitfalls in banks' offers are discussed in John W. Bowyer, "Watch Out for Those Fancy Price Offers," *The Independent Banker*, Vol. 30, January 1971, pp. 4–7.

[25]Dun and Bradstreet collected data on the attitudes of managers of small businesses regarding services provided by their local unit banks. The study revealed that the dissatisfactions of these businessmen were not confined to commercial loans but included unmet needs for conversion of overdrafts into loans, an open line of credit for emergency service, night depositories, Saturday banking hours, and other services.

competition of many unit banks be eliminated? Bank managers can consider these questions in terms of the bank's operating efficiency and ability to serve its customers effectively. For public officials, the adequacy of banking competition has become the paramount issue.[26]

Any purely geographical limitation is bound to be arbitrary and confining.[27] National corporations require nationwide banking services, and to an increasing extent, the larger banks provide such services through traveling officers who call on businesses in all parts of the country. Not even the largest bank, however, is big enough to accommodate alone any of the one hundred largest corporations in the nation. All of these use many banks, and most even use two or more in major financial centers.[28]

It is likely that the larger banks in the major financial centers have more in common with each other than they do with the small community banks in the hinterlands of their own states. A nationwide branch system, composed just of such larger banks and serving the larger national corporations, might well be more logical than the union of the city banks with their country cousins. The trend, however, has not been in that direction. Where holding companies or branch banking is permitted, the city banks have already spread out into suburban and rural areas. Even the former purely "wholesale" banks in major financial centers have, in a number of instances, merged with "retail" banks.

The concept of regional banking has long held considerable appeal for those who recognize the economic need for and the potential economies of larger banking organizations but who, at the same time, either harbor lingering fears of monopoly in banking or simply recognize the unfavorable popular and political climate. Regional banking, in effect,

---

[26]"There is no question that competition is desirable in banking, and that competitive factors should be considered in all aspects of the supervision and regulation of banks." Report of the Committee on Banking and Currency, House of Representatives, 86th Cong., 2d sess., 1960, on S. 1062, a Bill to Regulate Bank Mergers, p. 3.

[27]In testifying before the Senate Banking and Currency Committee in 1931, Governor Harrison of the Federal Reserve Bank of New York said, "There may be very much more reason why you should authorize branches within a hundred miles than within state limits. In the case of New York City, for instance, if you authorize a New York City bank to put a branch in White Plains, New York, and not in Newark, New Jersey, it would not seem a logical distinction to make." Operations of National and Federal Reserve Banking Systems, Hearings before a Subcommittee of the Committee on Banking and Currency, 71st Cong., 3rd sess., 1931, pursuant to S. Res. 71 (Washington, D.C.: Government Printing Office, 1931), p. 76.

[28]In a survey of forty large corporations, each having $1 billion or more in annual sales, the Bank Examinations Department of the Federal Reserve Bank of New York found that each of these companies distributed its borrowing over more than one and, in one case, as many as ten of the large New York City banks.

represents a compromise between the unit or purely local bank and its opposite extreme, statewide or even nationwide branch banking. A regional bank presumably can retain the local flavor but is large enough to benefit from the economies of size and the broadening of services discussed above.

Legal Aspects

Public concern with the adequacy of competition generally is expressed in the antitrust legislation of the late nineteenth and early twentieth centuries. The Sherman Act of 1890 prohibited restraints of trade and made monopolizing trade a misdemeanor. The difficulties of administering the Sherman Act led to the passage in 1914 of the Clayton Antitrust Act, Section 7 of which prohibits acquisitions of stock if the "effect of such acquisition may be substantially to lessen competition, or to tend to create a monopoly."

Prior to 1956, most Federal laws regulating bank mergers and the acquisition of banks by holding companies did not explicitly require the regulatory authority to consider the probable competitive effect of the acquisition of a bank. Although the National Banking Act of 1918 and the Banking Act of 1950 required the approval of mergers and acquisitions by one or more regulatory bodies, the only standard set was adequacy of capital. In effect, before 1956 bank mergers and acquisitions were primarily subject to control through state laws that provided for regulation by state agents or agencies using varying standards. Uncertainty about these standards and the bank-merger trend that developed after World War II led to agitation for more specific Federal controls over bank mergers and the formation and expansion of bank holding companies.[29]

After many years of discussion, bank holding company legislation was passed in 1956, and Federal control over mergers of all insured banks was legislated in 1960. Both laws require the supervisory authority to consider the competitive impact. The Bank Holding Company Act specifies that the Board of Governors of the Federal Reserve System should consider, among other things:

> ...whether or not the effect of such acquisition, or merger or consolidation would be to expand the size or extent of the bank holding company system involved beyond limits consistent with

---

[29]"Federal Laws Regulating Bank Mergers and the Acquisition of Banks by Registered Bank Holding Companies," *Economic Review* (Cleveland: Federal Reserve Bank of Cleveland), January 1971, pp. 18–27, presents an excellent review of the Federal laws and court cases pertaining to bank mergers and acquisitions.

adequate and sound banking, the public interest, and the preservation of competition in the field of banking.

The Bank Merger Act of 1960 provides that:

> ...the appropriate supervisory agency shall also take into consideration the effect of the transaction competition (including any tendency to monopoly), and shall not approve the transaction unless, after considering all of such factors, it finds the transaction to be in the public interest.

After the passage of the Bank Merger Act of 1960, all bank mergers involving insured banks were subject to the jurisdiction of one of three Federal agencies. Both statutes stressed three groups of factors: (1) banking factors such as management, earnings, and solvency; (2) convenience and need; and (3) prevention of excessive concentration of economic power. However, both acts were ambiguous regarding the relative weights to be attached to each of the three factors. The question of the applicability of antitrust laws to bank mergers was left open.

This issue was conclusively settled in the early 1960s. In the Philadelphia National Bank Case and the Lexington Bank Case, the Supreme Court ruled that bank mergers approved by Federal banking agencies could be challenged by the Attorney General under antitrust laws. In the former case, the court held that the proposed merger of two large Philadelphia banks, which would have resulted in a single bank controlling 36 percent of the bank deposits in a four-county area, was sufficiently anticompetitive to be in violation of Section 7 of the Clayton Act. In the Lexington Case, the Supreme Court declared that bank mergers were subject to the provisions of the Sherman Act.[30]

In 1966, the Bank Holding Company Act of 1956 and the Bank Merger Act of 1960 were revised along similar lines. In amendments to both acts, Congress affirmed the applicability of antitrust laws to bank mergers and acquisitions that would substantially lessen competition or tend to create a monopoly. Exceptions are allowed primarily when the anticompetitive effects are clearly outweighed by the probable effect of the transaction in meeting the convenience and needs of the community to be served. In the event of an approval, a thirty-day waiting period is required, during which the Attorney General may sue to prevent the proposed merger or acquisition.

Several Supreme Court decisions since the 1966 amendments provide additional insights into current judicial opinions relating to competition

---

[30]*United States v. Philadelphia National Bank et. al.,* 210 F. Supp. 348 (1962); 83 S. Ct. 1715 (1963) and *United States v. First National Bank and Trust Co. of Lexington et. al.,* 208 F. Supp. 456 (1962); 84 S. Ct. 1033 (1964).

in banking. A single opinion covering the Provident Bank Case and First City Bank Case indicated that the Department of Justice may challenge a bank merger on the grounds of a violation of the antitrust laws, regardless of the action of the regulatory agency. In addition, the defendant bank itself must demonstrate that considerations of convenience and need outweigh the anticompetitive effects of the merger.[31]

Two other key Supreme Court decisions were the Third National Bank Case and the Phillipsburg National Bank Case. In the former, the court made it clear that suitable weight should be given to considerations of convenience and need, but that the defendants have the responsibility of showing that the gains expected from the merger cannot reasonably be attained through other means. In the latter case, involving two banks with deposits of less than $30 million, the Supreme Court ruled that mergers between two directly competing banks, regardless of state boundaries and bank size, may violate the antitrust laws.[32]

The overall results of this mixture of legislative acts and judicial decisions are difficult to interpret. In the 1960s, only 3.1 percent of the 1,531 merger cases subject to regulatory approval were denied. Approximately 2.2 percent were taken to court, where roughly a third of the cases were won by the bank or settled by consent decrees. In the remaining cases, the acquiring bank either lost in court or abandoned its merger attempt.[33] The relatively small proportion of denials may be misleading, because there is some prescreening of applications, and many banks try to avoid mergers or acquisition that they feel may be denied.

There are still many unanswered questions about bank mergers and acquisitions. For example, the issue of the validity of using so-called concentration ratios—that is, percentages of market share—as criteria for assessing the competitive effects of mergers has not been settled.[34] The specific factors relating to the convenience and needs of the community to be served by the merged bank have not been spelled out in detail. Whether affiliation between banks that are potential competitors is a

---

[31]*United States v. Provident National Bank et al.*, 262 F. Supp. 297 (1966); 87 S. Ct. 1088 (1967) and *United States v. First National Bank of Houston et al.*, F. Supp. 397 (1966); S. Ct. 1088 (1967).

[32]*United States v. Third National Bank of Nashville et. al.*, 260 F. Supp. 869 (1966); 88 S. Ct. 882 (1968) and *United States v. Phillipsburg National Bank and Trust Co. et. al.*, 306 F. Supp. (1969); 90 S. Ct. 2035 (1970).

[33]Oscar Goodman, "Judicial Decisions and Litigation Affecting Competition in Banking," *Journal of Finance*, Vol. 26, No. 2, May 1971, pp. 615–46. Goodman found that in the 1960s the Federal Reserve Board rejected 10 percent of its 249 applications, the F.D.I.C. rejected 1.8 percent of its 433 applications, and the Comptroller rejected 1.8 percent of its 849 applications.

[34]For example, in the Brown Shoe Case, a single firm's control over roughly 3 percent of the market was held to be anticompetitive.

violation of the antitrust laws is still unresolved.[35] Furthermore, each of the three Federal regulatory agencies appears to employ a different set of standards for evaluating the merger proposals over which it has jurisdiction.

Competition in Banking

Much of the confusion about the standards for bank mergers and acquisitions derives from the fact ·that the concept of competition itself is changing. Perfect competition in the classical sense was virtually eliminated from most of our business enterprise long ago. It is disappearing rapidly from banking as well, wherever even limited branching is permitted. A large number of small banks may possibly have provided adequate competition in the past. Each had roughly equal competitive power and provided alternative choices of approximately equal facilities, because none was equipped to render much more than the rudimentary banking services required by a relatively simple economy.

The classical economist contrasted competition—in the sense described above—with monopoly, as good is contrasted to evil. What has developed, and is still developing, is neither. The emerging banking structure is constituted of a smaller number of larger banks in much keener competition with each other and with a number of smaller banks as well. The larger banks tend to broaden the scope of their services more and more; the smaller banks tend to specialize in the kinds of business in which they can compete most effectively.

This development is itself the result of competition. An expanding economy, a growing population, improvements in transportation and communication, and the integration of business into large national corporations have all called for numerous new and improved banking services that the nonspecialized small bank was not and is not capable of performing adequately.

Banks compete with each other (and with many other financial organizations) to render the banking and financial services demanded by all segments of the public. These are many and varied—far more so than in the past. Dozens of banking services common today, from drive-in tellers to account reconciliation, were unheard of forty years ago. The extension of credit is, of course, the basic banking service, but the forms and varities of loan arrangements, from term loans to boat loans, have multiplied beyond the wildest imagination of any past generation of commercial bankers and will continue to evolve. To serve a dynamic

---

[35] "Justice Likely to Appeal Colorado Holding Company Defeat," *American Banker*, Vol. 136, No. 138, July 20, 1971, pp. 1, 23.

economy, the banking structure must remain flexible and must find the resources, primarily of management and organization, to meet even more challenging demands in the future. Only banks that can develop such services will prosper in a competitive banking world.

One cannot stress too often that to compete in banking is primarily to render banking services more effectively than one's competitors. Success in doing so attracts depositors, the wise investment of whose funds yields the profits of the banking business. Rate or price competition is rare in banking except in the sense that rate changes by one bank are generally quickly followed by its competitors. The real nub of competition is the ability to attract and satisfy customers, large and small.

Large banking organizations can specialize in many fields; small banks can specialize effectively only in a few. Thus, larger size, in itself, has become a means of competing more effectively because it broadens the scope of a bank's ability to render service and therefore adds a measure of competitive success (sometimes overrated) that tends to attract large customers.

Most informed persons would agree with this analysis up to a point— the point at which each person feels that banks have become overwhelming in size or that the number of banks has become too small. Perhaps our economic and political heritage has led us to look at competition too much as an end in itself or (in banking) as the means of preventing the evil envisaged as some sort of financial stranglehold on the economy by a concentrated "money power." It is more useful and realistic to look upon the actual results of the concentration that has already taken place. In so doing, one can find little evidence of evil and considerable evidence of public benefit. In general, the largest banks have developed and offered a wide variety of improved services and have paid the maximum rates of interest and charged the lowest rates on loans as well. Their ability and willingness to do so result not only from their somewhat greater operating efficiency but, more importantly, from the fact that they generally face more direct and aggressive competition from other large banks and the smaller specialists than do small banks doing a general banking business in relatively isolated communities.

There are, furthermore, two aspects of banking competition that are frequently overlooked. Even the largest bank is small in comparison with its largest customers. The big national corporations, with their huge holdings of cash and liquid assets, are in a dominant position when they come to even the largest banks in the country to negotiate loan rates and terms or to ask for special services. In addition, nearly every aspect of commercial banks faces strong competition from other financial institutions. On the deposit side are the savings banks and savings and loan associations, which are generally permitted to pay higher rates. On the asset side are a host of institutional lenders, insurance companies, pension funds, savings institutions in the mortgage market, commercial factors, finance companies, and, in many communities, even individuals. The acceptance and commercial paper markets compete for prime borrowers with increasing intensity.

If the preservation of competition in the field of banking is to be a meaningful criterion for judging merger or holding company applications, the supervisory authorities cannot rely on size or number of banks alone. The so-called concentration ratios do not, in themselves, tell the whole story. Rather, the authorities should seek to preserve or foster a competitive pattern in which no one bank overshadows all others and a reasonable number of choices of alternative banking facilities are maintained at various size levels, for the entire range of banking services, at reasonably convenient locations within meaningful market areas. At the same time, they should permit sufficient consolidation to allow commercial banks to compete effectively on a wide scale and not be overshadowed by their largest customers.

The Bank Holding Company Act of 1956 specifically refers to the convenience, needs, and welfare of the community to be served. In a broad sense, this criterion encompasses the maintenance of soundly managed, progressive banks. It will be in the public interest, therefore, to sacrifice in some degree the existence of a larger number of banks if the consolidation results in more effective banking services, lower costs, better management, provision for management or ownership succession— so long as a reasonably balanced pattern of competition is preserved.

THE STRUCTURE OF BANK SUPERVISION

Banking is more closely regulated in the United States than in most other developed countries in the world. At the same time, no other country has as many banks in relation to its population. These facts are not unrelated. On the contrary, the degree and character of bank regulation in the United States spring directly from the nature of our banking structure. The American system of bank regulation has developed over the years in response to the desire for a sound banking system that is also responsive to the credit needs of a dynamic economy. To assure the continuance of such a system should still be one of the basic responsibilities of bank regulatory authorities.

All banks derive their powers from the banking laws, which are, in this sense, permissive. At the same time, the banking laws grant only specifically limited powers and are thus also restrictive. The restrictions are designed to prevent, if possible, our thousands of individual banks from making the mistakes that led to bank failures in the past.

The state and Federal banking authorities are concerned with both regulation and supervision; they administer the banking laws, promulgate and interpret regulations issued thereunder, and exercise impersonal and objective judgments about bank policies in furtherance of the public interest. They use the examination process to keep themselves informed of both the legality and the soundness of individual banks' operations.

In the historical development of the American banking structure, a multiplicity of regulatory agencies has arisen at both the state and Federal levels. Under the concept of dual banking, national banks are chartered and supervised by the Office of the Comptroller of the Currency, and state banks are chartered and supervised in the first instance by the banking authorities of the respective states. Most state-chartered banks, however, have come under Federal supervision and regulation of one kind or another. In becoming members of the Federal Reserve System when it was established, most of the larger state banks submitted themselves voluntarily to many of the restrictions imposed by law on national banks and to examination and supervision by the Board of Governors of the Federal Reserve System.

With the advent of Federal deposit insurance, nearly all the remaining state banks accepted supervision by the Federal Deposit Insurance Corporation as a condition of insurance. There remain fewer than two hundred nonmember, noninsured commercial banks not subject to any direct Federal supervision.

The three Federal regulatory agencies, moreover, have overlapping jurisdictions. The extent of this overlapping is shown in Chart 1. National banks, for example, while chartered and supervised solely by the Comptroller of the Currency, are required to be members of the Federal Reserve System, and their deposits are insured by the Federal Deposit Insurance Corporation. Although the latter agencies seldom exercise their power to examine national banks, they review reports of examination made by national bank examiners. National banks are also subject to some state laws, such as those governing branching authority, legal holidays, and so on.

The crisscrossing of regulatory responsibility is further illustrated by the rules with respect to changes in banking structure. All holding company transactions, including those involving nonmember banks, are under the jurisdiction of the Board of Governors of the Federal Reserve System. The establishment of *de novo* branches requires the approval of the chartering authority, state or national, and for state banks the additional approval of either the Board of Governors or the FDIC, depending on membership status. Merger applications follow the same course, except that each of the three Federal agencies must seek the advice of the other two and of the Department of Justice with respect to the competitive factors involved.

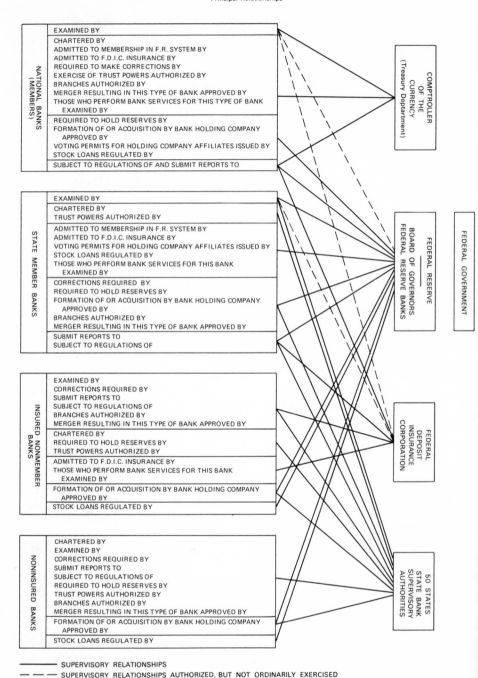

SUPERVISION OF THE COMMERCIAL BANKING SYSTEM
Principal Relationships

NATIONAL BANKS (MEMBERS)
- EXAMINED BY
- CHARTERED BY
- ADMITTED TO MEMBERSHIP IN F.R. SYSTEM BY
- ADMITTED TO F.D.I.C. INSURANCE BY
- REQUIRED TO MAKE CORRECTIONS BY
- EXERCISE OF TRUST POWERS AUTHORIZED BY
- BRANCHES AUTHORIZED BY
- MERGER RESULTING IN THIS TYPE OF BANK APPROVED BY
- THOSE WHO PERFORM BANK SERVICES FOR THIS TYPE OF BANK EXAMINED BY
- REQUIRED TO HOLD RESERVES BY
- FORMATION OF OR ACQUISITION BY BANK HOLDING COMPANY APPROVED BY
- VOTING PERMITS FOR HOLDING COMPANY AFFILIATES ISSUED BY
- STOCK LOANS REGULATED BY
- SUBJECT TO REGULATIONS OF AND SUBMIT REPORTS TO

STATE MEMBER BANKS
- EXAMINED BY
- CHARTERED BY
- TRUST POWERS AUTHORIZED BY
- ADMITTED TO MEMBERSHIP IN F.R. SYSTEM BY
- ADMITTED TO F.D.I.C. INSURANCE BY
- VOTING PERMITS FOR HOLDING COMPANY AFFILIATES ISSUED BY
- STOCK LOANS REGULATED BY
- THOSE WHO PERFORM BANK SERVICES FOR THIS BANK EXAMINED BY
- CORRECTIONS REQUIRED BY
- REQUIRED TO HOLD RESERVES BY
- FORMATION OF OR ACQUISITION BY BANK HOLDING COMPANY APPROVED BY
- BRANCHES AUTHORIZED BY
- MERGER RESULTING IN THIS TYPE OF BANK APPROVED BY
- SUBMIT REPORTS TO
- SUBJECT TO REGULATIONS OF

INSURED NONMEMBER BANKS
- EXAMINED BY
- CORRECTIONS REQUIRED BY
- SUBMIT REPORTS TO
- SUBJECT TO REGULATIONS OF
- BRANCHES AUTHORIZED BY
- MERGER RESULTING IN THIS TYPE OF BANK APPROVED BY
- CHARTERED BY
- REQUIRED TO HOLD RESERVES BY
- TRUST POWERS AUTHORIZED BY
- ADMITTED TO F.D.I.C. INSURANCE BY
- THOSE WHO PERFORM BANK SERVICES FOR THIS BANK EXAMINED BY
- FORMATION OF OR ACQUISITION BY BANK HOLDING COMPANY APPROVED BY
- STOCK LOANS REGULATED BY

NONINSURED BANKS
- CHARTERED BY
- EXAMINED BY
- CORRECTIONS REQUIRED BY
- SUBMIT REPORTS TO
- SUBJECT TO REGULATIONS OF
- REQUIRED TO HOLD RESERVES BY
- TRUST POWERS AUTHORIZED BY
- BRANCHES AUTHORIZED BY
- MERGER RESULTING IN THIS TYPE OF BANK APPROVED BY
- FORMATION OF OR ACQUISITION BY BANK HOLDING COMPANY APPROVED BY
- STOCK LOANS REGULATED BY

COMPTROLLER OF THE CURRENCY (Treasury Department)

FEDERAL RESERVE BOARD OF GOVERNORS FEDERAL RESERVE BANKS

FEDERAL GOVERNMENT

FEDERAL DEPOSIT INSURANCE CORPORATION

50 STATES STATE BANK SUPERVISORY AUTHORITIES

————— SUPERVISORY RELATIONSHIPS
— — — — SUPERVISORY RELATIONSHIPS AUTHORIZED, BUT NOT ORDINARILY EXERCISED

CHART 1 (Source: Federal Reserve Board)

Who actually does the administrative chores? Each of the three Federal agencies has a Washington office with staff members engaged in various aspects of regulatory work. The Comptroller of the Currency maintains a regional chief national bank examiner with a staff of examiners in each of the fourteen national bank regions. Fourteen regional supervising examiners with their respective staffs are employed by the FDIC. Each of the twelve Federal reserve banks includes an examination department, headed by a vice-president and charged with the responsibility of supervising the member banks in that particular district. Each state has a banking commissioner (or person with a similar title) responsible for its regulatory activities.

The organization of bank supervision has been a subject of intense discussion. To the outside observer, the present tripartite Federal supervision must seem as if it would inevitably result in overlapping and inefficiency. From time to time, proposals have been advanced and legislation introduced in Congress to centralize Federal bank supervision in one or another of the existing agencies or to create a new centralized agency with overall supervisory responsibility. These proposals have never been adopted, however, because many people feared that centralization of so much power would lead to arbitrary and perhaps stifling bank supervision and because the present system, hodge-podge as it seems, has worked out well in practice.

During most of our recent history, cooperation among the three Federal agencies, and between them and the state bank supervisors, kept duplication of effort to a minimum. The concept of a dual banking system, although never clearly defined, provided a frame of reference in which reasonable men could work out a common philosophy. Under this system, in essence, the several states had the primary say in questions regarding the banking structure, and the Federal supervisors concerned themselves principally with the adequacy of bank examination procedures, compliance with Federal banking laws and regulations, and general banking safety and solvency.

The standards of the three Federal examining agencies were reasonably uniform. Banks were free to move from one supervisory authority to another by changing the form of their incorporation or by electing membership or nonmembership in the Federal Reserve System. Limited competition among the agencies tended to improve examining techniques and coverage. All this worked very well until the legislation discussed above involved the Federal agencies in cases pertaining to mergers and holding companies. As a result, the potential for conflict among the various Federal and state authorities has increased.

Over the years, a number of proposals have been advanced to centralize Federal bank supervision. The Commission on Money and Credit recommended that the Federal Reserve System be the one Federal supervisory authority. The Advisory Committee to the Comptroller of the Currency recommended that all supervisory, examination, and regulatory authority relating to national banks and all authority pertaining to the formation and expansion of bank holding companies be transferred to the Comptroller of the Currency and that all supervisory, examination, and regulatory authority over state-chartered insured banks be transferred to the Federal Deposit Insurance Corporation. Governor Robertson of the Federal Reserve Board advocated a new five-man Federal Banking Commission that would have full responsibility for all Federal supervisory authority, deposit insurance, and Federal responsibility for structural change.

Despite the logic of uniform administration of Federal law with respect to banking, bankers have consistently objected to centralization of this Federal authority. In mid–1971, the Presidential Commission on Financial Structure and Regulation was urged by a special Committee of the American Bankers Association to "oppose consolidation of the Federal bank regulatory agencies and to concentrate instead on ways of improving the present tripartite regulatory structure." The ABA concluded that "there is little doubt that centralization of Federal bank regulatory authority would mean an end to the dual banking system." It is claimed that the tripartite system has contributed to making the banking industry "the most dynamic and innovative of all regulated industries."[36]

Most people discussing this problem have somehow missed the essential difference between bank supervision and regulation, on the one hand, and the approval of structural changes, on the other. The tripartite system has indeed provided flexibility of supervision and prevented the concentration of the examining and regulatory power that bankers justifiably fear. However, there has never been adequate justification for a national bank to be permitted to open a branch or to acquire another bank through merger under circumstances in which a state-chartered member bank or an insured nonmember state bank would be denied the same privilege. There is one law governing all Federally insured banks, and it should be administered consistently.

To solve this problem, Howard Crosse suggested a modification of Governor Robertson's plan that would leave the examining and regulation of banks in the three agencies as they are now and establish a Federal Banking Commission to pass on structural changes only. Such a Commission, it was suggested, should consist of representatives from each of the three regulatory agencies and perhaps two additional public

---

[36]*Capital,* July 13, 1971, pp. 2–3. News reported weekly by the American Bankers Association.

members who might bring broad legal and economic experience to the deliberations over structural change.[37]

In the final analysis, the soundness of individual banks should be the basic concern of the regulatory authorities; the adequacy of our banking structure is a question of broader public policy that should not be decided within the narrow confines of three competing bureaucracies.

---

[37] Howard D. Crosse, "A Plan for Banking Supervision," *Banking*, Vol. 56, No. 2, August 1963, pp. 42–43.

3
THE STRUCTURE OF A BANK

A commercial bank is much more than a building. It is an organization that combines human effort and financial resources to perform the banking function required by the community it serves and to earn an adequate return on its owners' investment. The character of a bank or banking office reflects the personality and purposes of its management, the objectives it has set for itself, and the methods it has chosen to carry out those objectives. A person who is in frequent contact with banks, such as a bank examiner, can sense the personality of a bank almost as soon as he enters its lobby. In some banks, he finds alertness, in others, indifference; in some, a sense of mission, in others, an air of smug self-importance.

In some small part, these impressions can be derived from the physical appearance of the bank. Low, inviting counters and tasteful decorations bespeak a certain warmth; old-fashioned, floor-to-ceiling cages, in the few places where they are still found, may well represent an ultra-conservative approach to lending as well as to changing times. These impressions are mostly a reaction to the attitudes of officials and employees: the helpful guard, the cheerful teller. These outward appearances are not accidents. They are the product of management decisions and policies, and they lie at the heart of a bank's willingness and ability to perform its functions well. The character of a bank—its appearance, its policies—reflects its organization and is a vital determinant of its ultimate success or failure.

The structure of a bank, in the dynamic sense, encompasses various characteristics that shape or determine its individuality. Among these are its size, the markets it serves, and its own institutional organization. These characteristics are interrelated aspects of a bank's nature that can be separated only for the purpose of study and discussion.

SIZE

In this country, banks range in size from those with deposits of less than $1 million to the very largest banks with deposits in the billions. Size, of course, is relative, but by any reasonable measure the small bank is still the typical bank in the United States. Over half of the nearly 13,800 commercial banks in the United States have deposits of less than $10 million. These are small banks by today's standards. About 5,200 additional banks have deposits of between $10 million and $50 million and could be designated as small-to-medium-sized institutions.[1]

For the sophisticated, city-dwelling student of finance, a really small country bank has to be seen to be believed. To anyone who grew up in a rural community and still remembers the general store, the operations of a small bank are nostalgically familiar. It is a friendly place where every customer is known, usually by his first name. The chief executive officer is as likely as not to be found at a teller's window or proving the incoming exchanges. His desk will be piled high with banking literature and the latest banking regulations, which he has no time to read, but his knowledge of the bank's clientele is intimate and extensive.[2]

Major decisions in such very small banks are usually made not by the active management but by the directors, who are the prominent and usually prosperous businessmen and farmers of a rural community. The president is frequently a local merchant who spends little time in the bank but is available for consultation to the chief operating officer. As a merchant, he is thoroughly familiar with the credit standing of every citizen in the community. He has their accounts on his own books as well as on those of the bank. Typically, he has a fairly large stockholding

---

[1]*Annual Report of the Federal Deposit Insurance Corporation, 1971* (Washington: Federal Deposit Insurance Corporation, 1972), p. 189.

[2]Edward H. McMahan, Hearing Examiner, *Report and Recommended Decision,* in Re Application of BACOHIO CORPORATION Pursuant to Section 3(a)(2) of the Bank Holding Company Act of 1956, for approval of acquisition of up to 100 percent of the voting shares of The Hilliard Bank, Hilliards, Ohio. (Docket No. BHC-56) heard in Columbus, Ohio, May 31-June 2, 1960. The examiner's findings of fact with respect to The Hilliard Bank constitute a classic description of a small bank (deposits of $2,900,000).

in the bank, and whatever he receives in salary is less important to him than an increase in the value of his investment.

Small banks fill an important need in the small communities they serve, but they seldom serve those communities to the fullest extent possible. Their loan-deposit ratios are below average, they are seldom interested in consumer lending, and they have neither the time nor the technical knowledge to accommodate an unusual or complicated request for credit.[3]

Small banks tend to be director-managed, because they do not earn enough to afford top-grade operating management in today's competitive market for banking talent. A study of thirty-two banks in the Second National Bank Region that had total deposits of under $5 million showed that the median salary of the highest-paid officer was slightly less than $10,200 per annum and that this was seldom supplemented by any pension or insurance benefits. The average age of these officers was fifty-seven years. In other words, near the peak of their earning power, the officers of these small banks were being paid less than a junior bank examiner or a senior clerk in a large bank. In most cases, these salaries were substantially lower than those paid by large branch banking organizations to the managers of comparable offices. The second officer in these thirty-two banks was paid, on the average, $7,900 per annum, less than large banks pay college-graduate trainees with no banking experience whatsoever.[4]

In most of these banks, the examiner rated the management as ranging from fair to poor.[5] In many of the cases, the examiner considered

---

[3]McMahan, *op cit.* "The bank has never offered any consumer credit program ...it has turned away installment loan applications because the cashier has so many duties he is physically unable to handle them.... The cashier is reluctant to make any loans when it appears that out of the ordinary procedures will have to be followed to handle or collect them. In his own words he says he prefers 'to make a loan and collect it when I make it.'" (Finding No. 15, p. 12.)

"In February, 1951, the most substantial business establishment at Hilliards presented negotiable warehouse receipts on soybeans to the bank in an effort to secure funds to finance the soybean crop. They were turned down by the bank and moved their account to a Columbus bank in order to secure adequate financing for their business." (Finding No. 17(a), p. 13.)

"A real estate broker in Hilliards refers to the continuing growth of the community over the past few years, and points out that there is only one general banking facility. He states that the service which the bank...can provide the community is entirely inadequate." (Finding No. 17(c), p. 13.)

[4]Charles M. Van Horn, "Officers' Salaries: New York National Banks," Unpublished remarks made at 41st Annual Meeting of the New York State Bankers Association, 1969.

[5]National Bank Examiners frequently characterize such management as being "of mediocre ability but sincere in effort."

the problem of management succession to be an immediate one. In most of the remaining instances, the problem was present but not acute, only because the managing officer had not yet reached the age of sixty.

The inability of small banks to attract and keep highly competent management is inherent in their limited earning power. The problem is particularly acute for the very small bank but is still present in a significant number of the commercial banks in the United States with deposits under $10 million (over half of all banks are in this size category). In 1971, for example, insured banks with deposits of from $2 million to $5 million had average operating income (before expenses and taxes) of 6.0 percent on total assets and spent an average of about 23 percent of gross earnings on salaries and wages.[6] Thus, a bank with resources of $5 million might earn about $300,000 and have about $70,000 with which to compensate a staff of four officers and six to ten clerks. Such a bank might pay from $15,000 to $20,000 for a top man and perhaps $9,000 to $15,000 for a second man; however, after the clerical personnel have been adequately compensated, there is usually too little left over for junior officers of the caliber that would assure competent management succession from within the organization. In even smaller banks, the problem is more acute. One result is that the better junior officers all too frequently leave small banks to obtain higher remuneration and wider opportunity in larger banks.

Many small banks persist—partly because of the sentimental attachment of important segments of the American public to home-town unit banking and partly for other psychological and economic reasons. The directors of small banks, who are usually also the principal stockholders, take a great deal of pride in the banks they direct and a paternalistic view of the communities they serve.[7] They have the time and the knowledge of local affairs to supply management at the relatively low cost of directors' fees, and they manage most small banks safely and soundly, if not progressively.

Small banks can still justify their existence in terms of profitability partly because their salary scales are low and partly because a greater proportion of their net profits are taxed at a relatively low rate (Federal

---

[6]*Annual Report of the Federal Deposit Insurance Corporation, 1971* (Washington: Federal Deposit Insurance Corporation, 1972) p. 221.

[7]McMahan, *op. cit.* "The President is Minar W. Schofield, age 75, who has been engaged in farming all his life on the farm operated by his father and grandfather. His father was one of the founders of the bank and its first president...Dr. Jesse Jasper, a physician, and Jack Alder, owner of the Chevrolet agency in Hilliards, whose grandfather was one of the founders of the bank, are the two other shareholders who, together with the officers, compose the Board of Directors." (Finding No. 2, p. 7.)

income tax specifies a rate of 26 percent on corporate profits up to $25,000 and 48 percent on corporate profits above that amount).[8]

Because of these advantages, the net profits of banks with deposits of under $5 million compare favorably with those of larger banks (see Table 3). For example, in 1970, profits as a percentage of assets for the smaller banks exceeded those for the larger banks and their return on invested capital was lower only because of the smaller banks' higher capital ratios.[9]

Although small banks are numerous and profitable despite their management problems, it is the large banks that control the major portion of the nation's banking resources. As shown in Table 3, banks with total

TABLE 3

SIZE AND PROFITABILITY OF INSURED COMMERCIAL BANKS
DECEMBER 31, 1971

Deposit Size ($Millions)	No. of Insured Commercial Banks	Percentage of Total Deposits	Operating Income as Percentage of Assets	Net Profit as Percentage of Assets	Net Profit as Percentage of Capital Funds	Capital as Percentage of Total Assets
Under 1	146	.02	5.96	.92	5.65	16.28
1 to 2	732	.22	6.05	.91	8.01	11.30
2 to 5	3,004	1.92	6.01	.87	9.61	9.08
5 to 10	3,333	4.48	5.94	.90	11.10	8.11
10 to 25	3,756	10.77	5.97	.90	12.07	7.48
25 to 50	1,404	9.09	5.92	.88	12.29	7.16
50 to 100	608	7.80	5.96	.86	11.93	7.17
100 to 500	479	18.17	5.74	.84	11.70	7.21
500 to 1000	85	10.85	5.81	.84	11.55	7.25
Over 1000	63	36.68	5.45	.76	10.44	7.26

Source: *Annual Report of the Federal Deposit Insurance Corporation, 1971* (Washington: Federal Deposit Insurance Corporation, 1972), pp. 189–222.

deposits of $50 million or more held over 70 percent of the aggregate deposits of all insured commercial banks at the start of 1972.

---

[8]According to average operating ratios, a bank would have to have deposits in excess of $2,300,000 before any of its operating earnings would be subject to taxes at the higher rate. Inclusion of tax-exempt income would increase this figure.

[9]Two recent studies of the probability of small banks are by Ernest Kohn, *The Future of Small Banks* (New York: New York State Banking Department, 1966), and Nancy H. Mead, *The Performance of Small Banks* (Washington: The American Bankers Association, Research Paper No. 5, 1970).

Only the very large commercial banks—probably those with resources of over $500 million—can adequately serve the needs of large national corporations or engage to a significant degree in such activities as the underwriting of municipal securities, active trading in money-market instruments, or participation in the rapid expansion of international banking. Even so, the large national corporations nearly always use the facilities of several banks.

As banks become larger, they acquire a greater degree of flexibility, but at the same time their management problems become more complex. Fortunately, they are able to attract the necessary competence to deal with the greater complexities. Most of the discussion of the formation of commercial bank policy in subsequent chapters is pertinent primarily to the bank with resources of at least $10 million. Until a bank reaches approximately that size, it cannot afford management specialization for studying its problems separately. There is little point in designing an organization chart for the very small bank where the cashier plays all of the executive and some of the clerical roles. By contrast, organizational responsibility needs to be clearly defined in larger banks, where personnel administration, for example, is a separate function.

Large size brings its own special problems. The cashier of a $2 million bank not only knows most of his customers intimately but works in constant close association with the people under his direction. In large banks, not only do the customers tend to become impersonal individuals known chiefly through the medium of account numbers of financial statements and credit checkings but even the employees lose their individuality for the senior officers. In very large banks, it is not unusual for the officers themselves to complain that they have little personal contact with the "head man," who is often also the mysterious fountainhead of policies that may seem arbitrary and unrelated to the reality of the officers' daily and practical problems.

Larger banks, in short, require decentralization and delegation of managerial authority. Such decentralization and specialization call for greater management skills. At the same time, the greater earnings and economies that derive from size and specialization should provide the means to attract and train officers of the requisite caliber.

MARKETS SERVED

The structure of a bank is shaped in a number of ways by the community it serves. The credit needs of that community largely determine the fields of lending in which a bank specializes, and the nature of the community determines the other banking services expected. Rural banks tend to engage in farm lending, whereas suburban banks specialize in mortgage loans and consumer credit. A bank's costs are also affected by its location. Salaries, as shown above, tend to be lower in small, rural communities and higher where there is active competition from industry or government for clerical personnel.

Location affects a bank's needs for liquidity. For example, banks in resort and farm areas tend to have wider seasonal swings in loans and deposits than do banks of comparable size in suburban areas. In similar fashion, a bank's exposure to risk may be increased by the lack of diversification in the business of the community it serves. One of the advantages of regional branch banking systems is their ability to average out the problems of the particular localities that they serve.

It is the specific locality served by a bank rather than any marked differences among broad geographical areas that affects its operations. For example, comparisons between similar groups of banks in New York and Iowa or Kansas show only minor variations in their operating results or ratios of asset distribution. The differences among individual banks even in neighboring localities are usually far greater. One of the important tasks of bank management is to keep fully aware of local banking needs and seek to contribute in every appropriate way to the health and growth of the community that the bank serves.

Character of Business

Although the character of a bank's business is largely determined by the community it serves, within large communities some banks specialize in serving particular segments of the market for banking services. Among the big banks in New York City can be found the predominantly wholesale banks, which deal largely with other banks and national corporations. Their character is entirely different from the equally big (or even bigger) banks that, through extensive branch networks, do a retail as well as wholesale banking business. By the same token, the smaller banks that serve only particular neighborhoods or trades within the city have a still different character.

Whenever there are two or more banks serving the same community, such specialties are likely to be found. One bank will stress trust services, another, consumer lending or service tailored to the needs of smaller businesses. One bank will aggressively seek savings deposits, another will concentrate on commercial lending. This kind of specialization reflects the predilections and special skills of management and represents still another facet of a bank's individuality.

MANAGEMENT ORGANIZATION

Size, location, and the special nature of a bank's business may delineate the potentialities of a bank, but its own organization determines its individual character. Banks of like size, located in similar communities and doing about the same kind of business, still differ markedly in individual character and, what is even more significant, in results. Some banks grow and prosper in areas with seemingly low potential, while others stagnate in thriving communities. The difference lies at the heart of the problem of bank management.

The organization of a bank, in the sense that it is used here, is the unique management arrangements that have been devised and used by an individual bank to enable it to perform the banking function in its community or trade area. This organization includes those too often silent and neglected partners, the bank's shareholders, who have placed their capital at risk in the hope of profit to be derived from the lending and investing of deposits. To perform its functions well, a bank also needs a balanced combination of sound direction and competent executive management. All three elements in the organization of a bank—shareholders, directors, and officers—have vital roles to play if the individual bank is to develop its capabilities to the fullest extent.

Board of Directors

Ideally, direction should originate from the directors of a bank, who have the responsibility for determining its policies and the opportunity of doing so in ways that will make it effective in the community and profitable for the stockholders. The Board of Directors, therefore, appropriately heads the organization charts that depict the management arrangements devised by most banks.

A great deal has been written about the duties and responsibilities of bank directors, much of it by the courts. In a leading case, Judge Finkelburg stated:

> Briefly summarized, I understand the law on this subject to be as follows:
>
> (1) Directors are charged with the duty of reasonable supervision over the affairs of the bank. It is their duty to use ordinary diligence in ascertaining the condition of its business, and to exercise reasonable control and supervision over its affairs.
>
> (2) They are not insurers or guarantors of the fidelity and proper conduct of the executive officers of the bank, and they are not responsible for losses resulting from their wrongful acts or omissions, provided they have exercised ordinary care in the discharge of their own duties as directors.

(3) Ordinary care, in this matter as in other departments of the law, means that degree of care which ordinarily prudent and diligent men would exercise under similar circumstances.

(4) The degree of care required further depends upon the subject to which it is to be applied, and each case must be determined in view of all the circumstances.

(5) If nothing has come to their knowledge to awaken suspicion that something is going wrong, ordinary attention to the affairs of the institution is sufficient. If, upon the other hand, directors know, or by the exercise of ordinary care should have known, any facts which would awaken suspicion and put a prudent man on his guard, then a degree of care commensurate with the evil to be avoided is required, and a want of that care makes them responsibile. Directors cannot, in justice to those who deal with the bank, shut their eyes to what is going on around them.

(6) Directors are not expected to watch the routine of every day's business, but they ought to have a general knowledge of the manner in which the bank's business is conducted, and upon what securities its larger lines of credit are given, and generally to know of and give direction to the important and general affairs of the bank.

(7) It is incumbent upon bank directors in the exercise of ordinary prudence, and as a part of their duty of general supervision to cause an examination of the condition and resources of the bank to be made with reasonable frequency. . . .[10]

Thus, it has been well established that the legal responsibility for the operations of a bank rests with its directors and that they "are under a duty to use ordinary care and prudence in the administration of the affairs of the bank and if through their failure to do so a loss to the bank results, they may be held liable for such loss in a civil action for damages."[11] This legalistic concept of responsibility, important and binding as it is, only scrapes the surface of the directorial function.[12]

The first responsibility of the directorate is to define the business of the bank and to determine its objectives for the stockholder, the depositor, and the community it serves. Herein lies the importance of a clear understanding of the banking functions discussed in Chapter 1. If the directors are aware, in general terms, that it is the essential business of a bank to supply the legitimate credit needs of the community, it is a natural

---

[10]Rankin v. Cooper, 149 Fed., 1010, Briggs v. Spaulding, 141 U.S. 132, and Gibbons v. Anderson, 80 Fed. 345.

[11]*Duties and Liabilities of Directors of National Banks,* Form 1417, Treasury Department, Office of the Comptroller of the Currency.

[12]The booklet *A Bank Director's Job,* published by the American Bankers Association (Washington, 1964), contains a discussion of eighteen areas of bank directors' responsibilities. It should be read by all bank directors.

second step for them to determine what kind of loans and how many of each the bank should make. The directors will thus formulate a lending policy in accordance with the bank's objectives.

If the directors are aware that deposits are the raw material of the bank's lending and investment business, they will be in a better position to establish the bank's objectives with respect to the deposit and other services it should render to its customers. These considerations will have important bearing on banking hours, physical facilities, and the rate of interest paid on savings deposits. If the directors are conscious of their responsibility to shareholders, they can more effectively consider and plan the level of profits required to keep the bank's capital attractive to the public and still maintain a competent and adequately paid staff. Objectives can and should be set with respect to public relations, personnel training and development, and community progress. Directors should also be aware of the risks in banking, discussed in the following chapter, and establish objectives for minimizing those risks for the bank they are directing.

Having determined the objectives, the directors must next measure the bank's accomplishments. One way of doing this is by self-comparison. Most directors are furnished with monthly and other periodical statements of the bank, which form a basis for judging the bank's progress. It is especially helpful to chart or graph the principal asset and liability accounts and the chief components of the bank's earnings, so that self-appraisal may be visual as well as statistical.

A second method of measuring a bank's accomplishment is to compare it with similar banks. All supervisory authorities and many banking associations publish, at least annually, average ratio figures of earnings, expenses, and asset distribution for banks in groupings of similar size. In making such comparisons, however, the director should not let himself be lulled into complacency merely because his bank is as good as the average. *Average* is but a synonym for *mediocre*, particularly when applied to bank statistics.

The most important but least frequently used method of measuring a bank's success is to compare its results with its clearly defined objectives. Every bank is required to publish its assets and liabilities periodically. As a part of establishing its objectives, each bank should also have unpublished figures for six, twelve, and perhaps twenty-four months ahead. The bank's results should be compared with these carefully planned budgets and significant differences between plans and results should be explained.

In establishing objectives and measuring accomplishments, bank directors should see to it that their banks have some form of cost analysis and carefully planned budgets. The directors should be thinking about the adequacy of the bank's capital and should be aware of its liquidity needs. They should also be formulating the bank's lending and investing policies and planning its new business development program and any projected large capital expenditures.

Directors also have to serve as the court of last resort, to which all unresolved problems and policy questions are referred. This is a responsibility that directors seldom escape, but they have the opportunity to avoid many emergency problems by careful forward planning. A periodic review of the organization and a clear delineation of responsibility, preferably in writing, will prevent many problems from arising. The establishment and supervision of effective personnel policies is a clear directorial duty.

Finally, the directors have the responsibility for developing managers and for assuring the adequacy of the rewards to management, the tools furnished to management, and management methods. They must, therefore, see to it that a well-functioning training program is kept in operation and that adequate salary incentives are provided. In addition, they must make certain that the staff has adequate space in which to work and that it is not handicapped by antiquated equipment and methods. The widespread failure of directors to meet this particular group of responsibilities has been an important contributing cause of bank mergers.[13]

It should be emphasized that it is the function of directors to direct and not to manage.[14] In small banks, directors may be required to make executive decisions because the bank cannot afford (or at least does not have) adequately trained executive management. Sometimes, however, the habit of managing tends to persist with the directors as the bank grows larger, and in too many moderate-sized banks the officers are not granted adequate executive authority to make on-the-spot decisions. Nevertheless, although directors ideally should not exercise executive authority, they should keep closely informed about the actions of the

---

[13]McMahan, *Report and Recommended Decision, Bancohio Corporation, op. cit.* The examiner's findings with respect to the management situation perfectly illustrate this point. "Since there is no assistant with authority to act for the cashier, and no employee trained to take his place, in the event of absence on the part of the cashier for a period of time, the bank, as presently operated, is without a credit or lending officer on active duty at such time.... The situation, as it is, has existed for some time, and although it is critical, and the directors recognize such, they continue to take no action.... They hesitate to take the steps they know they should take, because of the dread of responsibility with regard to enlarging the space so as to provide room for any addition to the Bank's staff, and because of the extra expense involved" (Finding No. 12, p. 11).

[14]The section entitled "Let Management Manage" in *A Bank Director's Job, op. cit.,* discusses the differences between making policy and administering it.

executive officers and remain vitally interested counselors to those officers.

A Board of Directors functions most effectively through committees or, if the number of directors is small, through the assignment of specific areas of knowledge to individual directors. In the case of large boards, it is customary to establish a smaller Executive Committee, which meets more frequently to review the bank's operations. Although certain outstanding directors may constitute the core of this committee, other directors should be required to serve on it in rotation. An examining committee and, if the bank exercises trust powers, a trust committee are required by law. Banks frequently have loan committees and sometimes investment committees. Too few banks, however, have directors' operations committees or business development committees.[15] For a board to function at its best, each of the important areas of the directors' responsibilities should be assigned to a special committee (or even to an individual director), whose plans and progress should be frequently reported back to the full board.

It is difficult to generalize about the composition of bank directorates. The size and location of the bank affect this aspect of a bank's nature as they do others. Larger banks tend to have more directors. Federal law sets a minimum of five and a maximum of twenty-five. According to a study made by the Federal Reserve Bank of Richmond for the Virginia Bankers Association several years ago, the typical $5 million country bank had an average of eight directors. In such banks, 45 percent of the directors were businessmen, 17 percent professional people, 13 percent farmers, 14 percent bank officers, and 11 percent retired and other. Twenty-five percent of the directors were over sixty-five years of age, 52 percent over fifty-five. This distribution probably was and still is typical of banks throughout the country.

Most successful and responsible businessmen and professional people enjoy being bank directors. A directorship in the local bank seems to carry an extra measure of prestige and tends to be among the last position that men relinquish as they retire gradually from full and active participation in business life. As a consequence, the aging of directors is a problem that many banks face. There is no certain age at which all men cease to think imaginatively and constructively, but the tendency to

---

[15]A country bank in New York State recently developed a "director-officer program." Each of its directors is assigned to work with the officers in one or more of twelve different areas: investments, loans and mortgages, records and building, personnel and salaries, business development, branch advisory, audit, methods and systems, cash and tellers, insurance, public relations, and installment loan policy.

resist change increases observably with age.[16] Because the ability to adapt to an ever-changing environment is a requisite of survival in the banking context as elsewhere, the problem of an aging board can be a serious bar to progress. Increasingly, banks are facing up to this problem by setting a retirement age for directors (usually around seventy). Directors reaching this age are designated honorary or emeritus. They continue to attend meetings and to give the bank the benefit of their experience, but they have no vote in final decisions of policy. What is more important, their places on the board are thus made available for younger and perhaps more progressive directors, the new blood that is needed to keep an organization alert to changing conditions in the community it serves.

Executive Management

Up to this point, our discussion has emphasized the role of the directors in establishing policy. Important as that role is, it is seldom performed (except in very small banks) without the active leadership and participation of the senior executive officers. It is the function of executive management not only to carry out policy but, even more importantly, to propose it.

The chief executive officer of the bank and often two or more of the senior officers fill a dual role as both officers and directors.[17] As officer-directors, it is their function to provide leadership and direction to the board. As professional bankers, the officer-directors can be presumed to have the technical training and experience to analyze the banking problems that face the institution and to present them to the full board in sufficient detail and with enough background for the board to determine policy wisely and effectively.

Competent management actively seeks the advice and counsel of the directors. It assumes the responsibility for keeping the directors interested as well as informed. It provokes discussion and works diligently to keep board meetings from becoming merely routine, seeking ways to present the bank's problems that will stimulate director participation. Management of this caliber is constantly seeking new directors who will

---

[16]In the late 1930s, when Federally insured mortgages were still an innovation, an informal survey of member banks in the Second Federal Reserve District showed that the proportion of such mortgages to total loans was roughly in inverse proportion to the age of the bank president.

[17]The president of a national bank is required by law to be a director (U.S.C. Title 12, Sec. 76). Similar provisions are contained in most state banking laws. When the president is inactive (as in many small banks), the cashier may or may not be a director. If he is not, one can be certain that the bank is director-managed.

add varied viewpoints to the counsel of the board, directors who will bring new ideas as well as new business to the bank.

By contrast, some bank officers seem to mistrust their directors. They like to keep the number small and to avoid different viewpoints on the board in order to escape what they would term controversy or interference. They try to insulate the board from bank examiners and other outside influences, apparently for fear that management policies or practices may be questioned. Life may be easier for the senior executive if he knows that the board meetings will hold no surprises and no searching or perhaps embarrassing questions, but this is a shortsighted approach that will eventually slow down the bank's progress.

When policies and objectives have been established by the board under the leadership of senior management, it becomes the duty and responsibility of management to carry them out. In general terms, the fundamental principles of good bank management call for a clear definition and explicit delegation of management responsibilities. These are often depicted on an organization chart, but such a chart bears the same relationship to reality as a two-dimensional photograph bears to a human personality. It is the way in which the officers and directors work together to build a structure based on a combination of teamwork and individual responsibility that will give each bank its unique personality.

Stockholders

Part of a bank's special character is related to the distribution of its stock. A bank's stock may be closely held by a single individual or a relatively small group, such as the Board of Directors, or it can be widely distributed in the community or country. The directors and management of many small banks and even of some fairly sizable ones deliberately seek to maintain close control. In other banks, management seeks to distribute the stock as widely as possible in the community. Such wide distribution in small lots tends to make a bank more community-minded. Ownership succession is facilitated, and a bank's ability to remain independent is enhanced.

A large group of informed and loyal stockholders can be a valuable asset in a bank's public relations and business development programs. Bank directors who represent numerous small shareholders are more likely to put the interests of the bank and the community before their own and to look upon their directorships as public service. Although these comments are broad generalizations to which many exceptions can be found, in recent years, most of the banks that the supervisory authorities would consider "problem banks" have been institutions owned or controlled by a single individual or a small group.[18]

THE BALANCE SHEET

A final aspect in the structure of a bank is the composition of its assets and liabilities. An examination of how a bank has obtained funds, for example, through the various types of deposits, Federal funds, or capital, and how it has used those funds it has obtained usually reveals significant information about management decisions and policies. Table 4 presents a simplified balance sheet for the hypothetical ABC National Bank as of December 31, 1973. The ABC Bank, like any other corporation, owns nothing itself. Every asset that the bank has must have been obtained with funds supplied by depositors, other creditors, owners, and so on. Bank assets represent uses to which the bank has put the money supplied by others, and bank laibilities, in essence, represent those who supplied the money to obtain the assets. The principal assets and liabilities are described in the following paragraphs.

Assets

Cash and amounts due from banks include coins and currency kept in the bank and the deposits kept by member banks at their district Federal Reserve bank. Banks that are not members of the Federal Reserve maintain similar reserves and clearing deposits at other commercial banks. Correspondent demand deposit balances (deposits kept in other banks to compensate for advice, collection, and other services) and checks in process of collection are also included in this category.

U.S. Treasury and agency securities include all U.S. government and U.S. government agency securities held by the bank, regardless of their maturity dates. These securities are valued at their original cost to the bank and not at their current market value.

State and municipal obligations and *other securities* include all secu-

---

[18]The problem of "dominated banks" is not a new one. Comptroller of the Currency Pole, testifying before a Subcommittee of the Senate Committee on Banking and Currency, indicated that supervisory persuasion was effective in some cases but "...in others, Mr. Chairman, where the board may be obdurate or the bank may be under the domination of a single person, which is very often the case, you can exact any sort of promise but performance is another thing." "Operations of the National and Federal Reserve Banking Systems," *Hearings Pursuant to Senate Resolution 71,* January 19, 1931, p. 5.

TABLE 4

BALANCE SHEET

The ABC National Bank
December 31, 1973
(000 omitted)

ASSETS

Cash and amounts due from banks	$ 9,144
U.S. Treasury and agency securities	3,802
State and municipal obligations	9,590
Other securities	147
Federal funds sold	1,000
Loans (less reserve for losses)	60,130
Accrued interest receivable	339
Bank premises and equipment (net)	2,370
Other assets	402
Total Assets	$86,924

LIABILITIES

Demand deposits	$32,378
Savings deposits	16,274
Time deposits	22,999
Federal funds purchased	4,000
Other borrowing	1,500
Accrued taxes and liabilities	2,338
Capital debentures	1,000
Capital stock	2,498
Surplus	2,623
Contingency reserves	305
Undivided profits	1,009
Total Liabilities	$86,924

rities in these categories, regardless of their maturity or credit rating, valued at what they cost the bank at the time they were purchased.

Federal funds sold are temporary (and in some cases longer-term) transfers of reserves made by the bank to other banks in need of reserves or money for other short-term use.

Loans include commercial and industrial loans; agricultural loans; loans based on the collateral of stocks, bonds, or other marketable securities; installment loans; mortgage loans; and other individually negotiated loans to all types of bank customers. Few banks classify loans according to expected repayment patterns or degree of risk.

Accrued interest receivable is the amount of uncollected interest the bank has earned on its securities and loans as of the statement date.

Bank premises and equipment are shown as the cost (after an allowance for depreciation) of the quarters and equipment used in the conduct of the bank's business.

Other assets is a catchall category for assets not specifically mentioned elsewhere and typically includes prepaid expenses and items pending collection or allocation to other accounts.

Liabilities

Demand deposits, savings deposits, and *time deposits* are accounts reflecting the primary forms in which funds are deposited in the bank. Total deposits nearly always constitute a substantial majority of all bank funds, although the proportion received in each of the three primary forms tends to vary widely. Further differences in the sources (for example, individual, commercial, public, bank, and so on), forms (for example, small consumer savings or large negotiable certificates of deposit), and maturity of deposits are not usually included in public reports.

Federal funds purchased represent temporary (and for some banks longer-term) borrowing of reserves by the bank from other banks with reserves of funds in excess of the amounts they are legally required to hold.

Other borrowing may include funds borrowed for short periods from the Federal Reserve discount window, funds larger banks have borrowed from their European branches, agreements to repurchase securities at a fixed price on some specified date, commercial paper, and so on. In recent periods of severe monetary restraint, these other borrowings have proven a significant source of funds for some banks.

Accrued taxes and other liabilities are funds set aside in the bank's accounting to pay taxes, interest on deposits, and other operating expenses incurred before the end of the accounting period but not yet paid. This account shows that the increases in assets it causes have not been earned for the stockholders but belong to governments, depositors, or others who will receive it soon. Generally, this account is never closed because new accruals replace accruals that are being paid.

Capital debentures (also called subordinated debentures or capital notes) represent indebtedness of the bank. The debenture or note holders receive a claim that is subordinated to the claims of depositors. For this reason, these debt instruments are now considered part of a bank's capital in the determination of its capital adequacy. Because funds raised in this manner are borrowed, there is no dilution of equity in the bank. However, banks issuing debentures have to be concerned with the payment of fixed interest and the repayment of principal at maturity.

Capital stock is the par (or nominal) value of the stock originally bought by the bank's shareholders or the par value portion of additional stock sold at a later date. It also includes the par (or nominal) value of stock distributed to stockholders in stock dividends.

Surplus consists of the sums payed by the shareholders in excess of the par value of the common stock both at the time of original issue and when additional common stock is sold at a price in excess of par value. This is called paid-in surplus. In most banks, the surplus account has been further augmented by transfers from accumulated earnings (undivided profits). National banks are required to make such transfers until surplus equals capital stock. In addition, in some states, the legal lending limit is based on the sum of capital stock and surplus, so that transfers from undivided profits to surplus increase the banks ability to meet the credit demands of its larger customers.

Contingency reserves are established by some banks against the possibility that unforeseeable losses will occur, such as an unanticipated trust department surcharge, or simply from their abundance of conservatism. Such reserves are a part of the stockholders equity. Some banks show their Reserve for Loan Losses as a capital (contingency) reserve. It is more properly deducted from total loans, even though there are no known loan losses at the moment. Reserves against securities established with the profits on securities sold are occasionally shown as a capital reserve but are more conservatively deducted from the securities account in anticipation of future losses.

Undivided profits includes all funds earned by the bank and not paid out as dividends or allocated elsewhere. This account is part of a bank's total capital, because earnings are actually owned by the shareholders of the bank, even if they have been left in the bank, temporarily or permanently, for the bank's use.

The ways in which a bank has obtained funds and how it has used these funds are reflected in these balance sheet accounts. The composition of a bank's assets and liabilities tells interested parties much about the bank's structure, its earnings, and the risks it has undertaken to attain these earnings.

PART II

BASIC CONSIDERATIONS IN BANKING

4

BANKING RISKS

The preceding discussion of the functions and structure of commercial banking does not emphasize sufficiently one essential element of the nature of banking—its risk. The specific bank policies to be explored in subsequent chapters must always be adopted with an eye for minimizing risks as well as maximizing return. A brief review of the principal risks of banking and an appraisal of their magnitude in the past will, therefore, serve as a useful backdrop for further discussion of specific policies.

Taking risks can almost be said to be the business of bank management. A bank that is run on the principle of avoiding all risks, or as many of them as possible, will be a stagnant institution and will not adequately serve the legitimate credit needs of its community. On the other hand, a bank that takes excessive risks or, what is more likely, takes them without recognizing their extent or even their existence will surely run into difficulty. Particularly in times of expanding business activities, some of the risks of banking may be obscured beneath the general economic prosperity, and banks may seem to take large risks without apparent penalty; however, the seeds of unwise banking will sprout inevitably into losses in the first serious business recession. They always have in the past.

In this chapter, we will analyze the nature of the principal banking risks and evaluate their past impact on banking. Subsequent chapters will be concerned with some of the management techniques that enable banks to guard against or minimize these risks.

THE CREDIT RISK

The most obvious risk in banking is the credit risk—the possibility that loans will not be repaid or that investments will deteriorate in quality or go into default with consequent loss to the bank. Few bankers ever knowingly make poor loans or investments. It is what occurs after a loan or investment is made that causes it to deteriorate in quality. Such adverse circumstances may sometimes be foreseen, as when obvious credit weaknesses are overlooked or ignored. However, many are unforeseeable. One cannot extend credit successfully on the premise of a major economic downturn in the foreseeable future. One cannot predict the impact of war or threats of war on the economy; one cannot even predict, very far ahead, changes in consumer demand that may affect the business of a borrower or even the business of an entire community. These risks to the quality of bank credit are always present.

Protection against the risks of lending and investing consists of maintaining high credit standards, appropriate diversification, intimate knowledge of the borrower's affairs, and alert collection procedures. These principles, as they apply to various kinds of loans and investments, are discussed in detail in Chapters 8 through 13.

RISKS ASSOCIATED WITH LIQUIDITY NEEDS

Another ever-present risk in banking is the possibility that customer demands for funds will require the sale or forced collection of credit-worthy assets at a loss. A depositor's demand for his money is one that a bank must meet promptly or go out of business. During a rapid economic decline, such as was experienced in the Depression of the 1930s, such demands come primarily from depositors seeking to convert their bank deposits into currency because of a general lack of confidence in banks. The danger of such money panics and their attendant runs on banks has been greatly reduced. Federal deposit insurance has become a stout bulwark of confidence, and greatly improved bank supervision and stricter banking laws have materially strengthened the banking structure. Nevertheless, bank management may still be called upon to meet depositors' demands for their money. In the credit crunches of 1966 and 1969–70, banks had to meet the withdrawal demands of depositors who were able to earn significantly higher returns on alternative investments.

The demands for funds that are made on banks in times of high economic activity are equally important to banking policy. In such times, bank depositors tend to use their funds more actively and banks are subject to heavy demands for loans from their customers. The increasing demand deposit turnover does not decrease the aggregate of demand deposits, but the rapid shift of deposits from one bank to another can prove embarrassing to the bank that loses them.

The increasing demand for loans is generally more significant than increasing turnover for commercial banks. In the process of increasing loans, the banking system creates new deposits for which additional reserves must be found. If the Federal Reserve System is following a tight monetary policy, which would be typical in a time of high economic activity, it may be unwilling to supply all of these reserves. As a result, commercial banks would have to meet part or all of their large loan demands from the sale of securities. Under the pressures of extensive demand for credit, interest rates rise, and the prices of fixed-interest obligations fall. Thus, the liquidation of investments to increase loans could be, and in recent times has been, a costly process. Such liquidation may be particularly costly if a bank is forced to sell bonds of intermediate or longer-term maturity, the price of which could be substantially affected by even modest changes in interest rates.

The amount of forced liquidation due to liquidity needs will vary widely among individual commercial banks. One might imagine that a bank could always refuse to make additional loans, and in some cases it could, but, when the request for credit comes from a depositor of long standing who normally maintains sizable deposit balances, the refusal to lend could easily lead to the withdrawal of deposits and the loss of a valuable customer. For example, a community bank in which the local municipality has maintained sizable balances for years could hardly afford not to accommodate the town's desire to negotiate bond-anticipation notes for a new school project. Even in the case of potential new customers, the bank has to consider its foregone opportunities for valuable, long-term business.

To protect itself against the risks associated with liquidity needs, a bank must maintain adequate liquidity in the form of assets readily convertible into cash at a minimum risk of loss. A discussion of how banks can estimate their liquidity needs, both short- and long-term, and of the provisions that can be made to meet these needs is contained in Chapters 8 and 9.

THE RISKS OF DEFALCATION AND THEFT

The credit risk and the risks associated with liquidity needs are normal banking risks. Unfortunately, there are other risks in banking from which not even the cash-in-vault is safe—the risk of defalcation (embezzlement) and the risk of theft by outsiders. The risk of defalcation is present in good times as well as bad and will remain a banking risk as long as banks employ people and as long as people are subject to the financial, social, and moral pressures of society. Internal controls and audits, along with adequate fidelity insurance, are essential to a bank's protection from the risks of loss and embarrassment resulting from the dishonest acts of its officers or employees. The risk of theft by outsiders can never be completely overcome, but can be reduced (both in incidence and potential loss) by taking adequate safeguards. Some of the ways of reducing these risks are discussed in Chapter 14.

RISKS ASSOCIATED WITH SOLVENCY NEEDS

Because of the small margin between return on assets and cost of deposits, a high proportion of deposits is essential for commercial banks to obtain an adequate rate of return on their ownership equity.[1] The consequence of the relatively low proportion of bank equity is that only a moderate percentage loss can be incurred on the assets before a bank's capital is impaired or wiped out. Some minimum amount of capital is, therefore, required to keep a bank in business. It is the bank examiner's job to appraise the risks in the bank's assets reflected in his classification of loans and to determine the adequacy of its liquidity provisions. Except when major losses develop suddenly and unexpectedly, as in the case of a large defalcation, the bank examiner will require that the bank raise capital long before its solvency is threatened. If losses estimated by the examiner impair the capital stock account *per se*, as distinct from surplus and retained earnings, a bank will be placed in receivership unless more capital is raised.[2]

PAST EXPERIENCE WITH BANKING RISKS

It can be claimed with considerable justification that the American financial system has been strengthened to the extent that banking panics and serious prolonged depressions will never again occur. It may be that the record of the 1930s is merely historical and has little practical significance. Nevertheless, the bankers who experienced the bank holiday

---

[1]Total capital accounts contributed slightly under 8 percent of total assets in 1971. Source: *Federal Reserve Bulletin,* 1971.

[2]U.S. Department of the Treasury, Comptroller of the Currency, *National Banking Laws and Related Statutes* (Washington: Government Printing Office, 1960).

of 1933, now steadily decreasing in number, were profoundly influenced by it, and familiarity with the record may serve as a salutory and sobering warning to those younger bankers who have never lived through a similar period. The bank officers of the late 1930s were not fools; they were intelligent men carried away by the spirit of the times. The same thing can happen to intelligent men again.

To point up this record, a study was made of fifty state member banks chosen at random in the Second Federal Reserve District. Each of these banks survived the Depression, although more than half of them were reorganized and required outside assistance in the form of additional capital funds or the removal of unacceptable assets. In 1929, these fifty banks had risk assets (assets other than cash and U.S. government securities) aggregating $373,325,000.[3] By 1933, the total of risk assets had shrunk to $258,809,000, a decline of approximately 30 percent. In this forced liquidation of assets, the banks took the following losses:

		Amounts (000 omitted)
Losses on loans		$ 9,590
Losses on securities		27,040
Other losses		2,287
	Total losses	$38,917
	Recoveries	3,659
	Net losses	$35,258

Net losses in the five years from 1929 to 1933 amounted to approximately 9.5 percent of the 1929 risk assets and about 30 percent of the risk assets liquidated during that period. This, however, was not the full extent of the banks' problem because in the examinations made during 1933 the remaining assets were classified[4] by the examiner as

[3]All figures from Reports of Examinations made during the year specified (Federal Reserve Bank of New York, confidential files).

[4]Examiners classify bank assets as "loss," "doubtful," or "substandard" (formerly "slow"). Estimated losses are required to be charged off immediately. Doubtful assets are usually considered to require reserves of 50 percent. Substandard assets are defined as "containing more than normal banking risk" but not necessarily a loss potential. In 1934, security depreciation was considered a "loss." Since 1938, depreciation on investment grade (relatively safe) securities has not been classified adversely, depreciation on lower-grade bonds not in default has been classified as "doubtful," and depreciation on stocks and defaulted bonds has been classified as a "loss."

follows:

	Amounts (000 omitted)
Security depreciation	$21,009
Estimated losses	12,080
Doubtful assets	5,899
Slow (substandard) assets	30,378
Total classified	$69,366

The total dollar amount of assets classified in the 1933 examination reports represented 27 percent of the remaining risk assets. The total of losses net of recoveries for the five years from 1929 to 1933 plus the classified assets in 1933 was about 28 percent of total 1929 risk assets.

The aggregate portrait of the effects of the Depression on bank assets does not quite tell the whole story, because it is an average picture. The following summary schedules from a 1934 examination report of a sample bank show in dramatic form some of the banking risks with which bank management and bank supervisory authorities had to cope.

SAMPLE BANK STATEMENT OF CONDITION
MARCH 23, 1934
(000 OMITTED)

Assets		Liabilities	
Loans	$30,830	Capital	$ 5,400
Mortgages owned	18,030	Surplus	3,000
Investments	14,370	Undivided profits and reserves	837
Banking house and fixtures (net)	3,830	Deposits	46,765
Other real estate	910	Bills payable	9,616
Cash and due from banks	3,754	Mortgages payable	193
Other assets	735	Mortgage participations outstanding	5,971
		Other liabilities	677
Total	$72,459	Total	$72,459

The problems of this sample bank in 1934 were not atypical. They were centered in stocks and bonds that had depreciated drastically in quality and market value and loans based on real estate values that had seemed most conservative ten years before but that, by 1934, had largely

ASSETS CLASSIFIED
(000 OMITTED)

	Slow	*Doubtful*	*Loss*
Loans	$13,658	$1,137	$4,022
Investments	804	31	5,226
Other real estate	826	30	55
Bonds and mortgages	4,346	–0–	101
Total	$19,634	$1,198	$9,404

RECAPITULATION OF CAPITAL
(000 OMITTED)

Total capital funds	
Capital	$5,400
Surplus	3,000
Undivided profits	232
Reserves	605
Total book capital funds	9,237
Less classified losses	9,404
Capital deficit	$ 167

CLASSIFICATION OF SECURITIES
(000 OMITTED)

	Book	*Allowed*	*Depreciation*
Group I bonds	$ 5,530	$5,435	$ 96
Group II bonds	2,822	1,449	1,373
Defaulted bonds	1,830	523	1,307
Stocks	3,936	1,485	2,450
Federal Reserve Bank	252	252	–0–
Total	$14,370	$9,144	$5,226

REAL ESTATE ACTUAL AND POTENTIAL
(000 OMITTED)

	Book
Other real estate owned	$ 910
Other real estate owned by affiliate (carried in loans)	3,265
Potential O.R.E. in loans	1,089
Potential O.R.E. in mortgages	1,403
Other real estate in name of affiliate or nominee	393
Other real estate in investments	350
Total	$7,410

faded into thin air. These values were to shrink still further in the next few years, and this bank took substantially more losses than the examiner estimated in 1934.

There have been many improvements in banking since the 1930s; nevertheless, banking still involves risks. The Federal Deposit Insurance Corporations' record of bank failures supports this contention. From the beginning of Federal deposit insurance through 1971, the Corporation has made disbursements to protect approximately 1.8 million accounts of close to $1.1 billion in 500 banks. Thirty-seven of these banks failed from 1966 through 1971.[5] In early 1971, the FDIC gave the largest dollar amount of financial help to a single bank in FDIC history.[6] Although analysis reveals that defalcation explains a substantial proportion of the bank failures in the period after World War II,[7] it is still clearly the task of bank management to be alert to unknown and perhaps unknowable eventualities as well as to protect themselves carefully against the risks of defalcation.

---

[5]*Annual Report of the Federal Deposit Insurance Corporation, 1971* (Washington: Federal Deposit Insurance Corp., 1972), pp. 227–34.

[6]In early 1971, the FDIC provided $100 million to the Fidelity Bank of Michigan, a new bank that was being formed to replace the insolvent and defunct Birmingham Bloomfield Bank of Michigan.

[7]Paul A. Meyer and Howard W. Pifer, "Prediction of Bank Failures," *The Journal of Finance,* Vol. 25, No. 5, December 1970, pp. 853–68.

5

BANK CAPITAL ADEQUACY

The ultimate strength of a bank lies in its capital funds.[1] Such is the consensus of writers on banking and of bank supervisors. But the problem of bank capital is not quite that simple. It is not merely a question of the more capital the better; rather it is how much capital for what reasons or purposes. The bank depositor (and the supervisor as his representative) may favor the maximum amount of capital as protection against the risks inherent in the banking business. The bank stockholder (or bank management as his representative) may, from the short-range viewpoint of maximizing profits, wish to operate with as little stockholders' capital as possible in order to gain the greatest leverage in earnings from the employment of deposits. The apparent conflict of interests between the stockholder and the public is not, however, as sharp as it might appear.

There is an element of public interest in the profitability as well as the safety of banks, because the public expects the stockholder to assume all the risk. Without profits, there would be no incentive for this risk taking. By the same token, it is in the interest of the shareholder to combine profitability with safety, because in the longer-run his invest-

---

[1]The capital funds of a commercial bank may include debt subordinated to deposits, preferred stock, common stock (par and surplus), retained earnings, and various equity reserves. The last three listed components are often called stockholders' capital or equity.

ment can remain profitable only if the bank stays in business. Closed banks pay no dividends. Adequacy of capital, therefore, will be found in some balance between these related but partly conflicting considerations. This chapter discusses capital adequacy, and Chapter 17 discusses the internal and external methods that a bank can use to increase its capital through enlightened financial management.

THE FUNCTIONS OF BANK CAPITAL

It has often been said that the primary function of bank capital is to protect the depositor against loss. Although such statements contain an element of truth, they do not adequately express the complete nature of the protective functions of bank capital funds. Most weak looking bank assets can be phased out with relatively little loss, given sufficient time, competent management, reasonable earnings, and the workings of the business cycle. Even the staggering losses of the 1930s were ultimately absorbed out of earnings when banks were not forced into liquidation. This is not to say that losses were not charged to capital funds; in the short-run, they were. And if too many losses are charged to capital, the bank's doors will inevitably be closed.

In the sense in which capital is described as a protection against the risk of insolvency, it is the ultimate protection. Capital funds will serve to protect the depositor when the bank is closed, but, if a bank has poor earnings, loose internal controls, and a large quantity of risky or speculative assets, the bank supervisor should step in long before the capital funds, as such, are severely impaired.

It is probably more meaningful, therefore, to look on the primary function of bank capital funds not as a cushion of excess assets that enables a bank to absorb losses and still remain solvent but rather as a factor, perhaps the most important factor, in maintaining the confidence a bank must enjoy to continue business and prosper. The primary function of bank capital is to keep the bank open and operating so that time and earnings can absorb losses—in other words, to inspire sufficient confidence in the bank on the part of depositors and the supervisor so that it will not be forced into costly liquidation. In this sense, capital serves to protect the stockholder as much as, if not more than, the depositor.

The fact that confidence is the vital ingredient of a bank's success should be self-evident. Depositors must be confident that their money is safe, and borrowers must be confident that the bank will be in a position to give genuine consideration to their credit needs in bad times as well as good. Above all, under the closely supervised private banking system of the United States, the continuing confidence of the bank supervisor is essential to a bank's continued existence.

Even the general public, which pays little attention to the financial statements of banks, has a vague idea that the strength of a bank is somehow related to the amount of its capital funds. Most banks, recognizing this awareness, proudly publicize not only the amount of their capital and surplus but also additions to them. The smaller segment of the public that understands and carefully reviews bank statements and annual reports pays considerable attention to capital. The corporate treasurer, in particular, focuses on this aspect of a bank's statement. In the past, some treasurers have devised their own methods of analyzing the adequacy of a bank's capital, although nowadays many of them use one or more of the bank supervisory approaches. These approaches will be discussed a little later. If the companies happen to be important depositors, they may insist that the bank furnish them with some information not otherwise published.

It is the bank supervisor, however, who most relies on the adequacy of capital as a factor in determining the degree of his confidence in a particular bank. This fact was never more clearly evident than immediately after the bank holiday in 1933, when every bank in the country came before the bar of supervisory judgment. It was the supervisor's appraisal of capital adequacy, more than any other factor, that determined whether and under what conditions a bank might be permitted to reopen.

The primary function of bank capital funds, therefore, is to reassure the public and especially the bank supervisor that the bank is in a position to withstand whatever strains may be placed on it. Adequate capital serves to keep banks open so that they may be able to absorb losses out of future earnings rather than out of capital funds themselves.

Bank capital has other functions, of course. As in any business, a part of the capital is needed to supply the working tools of the enterprise. This function is immediately evident in the organization of a new bank; the first expenditure of funds supplied by the stockholders goes for banking quarters and the equipment needed to begin operations.[2] The provision of working tools is a continuing function of bank capital, a responsibility of the stockholder. One cannot expect the depositor to supply the funds for new branch buildings or drive-in facilities. One of the problems considered in a subsequent discussion of how to measure the adequacy of bank capital will be the extent to which capital may be available to serve the other purposes and functions of capital funds, even though it is invested in bricks and mortar.

---

[2]This function of capital is recognized in Section 24 (A) of the Federal Reserve Act (U.S.C. Title 12, sec. 371), which limits the amount of a member bank's investment in bank premises to the amount of its stated capital unless specific permission is obtained to exceed this amount.

Another important function of capital is the representation of private ownership of commercial banks. The very existence of capital stock distinguishes commercial banks from the mutual savings banks and savings and loan associations that compete with commercial banks for savings. This structural difference entails a number of problems, such as tax treatment and reserve requirements, that have been in the forefront of public policy discussions for a number of years.

The question of who owns commercial banks is more important than the ownership of other business enterprises because banking is deeply tinged with public necessity. For this reason, commercial banks have been nationalized in many countries or actually organized by governments. One may well speak of the adequacy of the distribution of a bank's capital as well as its amount. Is ownership widely distributed, or is it concentrated in the hands of a few? The answer to this question has a good deal to do with the character of an individual bank and, at times, with the confidence the public may have in it.

The final function of bank capital is that of supporting the credit risks a bank is called on to assume in its normal business lending. Federal and most state regulations limit the maximum amount a bank can advance to any one borrower to a certain percentage of its capital. The desire for larger lending limits has inspired many banks to seek additional capital through the sale of stock or even through mergers with other institutions. Even more important, part of the confidence a bank's capital funds inspire is the assurance that it will be able to extend the credit that its community needs and to assume safely the risks involved.

CONDITIONS INFLUENCING CAPITAL ADEQUACY

The adequacy of bank capital is a dynamic concept. Capital adequacy is influenced by the prevailing and expected economic conditions of the entire economy and of the specific area served by the bank, by the quality and liquidity of the bank's assets, and by the quality of bank management. For example, assume that a bank operates in a prosperous economy, that assets are of excellent quality and possess adequate liquidity in relation to deposit volatility and economic conditions, and that management is sound. Under these favorable conditions, a small amount of capital would be adequate for the maintenance of solvency. An unfavorable change in any of these factors would increase the possibility of insolvency and would necessitate additional capital.

The public opinion of how much capital is adequate is equally important. If the depositors think the amount of capital is too small for a bank, they could withdraw deposits and force liquidation of assets. Thus, a solvent bank could suffer loss and liquidation when capital is inadequate for the maintenance of confidence.

People today certainly have more confidence in banks than they did forty years ago. The bank holiday of 1933 was in essence a lack-of-confidence crisis or panic that swept the country, closing good banks as well as bad. The panic was definitely accentuated by the public's long experience with bank failures even in times of general economic prosperity. As a result of the bitter experience of the 1930s, banking laws were substantially strengthened. Federal deposit insurance was inaugurated, and bank examining effort was greatly increased.[3]

The man in the street is probably not fully cognizant of the far-reaching implications of all of the legislative and supervisory buttressing of the banking structure that stemmed from the troubles of the 1930s, but he is very aware of deposit insurance. There have been few panic "runs" on insured banks since its inauguration, even when large defalcations have come to light. However, the informed public and the bank supervisor are much more cognizant of all that has taken place to strengthen banks generally since 1933. In a subsequent evaluation of the various measures of capital adequacy, the importance of these factors will be examined in detail.

No matter how much confidence one may have in the banking structure, however, or how much faith one may place in the management of a particular bank, the clear lesson of history is that conditions change and that managements age and are replaced. A floor of a given weight may be supported by either a thin column of steel or a thick masonry wall, but support is always necessary and cannot safely be removed. Bank capital supports confidence in banks in a very real sense; the quantity needed may be reduced by the improvement in tensile strength resulting from sound management policies, but the basic necessity for adequate capital support cannot be eliminated and should not be minimized.

LEGAL BASIS FOR CAPITAL ADEQUACY

Federal and state laws prescribe minimum amounts of capital required for the organization of a new bank. The minimum is usually related to the population of the bank's locality. In recent years, as a

---

[3]For example, the bank examining staff of the Federal Reserve Bank of New York in 1930 consisted of one examiner for each $360 million of member bank loans; today there is an examiner for each $60 million of loans.

matter of practical policy, supervisory authorities have usually required new banks to start with more than the legal minimum of capital.

Both Federal and state laws also have minimum capital requirements for the establishment of branches (where permitted). These legal requirements have little real significance for banking today, however. They were enacted at a time when banks generally were much smaller. They have not been revised upward, largely because the determination of capital adequacy has become a matter of administrative judgment rather than definitive law.

With respect to member banks of the Federal Reserve System, the basis for determining capital adequacy is laid in Section 9 of the Federal Reserve Act and Regulation H of the Board of Governors. The regulation requires that the net capital and surplus of a member bank "shall be adequate in relation to the character and condition of its assets and to its deposit liabilities and other corporate responsibilities."[4] The exact nature of the relationship between capital adequacy and the character and condition of a bank's assets is left to the judgment of the bank supervisor and bank management. The remainder of this chapter will be concerned with some of the considerations involved in arriving at such a judgment.

METHODS OF APPRAISING CAPITAL ADEQUACY

Beginning Ratios

Regulation H, as noted above, refers to the relationship of capital funds to both assets and deposits. Historically, the ratio of capital funds to deposits has had longer and wider public acceptance as a measure of capital adequacy. Early in the twentieth century, a rule of thumb developed that a bank should have capital funds equal to at least 10 percent of its deposits liabilities. This rough rule was enacted into the laws of some states and received a kind of official sanction in 1914, when the Comptroller of the Currency suggested it as the minimum ratio for national banks.

The 10 percent ratio was generally accepted and widely used until the years of World War II. During that period, bank deposits expanded rapidly as the result of bank purchases of U.S. government securities. To have maintained the 10 percent capital-to-deposit ratio in the face of balooning deposits that were largely created by U.S. government

---

[4]Nonmember insured banks must agree to maintain "adequate capital" as a condition of deposit insurance.

security purchases would have seriously impeded the financing of the war. Deposits in themselves contain no risk until they are used to make loans and investments. It became quickly evident, therefore, that capital adequacy should be related to a bank's assets and that the risks involved in holdings of U.S. government securities, the country's prime credit, were obviously different from other, more normal banking risks.

The ratio of capital to total assets was used by the Federal Deposit Insurance Corporation[5] and the Federal Reserve System[6] in the early postwar years. No generally accepted standard for adequately capitalized banks was developed for this ratio, although Federal Reserve System authorities suggested that an adequately capitalized bank would have capital equal to at least 7 percent of total assets, and the Federal Deposit Insurance Corporation used the national average of the ratio for all banks as the standard.[7]

The ratio of capital to total assets, like the ratio of capital to deposits, is unaffected by differences in risks associated with banks' differing asset structures. For example, two banks of equal asset size would require an identical amount of capital, even though one of them might have all of its assets in cash and short-term U.S. government securities and the other might have 85 percent of its assets in loans. Both ratios have the virtue of simplicity and for this reason are still frequently used as a first quick test of capital adequacy.

Ratios Reflecting Differences in Assets

Relating capital to risk assets is a means of taking into account the difference between cash and U.S. government securities and other kinds of assets. It was not long before students of the subject saw that the risks in the latter were not uniform. Some of them closely approximated the riskless character of short-term U.S. government obligations; others contained more than normal risk. A number of more or less scientific ratios subsequently appeared, each of which was inspired by an attempt to recognize the risks associated with various assets.

One of the earliest attempts at this new concept of capital adequacy

---

[5]*Annual Report of the Federal Deposit Insurance Corporation* for the year ended December 31, 1947, Washington, D. C., Table 22, p. 49. In this and subsequent reports, capital funds were related to "total assets" and to "assets other than cash and United States government obligations."

[6]Gaylord A. Freeman, Jr., "Does Your Bank Have Adequate Capital?" *The Texas Bankers Record*, September 1953, p. 31.

[7]*Ibid.* The FDIC standard lacks logic, because as the weaker banks improve their position, the standard must rise.

was made by the Comptroller of the Currency.[8] As the concept developed, it became known as the risk-asset ratio. This was conceived as the ratio of capital funds to total assets less cash, bank balances, and U.S. government securities. A ratio of one dollar of capital to five dollars of risk assets, or a risk-asset ratio of 20 percent, was originally considered sufficient.

This approach did not reflect the varying degrees of risk in a bank's remaining assets and was followed by the computation of an adjusted risk-asset ratio. This ratio not only relates capital funds to risk assets but also includes a secondary calculation, in which assets close to cash and U.S. government securities in their riskless nature are also deducted from total assets in the determination of risk assets.

This calculation of capital to adjusted risk assets was widely and regularly used by supervisory authorities as at least one test of capital adequacy. The standard usually applied was one dollar of capital funds to six dollars of risk assets. Slightly higher percentages of risk assets are tolerated if all other factors are favorable. This calculation as it now appears in Federal Reserve examination is reproduced below:

Total assets	$_____
Deduct:	
Total estimated losses	$_____
50% of assets classified as doubtful	_____
Cash and due from banks	_____
U.S. Treasury securities	_____
Securities of U.S. government agencies and corporations	_____
Public Housing Authority obligations (local issues)	_____
Federal funds sold	_____

---

[8]*Annual Report of the Comptroller of the Currency for the Year 1948*, p. 4. "For these reasons, our bureau in recent years has placed less stress upon the relationship between capital structure and deposits, emphasizing instead adequacy of capital in relation to several factors, particularly competence of management, and volume and quality of assets which necessarily involve some element of uncertainty, however slight. In order to expedite our procedures and perform our duties as efficiently as possible we have adopted certain rules-of-thumb for preliminary screening. One of the most useful of these is a ratio of capital funds to loans and investments other than United States government securities. When the capitalization of a particular bank, checked in this manner, apparently falls far short of the average, this is a signal for close analysis of relevant factors, such as the character of the loans and investments, the ability of management, local and regional economic conditions and trends, and the like. Even if loans and investments appear high in relation to capital structure at first glance, no criticism or corrective action will follow if it is ascertained that loans and investments are of high quality under the supervision of careful and intelligent management, and appropriate in the economic situation in which the particular bank is operating."

Securities purchased under resale agreement   _____
Loans or portions of loans   _____
   Secured by obligations of U.S. Treasury or U.S. government
     agencies and corporations   _____
   Secured by Public Housing Authority obligations (local issues)   _____
   Insured under the Higher Education Act   _____
   Insured under Title I of the National Housing Act   _____
   Insured under Titles II and VI of the National Housing Act   _____
   Guaranteed under the Servicemen's Readjustment Act   _____
   Guaranteed by the Small Business Administration   _____
   Insured by Farmers Home Administration   _____
   Secured by hypothecated deposits   _____
   Secured by dealers' reserves required by agreement   _____
Federal Reserve Bank stock   _____
Income collected, not earned   _____
        Total Risk Assets   _____   _____

                                                          \$_____

RATIO OF CAPITAL TO RISK ASSETS IS 1 TO _____

This simplified approach includes in riskless assets some in which the risk, although small, is nevertheless present. There is market risk even in government securities, particularly in the longer maturities, and there is some risk in every loan, no matter how well secured—risk, for example, that the collateral has not been properly endorsed or pledged. In addition, the risk in risk assets is not uniform. The risk-asset formula makes no distinction between a seasoned amortizing, residential mortgage and the bank's investment in fixed assets.

Capital Adequacy Analyses

Several capital adequacy analyses have been developed to meet these and similar objections to capital adequacy ratios. The Federal Reserve Bank of New York devised another approach to capital adequacy analysis[9]—an attempt to indicate the dollar amount of the minimum capital funds required by an individual bank on the basis of its own asset distribution. The amount of capital funds thus computed would be the minimum for a bank in which all other factors were favorable. The area of supervisory judgment would be the determination of how

---

[9]Federal Reserve Bank of New York, "A Measure of Minimum Capital Adequacy," December 21, 1952. This formula was devised by Mr. Crosse, then Assistant Vice-President in charge of Bank Supervision. It has been widely distributed through the Stonier Graduate School of Banking and was entered as Exhibit 178 in the hearings, "In the Matter of the Continental Bank and Trust Company, Salt Lake City," before the Board of Governors of the Federal Reserve System.

much more capital than the minimum an individual bank might need because of its peculiar circumstances. This approach is more selective than a straight risk-asset ratio.

For the purpose of this analysis, bank assets are divided into six rough groupings. These do not, of course, accurately reflect all the various shades or degrees of risk, but they appear to be the fundamental categories into which bank assets normally fall, and they provide a more selective basis than the simple distinction between risk and nonrisk assets used in the risk-asset approach.

To each of these six categories is assigned a specific capital requirement. Although these allocations are necessarily arbitrary, they are generally consistent with traditional banking and supervisory thought. They are designed to be large enough not only to absorb probable losses in each category of assets but also to provide enough additional capital to maintain supervisory confidence and keep the bank open. Just as bank credit men expect to find varying capital ratios in different kinds of commercial enterprises, so different kinds of banking business can be said, on the average, to require varying degrees of capital protection.

The first of these six asset categories consists of what may be called a bank's required reserves and its highly liquid assets. These include cash on hand, bank balances, and U.S. government securities maturing within five years. Other assets of comparable quality and very short maturity, such as bankers' acceptances and Federal funds sold, also belong in this category. Against these virtually riskless assets, no capital is required. There is, of course, some market risk even in short-term U.S. government securities, but ordinarily it is small enough to be readily absorbed by earnings.

The second category may be designated as minimum risk assets—loans and investments that have less than normal credit risk or that may be readily pledged or sold, although sometimes at a discount from face value. In this category are U.S. government securities with maturities of over five years, government-guaranteed loans and securities of government agencies, loans secured by similar assets and by savings passbooks and the cash value of life insurance, prime commercial paper, brokers, loans, and other assets of similar quality. Capital equal to 5 percent of these minimum risk assets is suggested. It will be seen that the assets included in this category are, for the most part, those that are considered riskless in the secondary computation used in the risk-asset ratio. Although the credit risk in such assets is minimal, it nevertheless exists. Banks themselves would not generally lend money to any enterprise with current liabilities exceeding twenty times its net worth, no matter how free from risk its operations might appear. Some minimum capital protection is advisable for all but those assets that are essentially cash or its equivalent.

The third general category is designated portfolio assets. These represent normal or usual banking risks. They include all of the remaining loan portfolio not adversely classified by the examiners and the rest of the investment-grade (rated Baa or above) securities (other than U.S. government bonds) maturing in more than five years. The suggested 12 percent capital requirement is considered minimum protection against the average or normal portfolio mix. It assumes that loans or securities containing more than normal credit risk will be listed in the examination report.

The fourth category includes substandard assets that have more than a normal banking risk because of the financial condition or unfavorable record of the obligor, insufficiency of security, or other factors. A 20 percent capital allocation is suggested for assets in this classification. Such assets do not necessarily contain an element of loss. Even the best-run bank will occasionally make loans or purchase securities that involve more than normal risk. But riskier business requires higher capital protection.

The fifth grouping consists of "work-out" assets. These include loans that the examiner has classified as doubtful, stocks, defaulted securities, and real estate assets that banks may not legally acquire except by foreclosure in satisfaction of debts previously contracted. Bank supervisors generally expect that such assets will be disposed of promptly. Against work-out assets, a 50 percent capital requirement is considered reasonable. A few state-chartered banks still legally hold common stocks, often written down to 1933 prices. Market appreciation on such stocks can serve as capital protection against the remaining book value.

The final category consists of assets classified as loss and fixed assets—premises, furniture, and fixtures. These fixed assets are not considered bank investments in a true sense. Rather they are regarded as the working tools of the banking business that should be provided by the stockholders. Costly and elaborate premises may attract business, but they provide little protection for the depositor. Bank buildings can be disposed of only when a bank goes into liquidation, and if this occurs in a serious depression, the real estate will not be readily salable. Viewing the bank as a going concern and seeking to ensure protection for depositors, the bank supervisor is chiefly concerned with the amount of capital a bank has in excess of its fixed assets.[10]

---

[10]The authors believe it would be preferable to require a lower allocation of capital against reasonable amounts of fixed assets. They believe that only fixed assets above a reasonable proportion of total assets should require the full 100 percent allocation of capital that supervisory authorities still tend to require for all fixed assets. However, in reopening banks in 1933, bank supervisory authorities often required a lower allocation for bank premises. One bank was reopened with "sound capital funds" of $1 million that included a bank building carried at $900,000.

Against these computed capital requirements are measured the bank's good capital funds. These consist of all capital funds, including capital and bad debt reserves.[11] In accordance with a 1938 general agreement among supervisory authorities, neither appreciation nor depreciation in investment-grade securities is considered in the calculation of capital funds. The analysis, by requiring a higher percentage of capital against longer-term securities, makes some provision for the greater risk of market fluctuation. The method was designed to permit a range of supervisory judgment between roughly 100 and 125 percent.[12]

A somewhat more complex approach to capital adequacy was subsequently developed by a staff group of the Board of Governors of the Federal Reserve System.[13] It combines a capital adequacy test with a liquidity test, requiring more capital for banks that are less liquid. This form is reproduced on pages 81a and 81b. The following explanatory notes are pertinent:

> A thorough appraisal of the capital needs of a particular bank must take due account of all relevant factors affecting the bank. These include the characteristics of its assets, its liabilities, and its management—as well as the history and prospects of the bank, its customers, and its community. The complexity of the problem requires a considerable exercise of judgment. The grouping and percentages suggested in the Form for Analyzing Bank Capital can necessarily be no more than aids to the exercise of judgment.
>
> The requirements indicated by the various items of the form are essentially "norms" and can provide no more than an initial presumption as the actual capital required by a particular bank. These "norms" are entitled to considerable weight, but various upward and downward adjustments could be made individually as the requirements are entered for each group of assets; but it is usually preferable, particularly for future reference to combine them and enter them as a single adjustment under Item 8, indicating on the Analysis Form or on an attached page the specific basis for each adjustment.
>
> The requirements suggested in the Analysis Form assume that the bank has adequate safeguards and insurance coverage against fire, defalcation, burglary, etc. Lack of such safeguards or coverage would place upon the bank's capital risks which it should not be called upon to bear.

---

[11]Reserves for bad debts established from pretax income in accordance with a formula permitted by the Internal Revenue Service.

[12]As a practical matter, a well-managed bank is not seriously questioned if its ratio falls somewhat below 100 percent, and banks with ratios above 125 percent would seldom be questioned.

[13]"Form for Analyzing Bank Capital," April 1956, entered as Exhibit No. 154 in the hearings before the Board of Governors, in the matter of the Continental Bank and Trust Company, Salt Lake City.

It should be noted that this form specifies a higher capital requirement for the first five hundred thousand dollars of the portfolio assets,
in effect stipulating relatively more capital for small banks.

> The extra requirement of 15 percent of the first $100,000 of port-
> folio, 10 percent of the next $100,000, and 5 percent of the next
> $300,000, as specified in Item 4, is a rough approximation of the
> concentration of risk (lack of diversification) which is likely in
> a smaller portfolio, and which is usually reflected in somewhat
> larger proportion of capital shown by most banks with smaller
> portfolios. This requirement is applied to all banks, but it is natu-
> rally a larger portion of the total capital requirements of banks
> with smaller portfolios. However, a particular portfolio, whatever
> its size, may in fact have either more or less concentration of risk
> than other portfolios of similar size. If there is in fact greater or
> lesser concentration of risk in the portfolio assets of a particular
> bank—as for example dependence upon a smaller or larger number
> of economic activities—it would be appropriate to increase or
> decrease the requirements correspondingly.

The most unusual feature of the Board of Governors' form is the
provision for a liquidity calculation and for additional capital requirements for those banks that do not meet the liquidity test. This additional
requirement is based on the theory that perfectly sound assets are
subject to shrinkage if they have to be sold in an adverse market or
forcibly collected. The liquidity calculation is explained as follows.

> The provision for 47 percent liquidity for demand deposits of
> individuals, partnerships and corporations actually represents
> 33-1/3 percent possible shrinkage in deposits, plus 20 percent of
> the remaining 66-2/3 percent. Thirty-six percent of time deposits
> I.P.C. represents 20 percent shrinkage, plus 20 percent of the
> remaining 80 percent. In both instances, the provision for 20
> percent liquidity for remaining deposits is to help the bank con-
> tinue as a going concern even after suffering substantial deposit
> shrinkage.
>
> Among possible special factors to be considered in connection
> with the liquidity calculation would be concentration or diversifi-
> cation of risk among deposits. This might be due to such things as
> dependence upon a smaller or larger number of economic activities,
> or preponderance of small or large deposits—large deposits usually
> being more volatile.
>
> Liquidity available for primary and secondary reserve assets is
> assumed to equal the amount of those assets less only the regular
> capital required thereon, since the regular capital specified for
> these assets assumes forced liquidation. However, the regular capital
> specified for other assets (i.e., those in Groups 2–4) is only a
> portion (approximately 40 percent) of that required for forced
> liquidation. Therefore, in determining the liquidity available from

FORM FOR ANALYZING BANK CAPITAL
(See Notes on Reverse Side)

April 1956

BANK: _____

LOCATION: _____

BASED ON REPORT OF EXAMINATION AS OF _____ DISTRICT NO. _____

(Dollar Amounts in Thousands)

	AMOUNT OUTSTANDING	CAPITAL REQUIREMENT		
		Per Cent	Amount	

(1) PRIMARY AND SECONDARY RESERVE

	AMOUNT OUTSTANDING	Per Cent	Amount
Cash Assets	$ _____)	0%	
Guar. Portion of CCC or V-loans	_____		
Comm. Paper, Bnk Accept. & Bnks' Lns	_____		
U.S. Govt. Secs:	}	0.5% $	
Bills	_____		
Certificates, etc. (to 1 yr.)	_____		
Other (1-5 yrs.)(Incl. Treas. Inv. Series A & B)	_____)		
Other Secs. Inv. Rtngs 1 & 2 or Equiv. (to 3 yrs.)	}	4.0%	
TOTAL	$ _____		

(2) MINIMUM RISK ASSETS

U.S. Govt. Secs. (5-10 yrs.)	_____		
Ins. Portion FHA Rep. & Modr'n Loans	_____		
Loans on Passb'ks, U.S. Sec. or CSV Life Ins.	_____		
Short-term Municipal Loans	_____		
TOTAL	$ _____	4%	

(3) INTERMEDIATE ASSETS

U.S. Govt. Secs. (Over 10 yrs.)	_____		
FHA and VA Loans	_____		
TOTAL	$ _____	6%	

(4) PORTFOLIO ASSETS (Gross of Res.)

Investments (not listed elsewhere)	_____		
Loans (not listed elsewhere)	_____		
TOTAL	$ _____	10%*	

*Plus 15% of 1st $100,000 of portfolio, 10% of next $100,000 and 5% of next $300,000.

(5) FIXED, CLASSIFIED & OTHER ASSETS

Bk. Prem., Furn. & Fixt., Other Real Est.	_____)		
Stocks & Defaulted Secs.	_____	100%	
Assets Classified as "Loss"	_____)		
Assets Classified as "Doubtful"	_____	50%	
Assets Classified as "Substandard"	_____	20%	
Accruals, Fed. Res. Bk. Stock, Prep. Expen.	_____	0%	
TOTAL ASSETS	$ _____		

(6) ALLOWANCE FOR TRUST DEPT. _____
(Amt. equal to 300% of annual gross earnings of Department)

(7) EXTRA CAP. REQD. IF ANY ASSETS IN GROUPS 2-4 USED FOR _____
LIQUIDITY (Zero if line C in Liquidity Calculation is zero, otherwise Total in line H)

(8) ALLOW. FOR SPEC. OR ADDIT. FACTORS, IF INFO. AVAILABLE
(+ or −) (See notes on reverse side)

(9) TOTAL CAPITAL REQUIREMENT (1 thru 8) $ _____

LIQUIDITY CALCULATION

47% of Demand Deposits i.p.c.	$ _____
36% of Time Deposits i.p.c.	_____
100% of Deposits of Banks	_____
100% of Other Deposits	_____
100% of Borrowings	_____
Allow. for spec. factors, if info. available (+ or −)	_____

A. Total Provision for Liquidity _____

B. Liquidity available from Prim. and Secondary Res. ("amt. outstanding" less cap. required thereon)

C. Liquidity to be provided from assets in Groups 2, 3 or 4 (zero if B equals or exceeds A, otherwise A less B)

D. Liquidity available from Min. Risk Assets (90% of "amt. outstanding" in line 2)

E. Liquidity to be provided from assets in Groups 3 or 4 (zero if D equals or exceeds C, otherwise C less D)

F. Liquidity available from Intermediate Assets (85% of "amt. outstanding" in line 3)

G. Liquidity to be provided from Portfolio Assets (zero if F equals or exceeds E, otherwise E less F)

* * * * * * * * * * * * *

Extra Capital Required on Any Assets in Groups 2-4 Used for Liquidity

6.5% of line C	_____
4.0% of line E	_____
9.5% of line G	_____
◄— H. Total Extra Cap. Req.	$ _____

---

(10) ACTUAL CAP., ETC. (Sum of Cap. Stock, Surplus, Undiv. Profits, Res. for Conting., Loan Valuation Res., Net unapplied Sec. Valuation Res., Unallocated Charge-offs, and any comparable items) (Exclude Depreciation and Amortization Reserves) $ _____

(11) AMOUNT BY WHICH ACTUAL IS: { MORE than requirement (10 minus 9) _____   +$ _____
or
LESS than requirement (9 minus 10) _____   −$ _____

(12) RATIO OF ACTUAL CAPITAL, ETC. TO REQUIREMENT (10 divided by 9) _____   _____ %

81a

A thorough appraisal of the capital needs of a particular bank must take due account of all relevant factors affecting the bank. These include the characteristics of its assets, its liabilities, its trust or other corporate responsibilities, its management--as well as the history and prospects of the bank, its customers and its community. The complexity of the problem requires a considerable exercise of judgment. The groupings and percentages suggested in the Form For Analyzing Bank Capital can necessarily be no more than aids to the exercise of judgment.

The requirements indicated by the various items on the form are essentially "norms" and can provide no more than an initial presumption as to the actual capital required by a particular bank. These "norms" are entitled to considerable weight, but various upward or downward adjustments in requirements may be appropriate for a particular bank if special or unusual circumstances are in fact present in the specific situation. Such adjustments could be made individually as the requirements are entered for each group of assets; but it usually is preferable, particularly for future reference, to combine them and enter them as a single adjustment under Item 8, indicating on the Analysis Form or an attached page the specific basis for each adjustment.

The requirements suggested in the Analysis Form assume that the bank has adequate safeguards and insurance coverage against fire, defalcation, burglary, etc. Lack of such safeguards or coverage would place upon the bank's capital risks which it should not be called upon to bear.

ITEM (4) — PORTFOLIO ASSETS

Concentration or Diversification.— The extra requirement of 15% of the first $100,000 of portfolio, 10% of the next $100,000 and 5% of the next $300,000, as specified in item 4, is a rough approximation of the concentration of risk (lack of diversification) which is likely in a smaller portfolio, and which is usually reflected in the somewhat larger proportion of capital shown by most banks with smaller portfolios. This requirement is applied to all banks, but is naturally a larger portion of the total capital requirements of banks with smaller portfolios. However, a particular portfolio, whatever its size, may in fact have either more or less concentration of risk than other portfolios of similar size. If there is in fact substantially greater or lesser concentration of risk in the portfolio assets of the particular bank--as for example dependence upon a smaller or larger number of economic activities--it would be appropriate to increase or decrease requirements correspondingly.

Drafts Accepted By Bank. — When drafts have been accepted by the bank, ordinarily the customers' liability to the bank should be treated as Portfolio Assets if the acceptances are outstanding, or the acceptances themselves should be so treated if held by the bank.

ITEM (5) — FIXED, CLASSIFIED, AND OTHER ASSETS

Rental Properties.— Bank premises, furniture and fixtures, and other real estate are assigned a 100% requirement as a first approximation, since these assets usually are not available to pay creditors unless the bank goes into liquidation, and even then they usually can be turned into cash only at substantial sacrifice. However, some properties which bring in independent income, such as bank premises largely rented to others, may be more readily convertible into cash by selling or borrowing on them, and in such situations it may be appropriate to reduce the 100% requirement by an amount equal to an assumed "sacrifice" value, such as, say, two or three times the gross annual independent income.

Stocks. — In the case of stocks, their wide fluctuations in price suggest a 100% requirement as a first approximation. However, in some cases it may be appropriate to reduce the 100% requirement against a stock by an amount equal to an assumed "sacrifice" value, such as the lowest market value reached by the stock in, say, the preceding 36 or 48 months.

Hidden Assets. — In some cases assets may be carried at book values which appear to be below their actual value, and may thus appear to provide hidden strength. However, any allowance for such a situation should be made with great caution, and only after taking full account of possible declines in values and the great difficulty of liquidating assets in distress circumstances.

ITEM (6) — ALLOWANCE FOR TRUST DEPARTMENT

Deposited Securities. — The requirement for the trust department should in no event be less than the amount of any securities deposited with the State authorities for the protection of private or court trusts, since such securities are not available in ordinary circumstances to protect the bank's depositors.

LIQUIDITY CALCULATION

Percentages of Deposits. — The provision for 47% liquidity for demand deposits of individuals, partnerships and corporations actually represents 33-1/3% possible shrinkage in deposits, plus 20% of the remaining 66-2/3%. 36% of time deposits i.p.c. represents 20% shrinkage, plus 20% of the remaining 80%. In both instances, the provision for 20% liquidity for remaining deposits is to help the bank continue as a going concern even after suffering substantial deposit shrinkage.

Among possible special factors to be considered in connection with the liquidity calculation would be concentration or diversification of risk among deposits. This might be due to such things as dependence upon a smaller or larger number of economic activities, or preponderance of large or small deposits--large deposits usually being more volatile.

Liquidity Available from Assets. — Liquidity available from primary and secondary reserves is assumed to equal the amount of those assets less only the regular capital required thereon, since the regular capital specified for these assets assumes forced liquidation. However, the regular capital specified for other assets (i.e., those in Groups 2-4) is only a portion (approximately 40%) of that required for forced liquidation. Therefore, in determining the liquidity available from such other assets, the amount of such other assets must be reduced by more than the regular specified capital.

Extra Capital Required. — This extra capital is to cover possible losses in forced liquidation of assets other than primary and secondary reserves in case they had to be used to provide liquidity. The 4% indicated for Line E amounts to an automatic addition to the 6.5% that has already been applied to Line C, and results in a total extra requirement of 10.5% of the liquidity to be provided from Intermediate Assets. Similarly, the total extra requirement on the liquidity to be provided from Portfolio Assets is 20%. If the same amounts of extra capital were stated as percentages of the assets to be liquidated rather than of the liquidity to be provided, the percentages would be smaller, namely, 6% of Minimum Risk Assets, 9% of Intermediate Assets, and 15% of Portfolio Assets.

such other assets, the amount of such other assets must be reduced by more than the regular specified capital.

This extra capital required is to cover possible losses in forced liquidation of assets other than primary and secondary reserves in case they had to be used to provide liquidity. The 4 percent indicated for Line E amounts to an automatic addition to the 6.5 percent that has already been applied to Line C, and results in a total extra requirement of 10.5 percent of the liquidity to be provided from Intermediate Assets. Similarly, the total extra requirement on the liquidity to be provided from Portfolio Assets is 20 percent. If the same amount of extra capital were to be stated as percentages of the assets to be liquidated rather than of the liquidity to be provided, the percentages would be smaller, namely, 6 percent of Minimum Risk Assets, 9 percent of Intermediate Assets, and 15 percent of Portfolio Assets.

This liquidity calculation used in the above analysis is based on uniform estimates of liquidity needs similar to the asset allocation plans reviewed in Chapter 9. It stipulates (as a first approximation, at least) a degree of liquidity roughly equal to the amount by which bank deposits shrank on the average during the Depression of the 1930s. Most informed persons would argue that this requirement is high in the light of Federal deposit insurance and the other factors that have strengthened banks and supervisory confidence in them. A more specific objection to this blanket approach is that, for the individual bank, liquidity needs (and therefore an adequate portfolio of liquid assets) vary throughout the year in response to seasonal or other periodical changes in the demand for and supply of funds. As a result, banks that may fully meet the liquidity tests of the Board of Governors' form of analysis at one period of the year may be deficient at another but still meet fully the liquidity test suggested in Chapter 8 at both times.

A unique feature of the Board of Governors' formula is its capital requirements for potential liabilities in connection with trust activities. Because trust assets are carried on the books of banks in many different ways (inventory cost, unit cost, and so on), the aggregate of trust assets is a poor measure of the risks involved. Trust fees, on the other hand, are roughly uniform and provide a reasonably comparable measure of trust activity and therefore of potential liability.

The provision of capital to the extent of three times gross income from all trust activities is admittedly an arbitrary requirement. Unquestionably, the operation of a trust department involves a bank in risk of loss—not only the risk of surcharge but also the risk of costly litigation and the uncertainties and possible unfavorable publicity involved in being sued for large sums, regardless of whether the suits are successful. The risk of loss in trust operations is probably greater in connection with personal trusts than with agency and corporate trust accounts, in many of which discretion is limited or clearly defined. Just how great the actual risk may be is virtually impossible to determine, because available records do not date back far enough to provide a factual basis of experience.[14] The Board of Governors' requirement coincides closely with the amount of capital held, on the average, by a number of large institutions that conduct only a trust business except for a minor amount of incidental deposit banking.

National bank examiners recently moved away from such formal analysis. The Comptroller's office issued the following policy statement:

> The Comptroller of the Currency will not hereafter rely on the ratios of capital to risk assets and to total deposits in assessing the adequacy of capital of national banking associations. These formulae, although of some value in assessing capital adequacy, do not take into account other factors of equal or greater importance. Henceforth, the capital position of the bank will be analyzed and appraised in relation to the character of its management and its asset and deposit position as a going institution under normal conditions, with due allowance for a reasonable margin of safety, and with due regard to the bank's capacity to furnish the broadest service to the public. These factors, which are necessarily imprecise, cannot be directly interpolated into any specific formula. The following factors will be considered by the Comptroller in assessing the adequacy of capital:
> (a) The quality of management;
> (b) The liquidity of assets;
> (c) The history of earnings and of the retention thereof;
> (d) The quality and character of ownership;
> (e) The burden of meeting occupancy expenses;
> (f) The potential volatility of deposit structure;
> (g) The quality of operating procedures; and
> (h) The bank's capacity to meet present and future financial needs of its trade area, considering the competition it faces.[15]

USEFULNESS OF ANALYTICAL METHODS FOR APPRAISING CAPITAL ADEQUACY

Analytical or statistical methods of computing capital adequacy represent attempts to standardize or systematize the more or less intuitive judgment of bank supervisors. Many supervisors would claim that they

---

[14]The experience of the Bank Examinations Department of the Federal Reserve Bank of New York since World War II is that few trust departments have had cash settlements or surcharges in excess of 1½ percent of gross commissions in any year. This, however, is admittedly short-range experience under generally favorable economic conditions.

[15]Part 14a issued under R.S. 324 et seq., as amended; 12 U.S.C. 1 et seq.

can gauge the adequacy of capital without benefit of such formulas. As stated in the preceding paragraph, the national bank examiners abandoned the use of formulas. Even experienced supervisors, however, find it difficult on occasion to convince bank management or directors of the soundness of their sometimes quite subjective views. They resort to statistical analysis to demonstrate the objectivity of their judgment, because a formula will convince managers that their bank's special situation is receiving equitable treatment.

Two considerations seem particularly helpful in evaluating the usefulness of the various analytical methods for appraising capital adequacy. First, what has been the experience of users of the various methods over time? Second, how do results obtained with various analytical methods compare at a particular point of time?

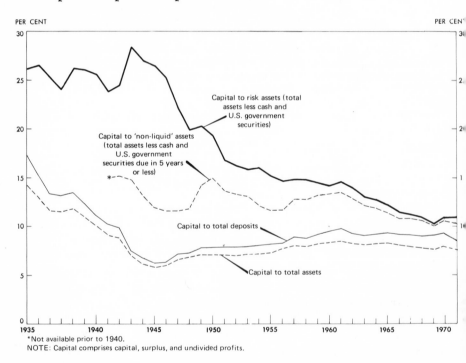

CHART 2 Conventional Capital Ratios, All Insured Commercial Banks, June 30, 1934–1971 (Source: Federal Deposit Insurance Corporation)

Chart 2 shows the postwar trends in four conventional capital ratios for all insured banks from 1934 through 1971. Although these percentages have declined drastically from the early 1930s, changes in the 1950s and the 1960s have been very modest. Capital as a percentage of total deposits or total assets has increased slightly, but capital as a percentage of risk or nonliquid assets was relatively stable in the 1950s and then declined slightly in the 1960s. The decline in the 1960s was primarily due to a reduction in bank holdings of U.S. government securities.

Generally, the different analytical approaches described in the preceding section provide roughly comparable results; in individual cases, however, the computed requirement may differ quite widely. A random sample of fifty banks was analyzed by each of the three principal methods, and the ratios were computed. The first column in Table 5 shows the average of each ratio for all fifty banks. The sample compares closely with national averages. In column 2, the capital of each of the

TABLE 5

COMPARISON OF CAPITAL FORMULAS

	1	2	3
	Actual	*Theoretical*	*Range*
New York formula	128%	100%	—
Board formula	116	91	68%–118%
Risk-asset ratio	1/6	1/7.4	1/3.4–1/12.0

fifty banks was theoretically increased or decreased to exactly the minimum requirement of the New York Federal Reserve formula, and the other two ratios were recomputed for comparison at the minimum level. Column 3 shows the range of individual banks at this average minimum.

Both the adjusted risk-asset approach and the Board form of analysis require, on the average, somewhat more capital than the bare minimum computed by the New York method. It should be noted, however, that this is a minimum, and that in actual practice, when all factors are taken into consideration, adequacy under this formula is usually in the range of 115 to 125 percent of the basic minimum.

In specific cases, the risk-asset ratio favors the bank with a relatively high investment in fixed assets. The Board of Governors' analysis form penalizes the bank that has a relatively small investment in short-term assets (whether it needs them or not). No one can authoritatively say that either of the methods is right, and that is why supervisors insist that, at best, any formula is only a screening device. Many banks and bank supervisors use several formulas for this purpose. Ultimately, the intangible factors of confidence will receive a great deal of weight in the determination of how much capital is adequate.

CAPITAL ADEQUACY IN PERIODS OF STRESS

Adequate capital tends to be enough to see a bank through a period of severe stress. Although circumstances like those of the 1930s may not recur, other adverse circumstances, unforeseen but equally disasterous, may. In order to shed some light on how banks might fare in a future period of equal strain, a sample of fifty banks (that survived the Depression of the 1930s) was chosen at random, and their loss experience during the ten years from 1929 through 1939 was subjected to careful analysis. Nineteen of the fifty banks went through this period without having to obtain additional capital. The other thirty-one did obtain additional capital in one way or another—through deposit waivers, stockholder assessments, sale of preferred stock to the Reconstruction Finance Corporation or others, or by other devices.

Available statistics permit the evaluation of the capital position of these banks only on the basis of an unadjusted risk-asset ratio—the ratio of capital funds to total assets less cash and U.S. government securities. Book capital position as of mid–1929 and as of the examination made in 1933 was measured in this way. All fifty banks were closed at least briefly during the bank holiday, and their reopening was a practical test of how much capital they needed at that time to obtain or regain supervisory confidence.

Not all the banks reopened at the same time. Reorganization took time, especially if additional capital had to be raised. For the purpose of determining how much additional capital a bank required, therefore, the total amount of additional capital funds acquired between 1933 and 1939 was taken into consideration. "Net sound capital" required to reopen in 1933, as that term is used here, includes the book capital funds and reserves of the bank in 1933 plus the additional capital raised through 1939 less estimated losses, security depreciation, and assets classified as doubtful in the examination report nearest to June 30, 1933. This figure for the fifty banks averaged 21.2 percent of risk assets. For the banks that were required to raise additional capital, the ratio averaged somewhat higher (22.8 percent) than for the banks that survived the bank holiday unscathed. For the latter, the comparable figure was 18.7 percent, reflecting perhaps a more favorable supervisory judgment of the ability of management or the quality of the assets.

These figures support, or at least explain, the general feeling among bank supervisors that a 20 percent primary risk-asset ratio is about right. But this is not the whole story. By 1933, these fifty banks collectively had been through a substantial liquidation. Their risk assets had shrunk from an aggregate of $373 million on June 30, 1929, to $259 million as of the examination date in 1933, a decline of 30 percent. In the process, net losses for the full years 1929 to 1933 had totaled $35 million or nearly 10 percent of their 1929 risk assets, and at the 1933 examination, the total of assets classified as loss or doubtful totaled another $38 million. The two together thus aggregated almost exactly 20 percent of 1929 risk assets.

Another way of looking at it would be to ask how much capital these banks would have needed in 1929 to survive the Depression without having to raise additional capital funds. The nineteen banks that accomplished this feat had a risk-asset ratio of 18.4 percent in 1929. The thirty-one that needed more capital had an average risk-asset ratio of only 15.5 percent in 1929. If the latter banks had held in 1929 all the capital funds they raised between 1933 and 1939, their risk-asset ratio would then have been 23 percent.

These signs, with remarkable unanimity, indicate the approximate sufficiency of a 20 percent primary or unadjusted risk-asset ratio in relation to the average character and risk of bank assets in 1929, the caliber of bank management in 1929, and the degree of public confidence from 1929 to 1933 in banks and the economic future. The bank supervisor may not be entirely convinced that 1933 will never return, but the objective student of banking can note many important changes in the banking scene since 1929. The need for capital today can be intelligently discussed in terms of 1929 only if one can appraise the changes that have since taken place in the factors affecting capital adequacy. Some of these are not easy to appraise statistically or objectively.

The development of Federal deposit insurance undoubtedly lessened the chances of wholesale loss of public confidence in banks, but even Solomon in all his wisdom would have difficulty translating this increased confidence into any given number of percentage points in a risk-asset ratio. Whether management is better today than it was in 1929 is a moot question. Those bank managers whose careers encompass 1933–34 are certainly wiser, but their ranks are rapidly thinning. It is always possible for a "new era" philosophy to creep back into banking—if it has not already done so (in some quarters, at least).

When it comes to asset quality, the advocates of lower capital requirements are on firmer ground. Fifty-eight percent of the gross losses incurred between 1929 and 1939 by the fifty banks in the sample studied were on securities—mostly corporate securities, which constitute a very minor portion of bank assets today. These securities comprised 20 percent of risk assets in 1929. Many of them were of a caliber that banks may no longer legally acquire.

Another large portion of bank losses resulted from the foreclosure of mortgage loans and the forced sale of the resultant real estate at sacrifice prices. These were mostly mortgages that had been on the books for years without amortization. Today, virtually all mortgages are being amortized. They are also being written for longer terms and frequently refinanced, so the average equity is not as large as one might suppose.

Loans against marketable collateral were another weak spot in the 1929 risk-asset portfolio. The margin requirements of the Board of Governors' Regulation U[16] effectively prevent the use of excessive bank credit for purchasing or carrying listed securities; but banks still lend against stocks for other purposes, and the market value of those stocks could fall rather sharply.

The asset quality of consumer credit, a substantial factor in many banks, is still largely untested. Banks' experience with consumer credit has been generally good, in spite of repeated liberalizations of terms. Some banks, however, ran into serious losses in the late 1960s and early 1970s when they went into credit cards blindly with mass mailings and inadequate (if any) credit checks.

Thus, despite the strengthening of the banking structure and despite obvious improvement in the quality of bank assets, it should be clear that not all risks have been eliminated from the banking business. The formulas used by the various supervisory authorities and their more or less flexible application reflect, to an important degree, the improvement that has taken place.[17] The previously noted decision of bank supervisors in 1938 not to take depreciation of investment-grade securities into account in computing a bank's capital position is, in itself, a substantial liberalization. In 1969, for example, when the yield on long-term government securities rose above 6 percent for the first time since the Civil War, the capital of many banks would have been seriously reduced if banks had been required to mark down to market values their still substantial holdings of government issues bearing only 4 percent coupons. Despite some inner qualms, the supervisors bravely ignored this situation, as they should have as long as the banks had adequate liquidity.

The public interest in safe banking, however, and the need to avoid forever a recurrence of 1933 require a conservative approach to the problem of capital adequacy. Bank shareholders should be equally interested in providing the assurance that the banks they own will be able to survive whatever adverse circumstances may possibly develop, and history bears abundant witness to the periodic recurrence of lean years.

---

[16]"Loans by Banks for the Purpose of Purchasing or Carrying Registered Stocks" (12 C F R 221).

[17]The average minimum requirement of the New York Reserve Bank formula represents a primary or unadjusted risk-asset ratio of 11.7 percent, compared with the original 20 percent standard.

SIGNIFICANCE FOR BANK POLICY

Whatever the analytical methods of the supervisors may be and however strong their moral suasion, the fundamental responsibility for capital adequacy rests with the directors and top management of each individual bank. It should be helpful for the directors and top management to understand the basis of the supervisory evaluation and to use one or more of the supervisory formulas at least as a measure of the trends in their capital positions. Not all banks will wish to go as far as to evaluate the risk in each and every bank asset, but all banks should go further than rough groupings, such as those in the New York Federal Reserve formula. Within the logical framework of that formula, capital allocations ranging from perhaps 5 to 15 percent could be used to distinguish among types of loans that the bank considers prime and those in which it recognizes normal or greater risk. Different amounts of capital might be allocated to different groups of securities as well to reflect variations in maturity dates, credit risk, and marketability. Such an evaluation of the risks inherent in the loans and securities of a particular bank would be an instructive exercise and could provide an effective review of lending and investing policies.

Just how much capital is enough can perhaps never be fully determined in advance of the hour of need. The bank supervisor has substantial responsibility in the area of capital adequacy and tends to react accordingly. Some more aggressive bankers try to keep the examiner unhappy but not agonized. However, from the viewpoint of management as well as of the supervisor, the risks of having too little exceed the costs of a moderate excess. In the review of the 1929–34 experience, it is perhaps significant that the nineteen banks that survived the Depression without having to raise additional capital had, in 1929, a capital ratio only 2.9 percent higher on the average than the thirty-one that needed recapitalization.

Adequate capital is not, of course, a substitute for sound lending and investing policies; it cannot take the place of experienced and progressive management of a well-conceived program of planning and control. It can only provide assurance to the public, the stockholder, and the supervisor that the bank has the strength and the wherewithal to survive circumstances and conditions that even the best management can never foresee. In a real sense, the provision of adequate capital is the price of the private enterprise banking system in the United States.

6

BANK EARNINGS

Bank earnings are the foundation upon which rest the two main pillars of banking strength—adequacy of capital and competence of management. The experience of the 1930s showed that even in the most serious and prolonged depression of our recent history nearly 95 percent of the losses taken by banks were absorbed through earnings over a ten-year period. Thus, earning power proved to be the first line of defense against the risks inherent in banking. In other words, bank earnings, current and accumulated, serve to protect a stockholder's investment in times of economic adversity, just as the bank's capital or owner's equity is the ultimate protection for the depositor.

In more normal times, bank earnings provide the return on capital investment in banks. It is for the sake of this return on his investment that the stockholder is willing to supply the capital that enables a bank to engage in the risky business of creating credit, and it is by retaining assets generated by earnings that the major portion of bank capital has been accumulated. Even when bank earnings are paid out as dividends, they tend to enhance the marketability and increase the value of the stock, thus enabling the bank to raise additional capital when needed.

Perhaps even more important to the strength and soundness of the privately owned banking system is the fact that adequate earnings are necessary as the wherewithal for banks to recruit and keep competent management. All too frequently, the complaint is heard that banks cannot afford to meet competitive wage and salary rates. But unless banks do attract able young men and women, the strength and caliber of the banking system will inevitably diminish. Only if they have ample earnings can banks afford to bid in today's highly competitive market for the best prospective talent.

TREND AND COMPOSITION OF BANK REVENUES AND EXPENSES

Bank revenues have been rising in recent years; however, bank expenses have been increasing even faster.[1] Chart 3 shows the growth of both revenues and expenses as percentages of assets during the past eleven years. Chart 3 also shows that earnings as a percentage of assets have declined slightly because of the higher growth rate of expenses during the decade. The steadily increasing size of bank assets, the larger portion of assets held in loans, and rising yields during most of this period have enabled banks to show a fairly steadily increasing level of net dollar earnings. After-tax earnings per share have also benefited from larger holdings of tax-exempt securities and, in some cases, from the leveraging of equity capital with debt (see Chapter 17).

Composition of Bank Revenues

At the present time, banks derive their revenues primarily from lending and investing and to a lesser extent from fees and charges received for services rendered. Chart 4 illustrates changes in the composition of bank revenues from 1946 through 1971. This chart indicates that interest and other fees from loans rose from 33 percent of total revenues at the end of World War II to 64 percent of total revenues in 1971. Interest on U.S. government securities declined steadily throughout the postwar period, but interest on other securities (primarily state and local securities) was a slowly rising proportion of total revenues. Total interest on investment securities accounted for roughly 24 percent of total revenues in 1971. All other revenues, including net fees from trust department activities, made up the remaining approximately 13 percent of total revenues in 1971.

Bank revenues are affected by shifts in the kinds of loans that banks

---

[1]In this chapter, the term *revenues* refers to gross return or gross earnings before any costs or expenses. *Earnings* or *income* refers to net income or net earnings after expenses have been subtracted from revenues. *Profitability* refers to the earnings as a percentage of equity capital.

PERCENTAGE
OF ASSETS

PERCENTAGE
OF ASSETS

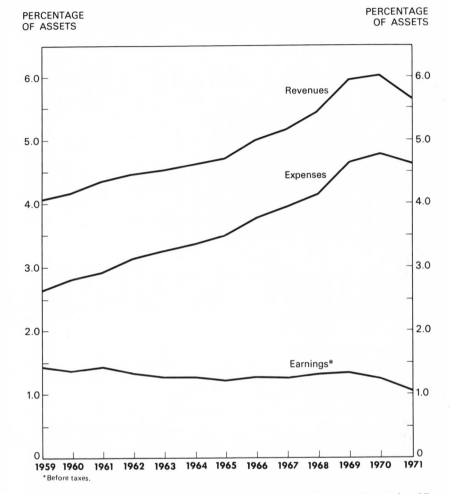

CHART 3 Revenues, Expenses, and Earnings as Percentages of Assets for All Insured Commercial Banks, 1960–71 [Source: *Annual Reports of the Federal Deposit Insurance Corporation, 1960–71* (Washington, D.C.: Federal Deposit Insurance Corporation, 1961–72).]

make. For example, the increase in the proportion of higher yielding consumer loans has increased the revenues from loans for many banks. This increase is at least partially offset, however, by higher expenses.

Composition of Bank Expenses

Chart 5 shows the relative growth of selected items of bank expense from 1946 through 1971. Until the mid–1960s, banks paid the largest

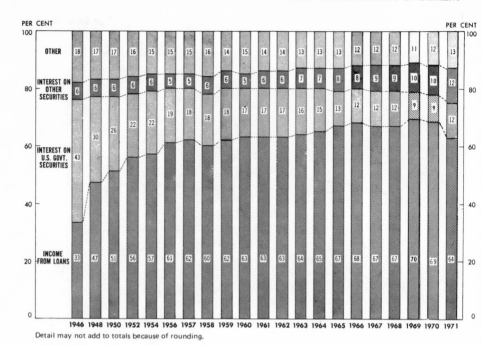

CHART 4 Composition of Revenues for All Commercial Banks, 1946–71 [Source: *Annual Reports of the Federal Deposit Insurance Corporation, 1946–71* (Washington, D.C.: Federal Deposit Insurance Corporation, 1947–72).]

portion of their revenues for salaries and wages. More recently, the cost of funds has been exceeding the cost of people, even though bank salary levels have been steadily rising. In 1971, commercial banks spent an average of 45 percent of their gross income in interest paid and only 28 percent on salaries and other employee benefits. This significant shift in cost elements results from the fact that demand deposits have been increasing more slowly than the demands for credit. Banks have had to rely more heavily on time deposits—and on other purchased funds in some situations—to try to meet expanding credit demands and to grow with the economy.

FACTORS AFFECTING BANK PROFITABILITY

The factors affecting the relationship between bank earnings and capital can be expressed in a simple profitability formula:

$$P = \frac{R - CL - CM - O - T}{C}$$

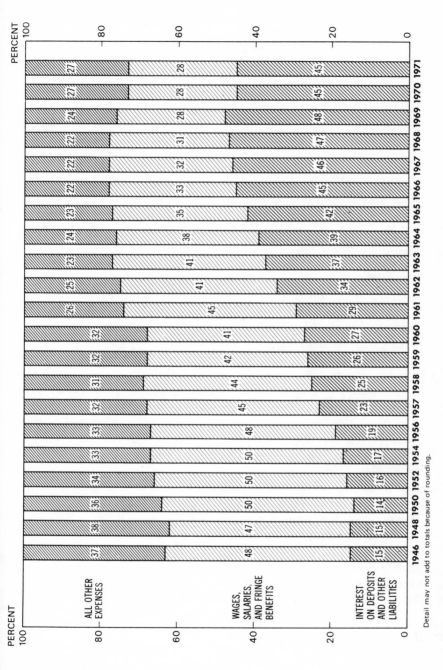

CHART 5 Composition of Expenses for All Insured Commercial Banks, 1946–71 [Source: *Annual Reports of the Federal Deposit Insurance Corporation, 1946–71* (Washington, D.C.: Federal Deposit Insurance Corporation, 1947–72).]

Detail may not add to totals because of rounding.

Where:

$$P = \text{Profitability}$$
$$R = \text{Revenues}$$
$$CL = \text{The cost of lending and investing}$$
$$CM = \text{The cost of money}$$
$$O = \text{Overhead}$$
$$T = \text{Taxes}$$
$$C = \text{Equity capital}$$

The profitability of a bank can be increased only by an expansion of revenues or a reduction in one or more of the other factors. However, these factors are interrelated in various ways; a change in one affects at least one or more of the others. For example, if management decides to switch funds from Treasury bills to installment loans, revenues will be increased, but so will expenses. At the same time, the greater risk in consumer loans may require more capital. It is the continuing task of bank management to balance these factors in order to maximize earnings in relation to capital over time. This balance should be within prudent risk limits and in the framework of the financial needs of the community or banking markets it serves.

Several aspects of management are involved. The first, often called asset management, is the allocation of funds to various asset categories to provide adequate liquidity, serve the credit needs of the bank's customers, and maximize the income from its investments. In recent years, as banks have relied more heavily on time deposits and purchased money of various kinds, the acquisition of funds has assumed as much importance as their use. We might more accurately label this phase of bank policy liability management. The need for coordination between asset management and liability management has led to the current term *balance-sheet management* for the first aspect of management.

A bank can also increase its earnings by expanding its services and making them more profitable. Service charges on deposit accounts are one example. Trust fees are another, although not all small trust departments can be operated profitably. More recently, banks have been expanding into other areas of financial services either directly or through holding company subsidiaries (see Chapter 2). Many bank managers believe that much of the future growth in bank earnings lies in this direction.

Management of these related enterprises as well as the running of the bank itself might be called operating management. This second aspect of management is primarily comprised of expense reduction and control, all phases of efficiency and productivity, and minimizing the overhead factor in the profitability equation. Operating management may also contribute to reducing the cost of money, because demand deposits have a definite cost in services rendered, even though no interest is paid on them. Most banks recognize this function by placing a senior officer in charge of operations. His realm usually includes personnel, accounting, and data processing and often includes systems design and review, budgeting, and planning.

The third aspect might be designated financial management, which includes capital planning and an overall view of the bank's tax picture. The Board of Directors and senior management generally have primary responsibility for this aspect.

These aspects of bank management overlap, of course. They eventually come together in the chief executive officer and the Board of Directors, whose task it is to juggle all the factors in the profitability equation in the light of a continually changing financial and economic scene. Many of the ingredients of a bank's profitability are beyond its immediate control. Interest rates, for example, are determined by monetary and fiscal policy and tempered by competition. Salary scales are determined in the local labor market. Taxes are decreed by Congress. Within this broad framework, however, there is a good deal of room in which to maneuver.

THE OUTLOOK FOR BANK EARNINGS

If the steady rise in bank earnings over the past twenty years has been largely attributable to rising interest rates and a shift from investments with lower yields to loans and tax-exempt securities, and if interest rates fall, now that loan-to-deposit ratios have gotten about as high as they can go, what is the prospect for bank earnings? Although the cost of funds is likely to decrease as yields on loans and investments decline, salary costs and the other ingredients of overhead are likely to remain stationary at best or even to rise in an inflationary environment.

As the profitability formula shows, bank earnings represent the difference between revenues, which come increasingly from loans on the one hand and the aggregate of bank expenses on the other. This difference is often referred to as the spread, and it remains fairly constant in periods of both high and low interest rates.[2] All studies of banking looking for-

---

[2] E. Sherman Adams, "Key Factors Affecting Bank Earnings," *Banking*, Vol. 63, March 1971, pp. 34–36.

ward to the next ten years or more predict a very large demand for credit. The problem, as the forecasters see it, will be to find the funds to meet the loan demands of the future.[3] Intelligent bankers, conscious of the need to maintain the spread, are likely to price their lending at rates that will continue to cover their costs. The margin of profitability may continue to decline, but the volume will continue to increase.

Furthermore, in typical periods of recession, when loan demands slacken and interest rates fall sharply, the Federal Reserve usually increases the money supply. Bank deposits tend to rise, and banks add to their investment portfolios to take up the slack of declining loan volume. Falling rates (and rising bond prices) also provide the opportunity for *realizing* profits in securities that, at least in the larger banks, have substantially supplemented declining loan revenues during periods of recession. Banks taking advantage of this opportunity should realize that interest income is not increased and that the cost basis of securities is increased (meaning possible future opportunities to take losses) when they purchase other securities to replace those they have sold.

One cannot, of course, be too sanguine about maintaining the spread. Profit margins have been declining and may continue to do so. The challenge of the future will certainly include both the search for additional banking services that will produce fee income and the necessity for still further increases in the efficiency of banking operations.

EARNINGS FACTORS IN
THE INDIVIDUAL BANK

In all size groups, some banks are much more profitable than others. For example, Table 6 shows that banks with high earnings in 1970 tended to have higher revenues, lower expenses, and a considerably greater return on assets than the average for banks in similar size groupings. The factors that lead to greater earnings have been the subject of several recent studies.

In an attempt to identify these factors, Lyle Whitledge used a questionnaire approach to compare a selected group of thirty revitalized banks—banks with earnings well above average—with sixty-two stagnated banks with results known to be below par. He then made detailed case studies of several revitalized banks in an endeavor to determine what made the difference. His basic conclusion that "almost all stagnation is fundamentally traceable to inadequate leadership" bears constant repeti-

---

[3]Gerald C. Fisher, Ed., *Commercial Banking, 1975 and 1980,* (Philadelphia: The Robert Morris Associates, 1970).

TABLE 6

COMPARABLE EARNINGS OF COMMERCIAL BANKS, 1970

	Smaller Banks		Larger Banks	
	High Earnings[a]	*Average Earnings*[b]	*High Earnings*[c]	*Average Earnings*[d]
Total revenues as a percentage of assets	7.67	7.29	7.50	7.16
Total expenses as a percentage of assets	4.64	5.03	4.67	5.05
Earnings before taxes as a percentage of assets	3.03	2.26	2.83	2.10

[a] *Banks with deposits of $25 million to $50 million*
[b] *Banks with deposits of less than $50 million*
[c] *Banks with deposits of over $100 million*
[d] *Banks with deposits of over $200 million*

Source: *Functional Cost Analysis 1970 Average Banks* and *Performance Characteristics of High Earning Banks* (both available from the Federal Reserve Bank of New York, 1972). Raw data were furnished by 951 participating banks from the twelve Federal Reserve districts.

tion; but, like many broad generalizations, it is not a very specific guide to action. Effective leadership comes in many varied styles.[4]

John Haslem studied the differential effects of management and other selected variables on commercial bank profitability and the operating relationships through which these effects are transmitted and relative profitability is determined. Haslem defined *management effects* as the result of differences in bank objectives, policies, decisions, and actions. He concluded that the ability of management to earn on bank loans and investments appeared more important to relative profits than the asset mix or the effects of size and location.[5]

Another recent study was made by William Bryan under the auspices of the American Bankers Association Committee on Banking and Research with the cooperation of the Federal Deposit Insurance Corporation, which provided data on 1600 banks in the $10–25 million deposit category. Half of these were located in standard metropolitan areas and half were from outside such areas. Bryan started by eliminating statistically the factors affecting earnings that he believes are beyond the control of bank management. These include, among others, the ratio of

---

[4]Lyle A. Whitledge, *Vitalizing Banks* (Boston: Bankers Publishing Company, 1964), p. 28.

[5]John A. Haslem, "A Statistical Analysis of the Relative Profitability of Commercial Banks," *Journal of Finance*, Vol. 23, No. 1, March 1968, pp. 167–76.

time deposits to total deposits, the rate of interest paid on time deposits, the growth rate and size of the bank, and the wage bill for nonofficer employees. Having estimated the magnitude of nonmanagement effects, he then figured the profit potential of each bank. Next, Bryan compared the actual profits with those estimated and ranked each bank according to the size of its deviation. The larger a bank's actual profits relative to its predicted profits, the higher its ranking. He termed the upper 10 percent *successful* and the lower 10 percent *laggardly* banks.

On the basis of an elaborate questionnaire, he then examined the characteristics of both types of banks. He concluded,

> . . .there are substantial and numerous differences between successful and laggardly banks. It may be noted that successful banks achieved smaller earnings on government securities—even though they achieved a significantly greater yield on those governments they held. Their lower earnings on governments resulted from significantly smaller holdings.
> The chief contribution to earnings is from loans. Successful banks were distinctive in that they achieved significantly greater yields on loans and held significantly larger loan portfolios than did the laggardly banks. Finally, successful banks' portfolios contained significantly smaller cash holdings (including due from banks). Thus they were able to forego less earnings than did laggardly banks.[6]

Thus, Bryan found that superior balance-sheet management accounted for a major part of the difference between banks with high and low earnings. He found little or no significant correlation between success and structure, location, ownership, management characteristics, or money spent on advertising.[7]

These conclusions bear out the results of studies reported in the first edition of this book, except that the authors believe that a significant difference between the most profitable banks and the average lies in the ratio of total salary cost to gross income. Bryan considers staff salaries to be determined by salary scales in the local market and therefore beyond the control of management. However, the below-average costs of banks with high earnings often are not the result of low unit salaries; they reflect the ability of management to get the banking job done with fewer people. While others wait for the electronic age to solve bank operating problems, both big and relatively small banks with above-average earnings have demonstrated that the greatest savings are to be found not in better machinery alone but in more efficient procedures and more efficient management organization.

---

[6]William R. Bryan, unpublished study for the American Bankers Association Committee on Banking and Research.
[7]*Ibid.*

High productivity reflects not only simplicity of method but also the effectiveness of personnel training and the elimination of wasted time and effort, which in the aggregate still cost banks millions of dollars every month. For the attainment of maximum results and control over rising costs, a precise knowledge of the factors that go into each individual bank's revenues and expenses is essential.

ANALYSIS OF REVENUES AND EXPENSES

It obviously behooves the management of any bank that wants to be successful to carefully analyze the factors in its own profitability formula and to compare them with its past performance and, if possible, with the performance of other banks. Unfortunately, the traditional published figures of bank revenues and expenses, taken from the reports rendered to the supervisory authorities, leave much to be desired for comparative purposes.

Salary figures, for example, include trust department salaries for those banks that have such departments, so that comparison of their salary expense with that of a bank that does not operate a trust department becomes essentially meaningless. Of even greater significance, because it affects many more banks, is the fundamental difference between the operating costs of handling savings and demand deposits. The latter, because of their low rate of turnover, are substantially cheaper to process than active checking accounts. A bank with a large proportion of savings deposits, therefore, may show below-average salary costs when it is actually operating inefficiently. The published figures need to be subjected to closer analysis, and similar operations should be compared with each other.

Detailed analysis of revenues and expenses, often loosely referred to as cost analysis, serves a number of useful purposes. In the first place, bank management cannot successfully plan a broad lending and investing program unless it knows the net yield as well as the gross return on various types of loans and investments. There is no point, for example, in attempting to expand a consumer lending operation or entering some new phase, such as permissible overdrafts on checking accounts, until management is reasonably sure that the net return will be commensurate with the risk. The fact that such lending is considered profitable by other banks is no guarantee that it will be equally profitable in a particular bank.[8]

---

[8]An analysis of the revenues and expenses of one consumer credit department revealed that the net earnings of that active but inefficient department were less than the return on the bank's U.S. government securities, a fact that shocked management into remedial action.

Revenue and expense analysis is also vital to cost control and cost reduction. For this purpose, it is usually desirable for management to obtain departmental and branch office breakdowns of revenues and expenses so that particular segments of the bank's earnings can be made the direct responsibility of individual supervisors, department heads, or branch managers. Expense analysis can be used to relate expense to volume for determining per-item costs. Such figures are widely used as a basis for determining or justifying service charges and are also a measure of efficiency on the basis of which operating standards can be established. Finally, it is essential to determine functional costs, which can be defined as the direct costs of performing specific operations, such as bookkeeping or consumer lending. These costs provide a means for comparing systems and procedures, and they are the most nearly comparable costs among different banks.

Methods of Revenue and Expense Analysis

To a considerable extent, the purposes for which a bank analyzes its revenues and expenses will determine the form of the analysis. Many of these purposes are interrelated, and there is no reason why more than one approach should not be followed. Any analysis will, at best, involve a number of arbitrary decisions, and no one method can be said to be completely or scientifically accurate. For example, the allocation of senior officers' salaries to departments or functions and especially to item costs can be based only on subjective judgment.

One cannot accurately determine what the president of a bank spends his time thinking about. He himself would find keeping a record of his various activities intolerably burdensome, even for a few days. Moreover, such a record would be largely meaningless, because the work of senior management seldom follows established patterns. The president may spend a week working on a merger, half of the next week attending a bankers' convention, two days working out a complicated loan agreement, and the next day catching up on a pile of neglected and quite miscellaneous correspondence. Some of his most important contributions are made entirely outside of regular banking hours in the form of new business garnered on the golf course or the sudden insight that flashes across his mind as he is about to fall asleep.

In small- and medium-sized banks, even the work of the junior officer is equally varied. In the course of any business day, he may take loan applications, open new accounts, sell savings bonds or travellers' checks, and interview an equipment salesman, a representative of the bank's correspondent, and a wealthy customer who wants to know what stock

to buy. Such efforts cannot be accurately allocated to the cost of processing a check.

Even so, for many of the purposes for which banks analyze their
revenues and expenses, the inaccuracies of expense allocation are not
seriously detrimental. For comparing the bank's own performance year
by year and for most budgeting and cost control, consistent application
of well-thought-out allocations will be sufficient. For valid comparisons
between banks, however, reasonable consistency in allocating expenses
is essential. And, for some functional decisions involving nearly arbitrarily
allocated expenses, it may be preferable to refer to revenues and expenses
directly associated with the function.

The traditional method of cost accounting in banking has been to
distribute the revenue and expense accounts shown on the bank's general
ledger, first to departments and then to fund-using functions (lending or
investing) or fund-supplying functions (acquiring deposits and capital
funds). Either the estimated profitability of the department and function
or the per-item costs could be emphasized.

This is a fairly complicated process, at least on the surface, and for
many years cost accounting was used only by the larger banks. To bring
effective cost accounting within the reach of even the smallest bank, the
Federal Reserve Bank of New York in 1958 began developing a simplified
functional cost analysis, which has since been greatly expanded and is
now available to member banks in all twelve Federal Reserve districts.
The following excerpts from the summary published by the Federal
Reserve explain the methods used.

> Functional Cost Analysis is, by most cost study standards, a very
> simple system. Information about bank assets, income, expense,
> and item count is collected by member bankers with the guidance
> of uniform instructions. Although bankers must use judgment in
> making expense allocations, most of this judgment is required for
> the allocation of wages and salaries. Expenses not allocated by the
> banker are allocated by the computer on the basis of "experience
> factors" developed from expense data of participating banks. This
> technique has helped eliminate some inconsistencies of interbank
> comparisons.
>
> Development of comparative earnings information requires a uni-
> form method of allocating earnings to fund-providing functions
> and a uniform method of applying the cost of money to fund-using
> functions. Interbank comparability would suffer if different methods
> of asset allocations were used by participating banks. Therefore,
> FCA employs the "pool of funds" concept, in which the same
> portfolio yield is used in calculating income for each source of
> funds, and the same "cost of money" rate is charged to the different
> fund-using functions.

Pre-tax income is higher than that shown in other analyses of bank earnings since all tax-exempt income has been converted to a taxable basis. This is necessary to achieve interbank comparability of pre-tax earnings.[9]

In functional cost analysis, the *cost of money* is defined as "the cost of processing (including interest expense) demand deposits, time deposits, and net capital funds less any service charge or other income fee. It is calculated as a percent of available funds." *Available funds* are defined as "the sum of net capital and deposits," and are equal to the total of cash and amounts due from banks, loans, and investments.[10]

Having submitted its figures to the Reserve bank in its district, each participating member bank receives a report comparing its operations in its current year (1) with those of the previous year, (2) with the operations of a group of banks of similar size and ratio of time deposits to total deposits, and (3) with a group of banks with similar functional volume—that is, a comparable volume of consumer loans, mortgages, and so on. Each report also includes a wealth of information on the number of items processed, per-item costs, and break-even points on savings accounts and consumer loans. If used thoughtfully and with an understanding of the limitations of and possible inconsistencies in allocations, this information may reveal the bank's functional strengths and weaknesses.

Because a comparison with the average is seldom challenging, the Federal Reserve banks also publish annually the "Performance Characteristics of High Earning Banks" broken down by size groups and ratio of time deposits to total deposits. As stated in the introduction to this summary of the best performing 25 percent of participating banks, "The differences between your bank and the higher earners should be studied carefully and reconciled. In some areas you will find that your bank is doing as well as the banks in the superior quartile but in others there may be important differences in performance. Such a study enables the conscientious banker to set realistic objectives for individual functions and for his bank as a whole."[11]

Uses of Cost Analysis

A functional cost analysis is of little value unless it is used. Too often, even the bank managers who have taken the trouble to participate in

[9]*Functional Cost Analysis 1970 Average Banks.* Based on data furnished by 951 participating member banks in twelve federal Reserve districts available from the Federal Reserve Bank of New York, 1972, pp. 1–2.

[10]*Ibid.*

[11]"Performance characteristics of High Earning Banks," based on data furnished by 951 participating banks in twelve Federal Reserve districts (Federal Reserve Bank of New York, 1972).

such a program do not use the results effectively. They glance through the report, taking satisfaction in any favorable comparisons they may find but not assiduously pursuing the possible causes of their banks' apparent shortcomings. Even small deviations from optimum results can make a substantial difference in the profitability of large volume transactions. Progressive managers, therefore, will not be satisfied until they have at least explained all deviations from the results of the best performers. There may be some valid explanations, such as higher occupancy costs or a better level of compensation; but, if there are not, a careful study of operating procedures is called for.

PROFIT PLANNING

One of the principal byproducts of an analysis of revenue and expense should be a budget[12] or planned projection of the bank's operations into the future. A budget is much more than a simple forecast. It is a pattern to follow, a measure against which performance may be judged, a set of goals that an organization may strive to exceed.

Bank budgets do not start with revenues and expenses. They are derived from forecasts of the volume and character of the bank's assets and liabilities—the number and types of loans and the volume, variety, and degree of activity in deposits. When volume and activity have been projected, they can be combined with any other managerial projections to form an estimate of expenses and revenues to forecast earnings before and after taxes. One vital function of the budget is to divide the bank's operations into manageable and visible components so that management and the directors can see the results of each department or function. Budgets often provide for interdepartmental charges and credits that distribute the cost of services or the cost of funds to the departments using them.

When the budget is being prepared, last year's experience must be combined with next year's expectations. The attainment of budgeted results is not in itself as important as the explanation of the variance from what was expected. A budget should be a guide, not a straitjacket—an intelligently established set of goals, not a flat prediction. The goals that management is willing to set for itself provide powerful incentives for improved performance.

The initial budgets should come from the people primarily responsible for performance—the branch managers and department heads. Their

---

[12]The type of budget described in this section involves forecasting revenues, expenses, and the resulting profits on savings. Budgets can also be used to forecast liquidity and to assist in deciding whether to acquire fixed assets.

estimates should be checked by top management in the light of economic conditions, community growth, competitive factors, and comparisons with other banks in similar circumstances. It is the task of top management to see to it that budgetary goals are high enough to provide a realistic challenge to the entire organization. However, a budget imposed from the top will be ineffective unless those directly responsible for performance agree in good faith to the reasonableness of the goals set forth. Deviations from budgetary goals in either direction should require formal explanation, because the primary function of the budget is to act as a measure of management's ability to plan intelligently and to execute a plan successfully.

No bank is too small to have a budget, even if its form is relatively simple. Bank directors should insist on a budget, for it is the directors' most effective tool in the execution of their important function of giving guidance to the bank in its service to the community and its rewards to the stockholder.

LONG-RANGE PLANNING

In recent years, more and more well-managed banks have been looking ahead to periods longer than the next year. Long-range planning involves a good deal more than just projecting the budget for five years instead of one. Essentially, it consists of establishing longer-range objectives for the bank's organization, markets, staffing, and management succession, and ultimately its place in a rapidly changing banking structure—for example, does it want to remain independent or join (organize) a branch or holding company system.

To formulate long-range plans, bank management must take a close look at the markets it presently serves and what is happening to them. It must study the strengths and weaknesses of its people and physical facilities. It must relate these to costs and potential income, both present and prospective. It must, in effect, establish long-range objectives.

It is possible to translate these long-range plans into revenues, expenses, and earnings projections, and computer programs are available either on a time-sharing basis or through correspondent banks that enable management to make five-year or longer forecasts based on a variety of assumptions. But forecasting should never be confused with real planning; forecasting tells one where he may be, but planning tells him where he wants to be and how to get there.[13]

---

[13]There has been considerable emphasis placed on long-range planning for banks in recent years. Long-range planning has been the subject of numerous articles and conferences. One of the best concise summaries is Wray O. Candilis, *Long-Range Planning in Banking* (Washington: American Bankers Association, 1968).

PART III

BALANCE SHEET MANAGEMENT

7

ATTRACTING DEPOSITS

The purpose of this and the next six chapters is to discuss management policies and procedures relating to balance sheet management—asset management, liability management, and interactions between the two. The importance of attracting deposits, the major classifications of commercial bank deposits, and the growth and changing composition of these deposits are discussed in the first part of this chapter. This discussion is followed by suggested policies and techniques that can aid the individual bank in attracting deposits. Many of these policies and techniques are interrelated with the broader marketing policies discussed in Chapter 16.

INCREASING IMPORTANCE OF ATTRACTING DEPOSITS

For many years after the Depression of the 1930s, commercial banking could be classified as a *funds-using* business. The focus of bank policy was on asset management, more specifically on how to lend and invest a surplus of deposits. Although asset management is still important, the steady postwar rise in loan demand, the decline of commercial banks' proportionate share of financial intermediary liabilities (for example, savings and loan shares) during the 1950s and early 1960s, and the shortages of deposit funds in the late 1960s forced banks to place greater emphasis on attracting deposits, and terms such as *liability management* came into common usage. This shift can be seen in the more creative and intensive use of existing sources of funds and in the aggressive development of new sources of funds.

Furthermore, many banking forecasters believe that banking will become increasingly a *funds-gathering* business in the 1970s, with particular emphasis on the consumer market. Good loans will be easy to make, these forecasters say, in the face of a strong and rising demand for credit and a limited growth in the supply of money. The difficult part of managing a commercial bank will be finding the money to meet the demands for credit.[1] This involves actively seeking deposits in all the markets in which they may be found.

CLASSIFICATIONS OF DEPOSITS

Different classifications of deposits are attracted by varying techniques and have widely varying liquidity requirements and levels of profitability. The most meaningful classifications reflect ownership, security, and form of withdrawal. When classified by ownership, deposits may be private, public, or interbank. Private deposits are those owned by individuals, partnerships, corporations, and other private institutions. Public deposits are the deposits of all levels of government. Deposits of the Federal government are called Treasury tax and loan accounts. Interbank deposits are those of foreign banks, mutual savings banks, and commercial banks. Most interbank deposits are correspondent balances from other commercial banks.

Deposits can also be classified secured or unsecured. The most common kinds of secured deposits are public deposits. For example, commercial banks that accept Federal government deposits in excess of twenty thousand dollars must secure such deposits by pledging U.S. government bonds or other collateral approved by the Secretary of the Treasury. U.S. government securities, and sometimes the securities of the state and municipality, are usually required to secure state and local government deposits. The remaining deposits are unsecured in the sense that no specific assets have been pledged; however, all accounts are insured up to a maximum of twenty thousand dollars in banks that are members of the Federal Deposit Insurance Corporation.

Deposits may finally be classified demand, savings, or time deposits.

---

[1]One excellent description of the forecasted increasing emphasis on funds-gathering is "The Challenges Ahead For Banking: A Study of the Commercial Banking System in 1980," prepared by the Banking Department of Booz, Allen, and Hamilton, Inc., New York, 1971.

Demand deposits may be withdrawn by check or transferred to someone else by the depositor at any time without previous notice to the bank. It has been illegal since the early 1930s for a bank to pay interest on demand deposits. Savings deposits have indefinite maturity, receive interest, and can be withdrawn only by conversion into currency or demand deposits. Notice of withdrawal, usually thirty days legally, is normally waived. Savings deposits are often referred to as passbook savings accounts, because passbooks, containing the rules and regulations governing the account, are usually required for deposits or withdrawals. Time deposits are interest-drawing deposits left with the bank for a stated period of time. Because of the stated maturity, the interest rates on these deposits are usually higher than the rates on savings deposits. The two most prominent forms of time deposits are consumer certificates of deposit and negotiable certificates of deposit. A consumer certificate is issued for a definite period (from a minimum of ninety days to several years), is usually nonnegotiable, and can usually be renewed. A negotiable certificate of deposit is a formal, negotiable receipt for funds left with the bank for a specified period of time (usually from thirty days to a year); the bank pays interest if the funds are left until maturity. The deposit is payable only upon surrender of the properly endorsed receipt. A negotiable CD may be sold many times in the secondary market before it matures.

GROWTH AND CHANGING COMPOSITION OF DEPOSITS

Commercial bank deposits grew more slowly than other financial intermediary liabilities from the early 1900s through the early 1960s. The trend since the end of World War II is traced in Chart 6, and the record prior to 1952 is substantiated in Goldsmith's *Financial Intermediaries in the American Economy Since 1900.*[2] The decline in the relative importance of deposits prior to the 1930s is discussed in Goldsmith. The decline in the 1930s and 1940s appears to have been caused primarily by the lack of adequate demand for bank loans. Because they felt profitable use of funds was restricted, many banks actually tried to discourage deposit growth by paying minimum rates on time and savings deposits. Most large banks accepted time deposits only from individuals, charitable corporations, and foreign central banks. Deposit attraction became almost a forgotten art, because the economy was flooded with excess funds.

---

[2]Raymond W. Goldsmith, *Financial Intermediaries in the American Economy Since 1900* (Princeton, N.J.: Princeton University Press, 1958).

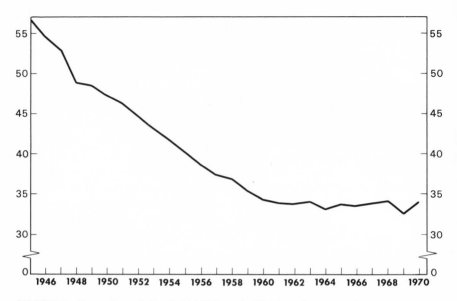

CHART 6 Proportion of Total Liabilities of All Financial Institutions Accounted for by Commercial Banks, 1945–70 (Sources: Federal Reserve Board; Life Insurance Institute; Federal Home Loan Board; *Finance Facts Yearbook; Best's Fire and Casualty Aggregates and Averages;* and *Weisenberg's Investment Companies.*)

The rapid growth of the demand for credit in the 1950s led to increased demands for commercial bank funds and increased interest rates. However, as illustrated in Chart 7, the growth of demand deposits during the 1950s was very slow. A major factor was the increasingly rapid turnover of demand deposits; rising interest rates encouraged depositors, particularly large corporations, to hold demand deposit balances at a minimum.[3] At the same time, most commercial banks were faced with increasing loan demands, especially from corporate borrowers seeking larger commercial loans. The slow growth in deposits and rapid growth in loans led to rapidly increasing loan-to-deposit ratios.

Although commercial banks were slow to react to the inadequate growth in deposits, by the early 1960s the need was obvious. The response came in several forms. First, commercial banks began to pay higher returns on their time and savings accounts. The proportionate decline in the differences among rates of financial intermediaries that accept deposits is illustrated in Chart 8. The Federal Reserve encouraged this improvement in the competitive position of commercial banks in the

[3]Richard T. Selden, *The Postwar Rise in the Velocity of Money* (New York: National Bureau of Economic Research, 1962), and George Garvey, *Deposit Velocity and its Significance* (New York: Federal Reserve Bank, 1969).

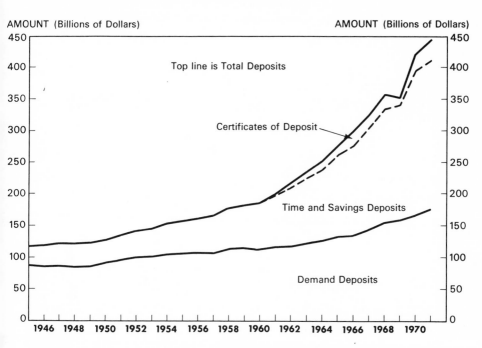

AMOUNT (Billions of Dollars)

Top line is Total Deposits

Certificates of Deposit

Time and Savings Deposits

Demand Deposits

1946 1948 1950 1952 1954 1956 1958 1960 1962 1964 1966 1968 1970

CHART 7 Size of Major Forms of Commercial Bank Deposits [Source: *Federal Reserve Bulletins* (Washington, D.C.: Federal Reserve Board, 1945–72).]

late 1950s and 1960s by raising the interest rate ceilings imposed on them by Regulation Q. Second, commercial banks began the aggressive use of certificates of deposit to attract both individual and commercial deposits. In particular, large banks, following the lead of First National City Bank of New York, began to use these certificates to actively solicit the time deposits of their corporate customers who had actively invested their excess funds in other money market instruments. The growth in large negotiable certificates of deposit is illustrated in Chart 7. Third, commercial banks began to emphasize the use of larger demand deposit balances from their loan customers.

The end result of these actions is seen in Charts 6 and 7. Commercial bank deposits showed rapid absolute growth and remained a constant proportion of the liabilities of all financial intermediaries from 1960 through 1965. The absolute growth slowed somewhat in 1966 because of the disintermediation[4] caused by market interest rates exceeding bank rates constrained by the Regulation Q ceilings. The growth resumed in

---

[4]*Disintermediation* refers to situations in which money that normally flows into banks and other financial intermediaries flows directly to the users of the funds.

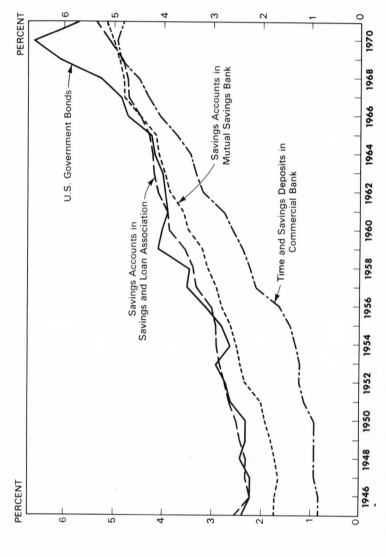

CHART 8 Average Annual Yields on Selected Types of Investments [Source: *Savings and Loan Fact Book, 1971* (Chicago: U.S. Savings and Loan League, 1971), p. 17.]

1967 and 1968; however, the disintermediation in late 1969 and early 1970 was more severe and caused an absolute decline as well as a proportionate decline in total deposits of commercial banks. From 1960 through 1970, total deposits of commercial banks increased from $186 billion to $396 billion, but were still roughly 34 percent of the liabilities of all financial intermediaries. As Chart 7 illustrates, most of the absolute increase in deposits was in time and savings deposits.

This increase in time and savings deposits was necessary. It has, however, changed the emphasis in management policies of many commercial banks. Some of the new time deposits are much more volatile (particularly to changes in interest rates) than past balances in demand and savings deposits, and management policies should reflect this.

POLICIES AND TECHNIQUES FOR ATTRACTING DEPOSITS

Although management and directors of individual banks do not have absolute control over the level of their deposits, they can nevertheless influence the amount their banks hold. Because deposits are so important to the profitable operation of a bank, most banks tend to compete aggressively for them. Among the factors determining the level of deposits in a bank are some that the individual bank usually cannot affect significantly. For example, monetary and fiscal policy, Regulation Q, and the level of general economic activity are exogenous factors that an individual bank must recognize but cannot control. The individual bank can control in varying degrees an intermediate group of factors—for example, the size and physical location(s) of the bank. Finally, the individual bank determines for itself such factors as its physical features and personnel, its marketing effort, the interest rates (within Regulation Q) it pays on time and savings accounts, the type of loans it is willing to make, and the level of services it offers its depositors. The major factors contributing toward attracting the principal types of deposits are discussed below.

Demand Deposits

The aggregate amount of demand deposits in this country at any given time is the result of Federal Reserve monetary actions controlling or limiting the money supply. Because banks are not permitted to pay interest on demand deposits, each bank must compete for its share on the basis of services rendered the depositor. It has long been held that the failure to charge for a service is not a payment of interest and this concept has led to the theory of supporting or compensating balances.

As depositors, particularly the larger ones, have become more sophisticated, and as alternative uses of money have become more profitable with rising interest rates, the corporate treasurer and the wealthy individual have learned to seek a specific *quid pro quo* in terms of service for every dollar of their demand deposits.

The most essential service compensated for by demand deposits is the collection and payment service in all its various forms. Every one who draws checks needs a bank account; everyone who receives checks needs a bank to collect them for him. The best service is rendered by the bank that can collect checks most quickly, thereby making funds available to the depositor earlier. Out of this need for faster collection has sprung a whole art of "funds mobilization" in which the Federal Reserve System has cooperated fully. These facilities include arrangements for sending large cash letters direct by air mail to Federal Reserve Banks in other districts (postage paid by the Federal Reserve) or to correspondent banks in major cities, bypassing the Reserve System entirely. Special carrier services have been established to bring checks into major cities more quickly than they can be delivered by mail. Locked-box arrangements have proliferated.[5] Some large banks have special departments whose function is to advise the corporate treasurer on the most effective way to mobilize his cash for short-term investment.

Whether it be funds mobilization for a large corporation or friendly service with a smile for the harried housewife, the cost of demand deposits is service. Ideally, banks should carefully calculate the costs of these services and assure themselves that the value of the related deposits compensates them for that cost and provides a profit margin. This is usually done by calculating a service charge representing the actual cost plus profit margin and offsetting this charge, in whole or in part, by an earnings credit. This credit is usually related to some money market rate representing the value of the funds to the bank. Both the service charges and the earnings credits are competitive rates, too often shaded, perhaps, in favor of the depositor.

The true net cost to the bank of services rendered depositors represents its cost of money for those deposits. Faced with higher costs in other markets for funds, most banks are willing to compensate the demand depositor by providing services at a charge somewhat less than net cost. Some banks waive service charges entirely even on individual accounts over some nominal amount, figuring that the cost of servicing

---

[5]Under a locked-box arrangement, remittances for a company's billings are sent directly to a post office box under the collecting bank's control, thus saving at least one day's handling and one day's collection time.

those accounts is less than the interest they would have to pay on time and savings deposits.[6]

It is very easy, however, to become entrapped by this philosophy, and a bank can easily find itself rendering a number of services in consideration of the same demand deposit account. The aggregate cost of these services may well exceed the value of the deposit. It becomes increasingly important, therefore, to look at each account relationship as a whole and, in recent years, computer programs have been developed to enable banks to measure the relative profitability of an account relationship in all its various facets. This involves coordinating in one computer printout all the services performed and their cost, average collected balances maintained by a given customer (including other related accounts he may control) and their value, as well as credit usage, if any. Small banks do not need a computer to look at their relatively few large deposit accounts in this fashion.

The basic relationship between demand deposits and services rendered is essentially the same whether the depositor be an individual, a business corporation, or a municipality. The most successful bank will be the one that can produce the needed services at the lowest cost and thereby market its services at the lowest price and still maintain an adequate profit margin.

Of almost equal importance in attracting demand deposits, particularly business accounts, is the willingness to lend. The availability of credit is an essential need for most businesses at one time or another, a constant need for some. When funds are in short supply (as they are predicted to be in the foreseeable future), banks will give preference to those customers who maintain demand deposit accounts with them. "Required supporting balances" are a part of loan pricing (see Chapter 11), but more than this the offer of credit accommodation is a primary factor in deposit soliciation. For this reason, banks frequently offer "solicitation" lines of credit to businesses with no present need to borrow and by the same token businesses maintain deposit balances in anticipation of their possible future need to borrow. One outstanding example of this relationship is the so-called back-up-line-of-credit supporting a corporation's sale of commercial paper. A company actively using the commercial paper to finance its current needs will obtain and advertise the availability of its unused bank lines of credit. These unused lines are typically supported by demand deposit balances of at least 10 percent of the credit available.

---

[6]This thesis is borne out, at least superficially, by the Federal Reserve Functional Cost studies that compute the cost of servicing demand deposits at approximately 2 percent per annum.

The willingness to lend, in short, is another vital service that banks are willing to perform for corporations or individuals who maintain or control important demand deposit balances. At times when money is extremely scarce, this relationship between deposit balances and the availability of credit seeps down even to the consumer lending field, and nondepositors will seek home mortgage loans in vain.

Passbook Savings

The passbook savings market is primarily a market of convenience. Competing mutual thrift institutions are permitted to pay higher interest rates than commercial banks (theoretically in the interest of channeling savings funds into the residential mortgage market) so that, in face of a rate disadvantage, all that commercial banks can offer is greater convenience. The full thrust of commercial bank advertising in this field has been on "one-stop" or "full-service" banking, and the fact that commercial banks, even when they are in close competition with strong mutual institutions, still have large amounts of savings deposits is evidence of the effectiveness of this marketing technique.

To compete effectively in the passbook savings market (with or without an actual passbook), banks will have to go beyond mere convenience and offer fringe benefits in the form of additional services to compensate for the lower permissable interest rates. A bank might offer lower charges on checking account facilities to savings deposit customers in some relation to the size of their savings accounts.[7]

Savings account banking offers many challenges to imaginative attraction of deposits. The specific purpose account is one of these. "Christmas Club" accounts have blossomed out into a wide variety of reasons to save—to pay taxes, insurance, finance vacations, and so on. A Philadelphia savings bank many years ago put different covers on the same passbook to differentiate among a "Stork Account," an "Education Account," a "Rainy Day Account," and a "Vacation Account." People save for reasons; interest earned is secondary. The reason may be general or specific, but the process should be made easy, attractive, and convenient.

Consumer Certificates of Deposit

Banking regulations permit the payment of slightly higher rates of interest on savings instruments with fixed maturities of at least thirty

---

[7]For example, some banks have offered a one dollar maximum service charge on demand deposit accounts to customers maintaining a five hundred dollar saving account.

days.[8] For savers who are interest conscious, the savings certificate may be an attractive alternative to passbook savings. Certificates are issued in a variety of forms to suit the needs and tastes of various classes of customer. They are usually sold in minimum denominations of one thousand dollars. Interest may be paid by check on a monthly or quarterly basis or, in some cases, accumulated to maturity. For customers who cling to the passbook concept, such certificates may be issued in the form of a special passbook.[9]

The most recent interest regulations permitting mutual thrift institutions to pay slightly higher rates of interest on similar certificates as well as on passbook savings has given them a competitive edge in the savings certificate market. Certificate buyers are *prima facie* interest rate conscious and the mutuals advertise their higher rates aggressively. Nevertheless, there are enough potential customers who will sacrifice a modicum of interest for the convenience of dealing with only one bank to make the promotion, or at least the availability, of the full spectrum of savings certificates worthwhile for a commercial bank that is actively seeking deposits.

Large Denomination Certificates

Under present regulations, certificates of deposit in minimum amounts of one hundred thousand dollars and with maturities of no less than thirty days and no more than eighty-nine days are not subject to interest rate regulation. Such certificates represent the most fruitful source of funds, especially when market rates of interest rise above the regulatory ceilings.

For the small- and moderate-sized bank, the market for large denomination certificates will be confined to those few of its own corporate customers who from time to time may have excess cash to invest. To be effective in this market, a bank must be large enough and well-known enough so that its certificates will trade in the secondary market at reasonable rates.

Although, in theory, most corporate treasurers will buy the certificates of any recognized bank at the highest rate obtainable, if rates are comparable they are more likely to acquire the certificates issued by one of their banks of account. In times of tight money, considerable pressure may be put on them by their banks to do just that. In more normal times,

---

[8]As a practical matter, maturities and automatically renewable options are generally limited to ninety days because of the cost of issuance and lower interest ceilings on shorter maturities.

[9]The term "Golden Passbook," originated by the Lincoln-Rochester Trust Co., was widely publicized and became almost generic in the industry.

the major banks post their issuing rates, and, if they are seeking money, telephone the corporate treasurers with whom they have established contacts. By the same token, the treasurer with funds to invest will call a number of banks and "shop the market." Actual rates are often negotiated slightly off the posted rates for large blocks of funds of especially desirable maturities.

From a deposit attraction standpoint, it is important that the banker get to know as many treasurers and other shoppers for such funds as possible. Although rate is always the primary factor, personal acquaintance is definitely a plus if rates are equal. The solicitation of large municipal deposits is carried out in the same way. In this case, however, willingness to acquire and hold the securities of the public entity is an additional important consideration.

The combination of all the factors discussed will determine a bank's effectiveness in attracting deposits. The following chapters discuss what a bank should do with the funds acquired.

8

LIQUIDITY—
CONCEPTS AND INSTRUMENTS

Bank asset management is the bank's allocation of the various funds it is able to attract and, as noted in the preceding chapter, is highly interrelated with the attraction of deposits and other liabilities. Many asset allocation decisions are based on the future availability of funds to the bank. Management's discretion regarding asset allocation varies considerably—the minimum amount of cash and deposits with Federal Reserve banks and, in some cases, correspondent banks is set by regulatory decision, but the amounts to be held in long-term state and local securities are a matter of management discretion. In meeting their liquidity needs, commercial banks have wide latitude in asset management and in recent years have begun to use the attraction of liabilities to assist in this task.

The problem of liquidity for commercial banks is essentially that of having available at all times sufficient funds to meet the demands for money that may be made on them. As stated in Chapter 4, *liquidity* is protection against the risk that losses may develop if banks are forced to sell or liquidate creditworthy assets in an adverse market. In this sense, liquidity is protective. In a more positive sense, *liquidity* can be defined as a bank's (or the banking system's) ability not only to meet possible deposit withdrawals but also to provide for the legitimate credit needs of the community (or the economy) as well.

The aspect of bank liquidity that has been most measured and discussed is the liquidity of the banking system as a whole—the ability of all banks or groups of banks to meet the credit demands that may be made on them. For the individual bank, the problem of liquidity can become quite acute, because transfers of deposits between banks, which do not affect the aggregate liquidity of the banking system, may be of major concern to the individual bank from which the deposits are withdrawn. The purpose of this chapter is to examine the concept of bank liquidity both from the viewpoint of the commercial banking system in its entirety and from that of the individual commercial bank and to review the instruments of liquidity available to the banking system. The following chapter will explore the measurement and forecasting of liquidity needs.

GENERAL MEASURES OF LIQUIDITY

Liquidity is frequently stated in terms of certain balance-sheet relationships. Chart 9, which shows the percentage distribution of bank assets by principal types in selected years from 1926 through 1971, provides some evidence of aggregate bank liquidity. Cash and U.S. government securities, which have traditionally been considered the

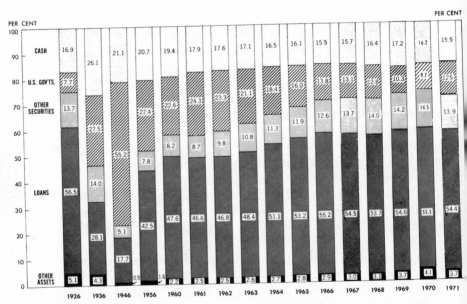

CHART 9 Percentage Distribution of Bank Assets by Principle Types, All Commercial Banks, Selected Years, 1926 to 1971 (Source: Federal Deposit Insurance Corporation)

primary sources of liquidity, have declined consistently in the period since World War II, while loans, which are traditionally considered among the least liquid assets, have grown consistently. However, if one goes back to the 1920s, present-day ratios do not appear unduly high.

The loan-to-deposit ratio is often used to demonstrate the degree to which banks have already used up their available resources to accommodate the credit needs of their customers. The presumption is that the higher the ratio of loans to deposits, the less able a bank (or all banks) will be to make additional loans. The loan-to-deposit ratio undoubtedly has a psychological effect on bank management. As the ratio rises, lending policies may become more cautious and selective. Obviously, the total of loanable funds, roughly measured by deposits, sets an upper limit to a bank's ability to make additional loans without recourse to more or less continuous borrowing. Chart 10 shows that the loan-to-deposit ratio for all insured banks in three size groupings of banks has risen throughout the postwar period. In 1969 and 1970, the loan-to-deposit ratio for banks with deposits of $100 million and over had risen above 75 percent.

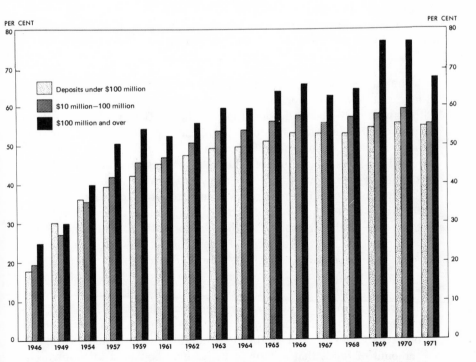

PER CENT

Deposits under $100 million

$10 million—100 million

$100 million and over

1946 1949 1954 1957 1959 1961 1962 1963 1964 1965 1966 1967 1968 1969 1970 1971

CHART 10 Loan-to-Deposit Ratios, by Size of Bank, All Insured Commercial Banks, Selected Years, 1946 to 1971 (Source: Federal Deposit Insurance Corporation)

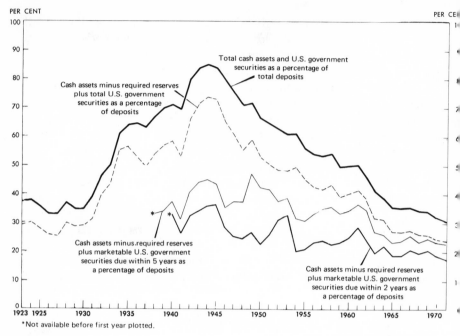

CHART 11 Ratios of Total Cash Assets and U.S. Government Securities to Total Deposits, All Member Banks, 1923–1971, Year End Figures (Source: Federal Reserve Board)

The ratio of loans to deposits reveals little, however, about the bank's other assets available for conversion into funds with which to meet withdrawals or to make additional loans. The relationship between short-term assets and deposits seems more significant for this purpose. Chart 11 shows four such ratios from 1923 through 1971.. The ratios for which required reserves are subtracted from cash assets and only limited maturities of U.S. government securities are treated as liquid are conceptually preferable. The four ratios tended to move together; the dominant trend is their nearly continuous decline since the end of World War II. One of the drawbacks of these ratios is that they do not reflect the proportion of U.S. government securities pledged to back public deposits and therefore not available to provide liquidity.

A ratio of liquid assets to deposits is a more accurate indicator of the amount of funds still readily available to a bank than is the ratio of loans to deposits. However, any such measure leaves out of consideration the flow of funds from loan repayments and from increases in other liabilities as well as the demand side of the equation—that is, the amount of funds that a bank or banks may be called to supply. The liquidity position of a bank is like a reservoir. It may be adequate, although nearly depleted, just before the season of heavy rains. Or it may be inadequate, although three-quarters full, just before the summer drought. To appraise the liquidity requirements of the individual bank, one needs to know more than is shown by these ratios. A method of making such an estimate will be discussed in the next chapter. First, however, it will be useful to look at the liquidity problem from a broader perspective.

ANALYZING THE DECLINE IN AGGREGATE LIQUIDITY

Charts 9, 10, and 11 all indicate that aggregate bank liquidity, as measured by traditional ratios, has been declining steadily since the end of World War II. During the Depression of the 1930s and through the war years, the Federal Reserve System supplied sufficient reserves to the market so that banks seldom had to worry about the availability of funds. Excess reserves, in fact, piled up in the banking system beyond the ability of banks to lend or invest them profitably. With the prices and yields of U.S. government securities effectively stabilized by Federal Reserve action, government bonds of any maturity were, for all practical purposes, liquid—that is, they could be readily sold without loss. Bankers literally forgot that a liquidity problem could exist.

Effect of Loan Expansion

With the return to more or less free markets after the Treasury-Federal Reserve "Accord" in 1951[1] and the rapid expansion in the private sector of the economy, the demand for bank loans began to ·rise sharply. In view of the inflationary potential of rapid credit expansion, the Federal Reserve System supplied reserves to the banks sparingly. Bank loans were expanding more rapidly than the overall economy, as measured by GNP, because of the shift from government to private economic activity. Meanwhile, deposits, particularly demand deposits, lagged behind the rise in GNP.[2]

---

[1]An agreement that freed the Federal Reserve from its obligation to support fixed prices for U.S. government securities. Board of Governors, *Annual Report for 1951*, p. 4.

[2]Between 1945 and 1971, loans at all commercial banks increased from 10.5 percent of GNP to 32.8 percent, while total deposits declined from 68.6 percent of GNP to 50.1 percent. The increase in loans accelerated in the 1960s; however, because of the rapid increase in time and savings deposits, deposits kept pace with economic growth in the 1960s. Source: *Federal Reserve Bulletins*.

To make the loans that were sought, therefore, banks had to reduce their holdings of U.S. government securities. Chart 9 shows that the percentage of total bank assets held in the form of U.S. government securities fell from 55.2 in 1946 to 27.4 in 1956 to 9.7 in 1970. These sales (and lack of purchases) resulted in substantially reduced prices (higher yields) for such securities. Bankers no longer considered longer-term U.S. government securities or other long-term securities liquid assets.

Effect of Changes in Loan Characteristics

Loan repayments should be considered as a factor in a bank's liquidity position. Over time, loan repayments constitute an important source of funds with which to make new loans (as long as total loans do not increase) and to repay deposits (to the extent that total outstanding loans decrease). If the rate of loan repayment is reduced, that is, if loan turnover diminishes, then liquidity is also reduced. Loan turnover tends to decline when the terms of repayment are extended.[3]

It has been many years since short-term, self-liquidating paper made up the bulk of loan portfolios in commercial banks. The integration of industry and commerce into larger and more extensive business organizations has long since eliminated much of the need for the kind of short-term credit that historically financed, in separate stages, the transfer of goods from raw material producer to fabricator, wholesaler, retailer, and consumer. Moreover, the increasing role of time and savings deposits has resulted in the availability of at least theoretically long-term funds. In any event, working capital loans and intermediate-term loans have assumed a position of considerable prominence in the vast growth of commercial bank lending since World War II. For example, in the early 1970s, intermediate-term loans averaged approximately 40 percent of the outstanding commercial loans at large commercial banks.[4] In addition, the growth of mortgage loans and consumer credit and particularly the tendency of banks to lengthen the terms of such loans have raised questions concerning many banks' ability to meet short-term credit needs in their communities in the event of a further upsurge in loan demand.

Commercial bank loans today are probably more liquid than they appear, however, because the regular amortization of term loans, mort-

---

3Federal Reserve Bank of Chicago, "Liquidity of Business Loans," *Business Conditions,* March 1961, pp. 9–10. Also, Federal Reserve Bank of New York, "Turnover of Business Loans at New York City Banks," *Monthly Review,* Vol. 44, No. 1, January 1962, p. 10.

4Loans of 160 commercial banks reporting weekly. *Federal Reserve Bulletins,* 1970–72.

gage loans, and consumer credit provides a steady flow of funds for relending. Although half of the business loans of New York City banks have original maturities of more than one year, it has been estimated that close to a third of the loans outstanding at any time fall due within a year. Experience shows that the average actual life of a twenty-five year mortgage is something under twelve years. Unfortunately, few banks have tried to determine what percentage of their loans will in all probability be repaid in given periods of time.

It is also probable that many of the so-called short-term loans historically made by commercial banks were short-term in name only. Ninety-day notes were all too frequently renewed over and over with little or no payment. The demand mortgages of the 1920s all too often were not reduced until they were foreclosed in the depths of the Depression. Experienced lending officers will freely admit that demand loans are generally among the slowest loans on their books.

One may conclude, therefore, that loan liquidity has not diminished perceptibly in recent years. It should be emphasized, however, that loan repayments do not supply funds for increasing the total of a bank's loan account or for meeting short-term deposit swings at times when loan demands are pressing on the bank's liquidity position. Loan repayments constitute an important source of protective liquidity over time but affect the current liquidity position only to the extent that net loan increases or decreases are predictable.

Effect of Increased Deposit Velocity

In addition to the fact that bank deposits have not grown as rapidly as the demand for bank credit, bank liquidity has been adversely affected by the increase in the turnover of demand deposits. As interest rates rose in the face of expanding demands for funds, the value of money rose, and—because banks could not pay interest on demand deposits and were limited in what they could pay on time and savings deposits[5]— there came into being, outside the commercial banking system, a vast market for liquid credit instruments, which assumed the character of near money.

During the postwar period, a substantial proportion of the liquid assets of individuals and corporations that had traditionally been held

---

[5]Until the spring of 1961, large banks in the principal money centers did not accept time deposits from domestic corporations as a matter of policy, largely because they feared a massive shift to such deposits from demand accounts. Since 1961, such time deposits have grown substantially (though irregularly and partially at the expense of demand deposits); however, the maximum rates that banks can pay on such deposits are limited by Regulation Q.

as demand deposits either came to be held outside the commercial banking system or were held in the form of time or savings deposits. In the
1950s, deposits of individuals in mutual savings banks (in areas where
they are found) and in savings and loan associations, whose interest
rates were not as closely regulated, grew at the expense of demand
deposits and more rapidly than time deposits in commercial banks.
Corporations, at the same time, invested the major portion of their temporarily excess funds in various money-market instruments. In the 1960s,
time and savings deposits at commercial banks grew more rapidly, but
demand deposits did not. The results of this pattern included a more
rapid turnover of demand deposits and interest sensitive time and savings
deposits, for which maximum rates are fixed by Regulation Q. Chart 12

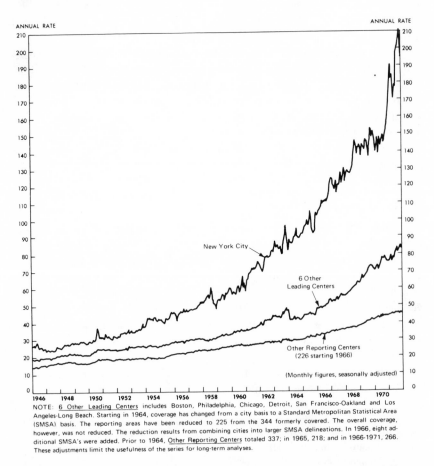

CHART 12 Turnover of Demand Deposits, 1946–1971 (Source: Federal Reserve
Board)

affirms the trend toward higher turnover of demand deposits from 1946 through 1971.

When a bank depositor elects to use his money to acquire some other form of liquid asset or money subsitute, the effect is a transfer of demand deposits, not a net decrease, if he acquires such assets from someone other than a bank. When a corporate treasurer, for example, draws a check on his bank to purchase Treasury bills from another nonbank holder, the existing demand deposit is merely credited to the account of a new owner, in all likelihood on the books of another bank. When an individual decides to save some of his money, whether currency or demand deposits, by placing it in a mutual savings bank, he is temporarily transferring to the savings institution the use of existing money. The first result will be an increase in amounts due from banks on the books of the savings institution.

On the other hand, if a depositor uses his money to purchase liquid or other assets from a commercial bank or to repay existing loans, the immediate effect is a reduction of bank demand deposits. When deposits decline, a portion of the bank's reserves become excess, and, in the absence of offsetting action by the Federal Reserve System, the commercial banking system can—and in times of high credit demand quickly will—use these excess reserves to recreate substantially the lost deposits by making new loans and investments.

When holders of demand deposits use them actively and invest them fully, however, the velocity of turnover of deposits rises. With this increased velocity, the level of deposits in each individual bank tends to fluctuate more rapidly and more widely. Surplus deposits not needed for working capital are quickly withdrawn for investment in other liquidity instruments, and the bank is unable to use these funds to make even short-term loans or investments. At best, a bank may sell the funds for a day or two in the Federal funds market. Increased deposit velocity has, therefore, had an adverse effect on bank liquidity that is not fully reflected by loan-to-deposit ratios or the ratio of short-term assets to deposits.

Effect of Pledging Securities

Commercial banks have to pledge securities to back most public deposits. In the early postwar years, this pledging requirement had little effect on banks' liquidity positions. By the 1960s, however, pledging requirements began to restrict the sale of securities as a means of meeting loan demands or deposit withdrawals. In the 1969–70 period of monetary restraint, in particular, commercial bank holdings of salable securities not pledged for public deposits were small; therefore, the role of securities was practically eliminated as a source of liquidity.

Effect of Liability Sources of Liquidity

The final factor affecting aggregate liquidity also became significant in the 1960s. During recent years, commercial banks have increasingly turned to liability sources of liquidity both to make loans and to meet deposit withdrawals. In periods of comparatively easy monetary policy, larger banks have been able to obtain a large amount of funds by issuing large denomination negotiable certificates of deposit[6] and, to a lesser extent, by borrowing Eurodollars or Federal funds. Aggressive smaller banks have obtained funds by bidding successfully on public deposits and by purchasing Federal funds. In periods of restraint (1966 and particularly 1969–70), larger banks tended to rely on holding company commercial paper, Eurodollars, Federal funds, sale of loans, note issues, and borrowing at the discount window. Table 7, which traces many of these sources from 1966 through 1971, supports the substantial reliance on liquidity sources. Smaller banks tended to use Federal funds and security repurchase agreements. In addition, some banks developed methods of satisfying loan demands without supplying the funds directly.[7]

The implications of using liabilities as sources of liquidity are complex. The traditional liquidity ratios, such as loans to deposits or liquid assets to deposits, become less accurate measures of bank liquidity. Banks have used and can continue to use large, negotiable certificates of deposit and nondeposit sources of funds to fill loan demands and meet deposit withdrawals. However, their ability to do so will depend in large measure on Federal Reserve policies. During recent periods of tight money, the Federal Reserve generally permitted money-market rates to rise above the maximum rates payable on time deposits. However, in June 1970, rate ceilings on CD's of one hundred thousand dollars and over maturing between thirty and eighty-nine days were removed entirely, providing much needed flexibility in the time of impending monetary crisis following the bankruptcy of the Penn-Central Railroad. Other liability sources came under varying degrees of regulatory restriction. In 1969–70, banks were able to purchase some kinds of liabilities, albeit at a high price, to meet liquidity needs, but there is no guarantee they will be able to do so in future years. The risk to bank management is that the supplies of

---

[6]In the sense that CD's can be bought or sold in the secondary market, they are purchased liabilities supplying liquidity. If one prefers to classify them as deposits that supply usable funds, he should be aware of the greater risk of outflow for CD's.

[7]All the major sources of liquidity are described later in this chapter and in Robert E. Knight, "An Alternative Approach to Liquidity," *Monthly Review*, Federal Reserve Bank of Kansas City (January, February, April, and May 1970). Knight estimates that in 1969, nondeposit sources of funds increased $17.2 billion for large commercial banks.

TABLE 7

SELECTED LIABILITIES OF LARGE COMMERCIAL BANKS[a]

(AMOUNTS IN MILLIONS OF DOLLARS)

As of Quarter Ended		Large Negotiable CD's[b]	Federal Funds Purchased[c]	Gross Liabilities of Banks to Foreign Branches[d]	Bank Related Commercial Paper	Loans Sold Outright[e]
1966	March	17,418	—	1,879	—	—
	June	18,312	—	1,951	—	—
	September	17,005	—	3,472	—	—
	December	15,668	—	4,036	—	—
1967	March	19,299	—	3,412	—	—
	June	19,135	—	3,166	—	—
	September	19,897	—	4,059	—	—
	December	20,330	—	4,241	—	—
1968	March	20,538	—	4,920	—	—
	June	19,256	—	6,241	—	—
	September	22,261	—	7,131	—	—
	December	23,468	—	6,948	—	—
1969	March	18,770	—	9,621	—	—
	June	15,252	12,799	13,269	1,245	—
	September	11,732	15,468	14,349	2,595	—
	December	10,919	13,472	12,822	4,294	—
1970	March	11,820	16,591	12,356	6,518	8,433
	June	12,976	17,758	12,701	7,603	9,688
	September	22,240	13,903	9,787	4,620	8,209
	December	26,075	18,775	7,669	2,349	4,625
1971	March	27,523	18,852	2,858	1,692	2,560
	June	28,527	19,053	1,512	1,733	3,058
	September	33,037	22,989	2,476	1,900	2,960
	December	34,018	26,046	909	1,973	2,940

a About two hundred weekly reporting banks are included. These banks account for roughly 60 percent of the assets and liabilities of all commercial banks.
b Issued in denominations of one hundred thousand dollars or more.
c Includes securities sold under agreements to repurchase.
d This is the commonly used measure of Eurodollar borrowings. Eurodollars also may be borrowed from branches in U.S. territories and possessions and from unaffiliated foreign banks.
e Amounts sold under repurchase agreement are excluded. Figures include small amounts sold by banks other than large weekly reporting banks.

Source: Federal Reserve Bulletins (Washington: Federal Reserve Board, 1966–71).

CD's and the various nondeposit sources of funds are likely to be inelastic or unstable and may disappear at precisely the time when liquidity needs are most acute.

LIQUIDITY NEEDS

The discussion above has been concerned with liquidity needs in general. More specifically, the liquidity needs of individual banks must be related to the demands made upon them for funds over periods of time. Some funds may be called for tomorrow, some may not be needed for a year or more, and additional liquidity may be needed for unforeseen or unpredictable demands as a margin of safety.

A bank obviously would not be operating efficiently if it held in cash today the funds needed to make loans two years from now. Therefore, just as the amount of liquidity is related to the size of the potential demand for funds, the form and maturity in which liquid assets are held should be related to the times at which demands for funds are likely to occur.

Liquidity and the Money Position

Every bank is required by law to maintain a portion of its deposits in the form of cash on hand, deposits at Federal Reserve banks, or demand balances due from specified banks. For banks that are not members of the Federal Reserve System, reserve requirements are established by the laws of the various states and differ widely. A member bank must maintain a minimum percentage of its demand and time deposits in the form of vault cash or deposits with the Federal Reserve bank of its district.[8] The reserve requirements are calculated as the minimum percentages of deposits held by banks during a "base" week and are satisfied by adequate average deposits plus vault cash in the appropriate Federal Reserve bank in the following week.

A bank's legal reserve is often considered its most liquid asset. Actually, it is not liquid at all in the sense in which *liquidity* has been defined here because it cannot be used (except for very brief periods) to pay deposits or make additional loans. When it is so used, it must be replaced almost immediately, except for the small portions freed by reductions in deposits.

A bank's legal reserve, however, does serve as a temporary buffer between the demand for funds being made upon it and its true liquidity

---

[8] Board of Governors of the Federal Reserve System, Regulation D, "Reserves of Member Banks" (Federal Reserve Act, Sction 19).

position. When depositors' checks are presented for payment, the immediate effect is a reduction in the bank's reserve account or correspondent balances. When loans are made, the proceeds are usually credited to a deposit account against which checks will be drawn. Thus, as loan proceeds are drawn down, the bank's reserve account or correspondent balance is reduced in exactly the same way as when other deposits are withdrawn. In the absence of offsetting credits, a bank must look to its liquid assets for funds with which to restore its reserve to the required amount within the reserve computation period.[9] Thus, a bank's money position immediately reflects the major portion of the demands for funds that may be made on it. Management of the money position (the techniques of which will be discussed in some detail in the following chapter) is closely related to but not a part of management of the liquidity position.

Short-Term Liquidity Needs

The holders of sizable deposit balances and the customers who borrow in substantial amounts influence the short-term liquidity needs of an individual bank to a degree that is directly related to their size. The needs of important customers for funds—intermittent, constant, or seasonal will impinge directly and substantially on their banks' liquidity requirements. Much of the management of a bank's liquidity position, therefore, will revolve around a knowledge of the needs and intentions of large customers and a preparation to cope with them. Alert bank management will endeavor to keep in close touch with those customers in order to learn their plans as early as possible. This is one important reason for bank officers to visit customers and to understand the nature of their businesses.

Seasonal factors that may affect the entire level of deposit supply or loan demand also influence short-term liquidity needs. Farm communities, for example, exhibit clear, recurrent, seasonal patterns of demand and supply of funds that are distinctly different from those of suburban communities. Some seasonality of loan demand and deposit flow is found in nearly every community. Certain industries borrow seasonally, and corporate needs for funds build up at tax dates. Most seasonal fluctuations can be quite accurately timed and appropriate liquidity provided on the basis of past experience. In planning for seasonal liquidity needs, bank managers can often closely tailor the maturity of the liquid assets to the probable timing of the demand for funds.

---

[9]In some states, reserve requirements must be met daily, and Federal Reserve banks expect their members to try to avoid large deficiencies on any one day, despite the averaging privilege.

Other Liquidity Needs

In addition to providing funds for the known and generally foreseeable short-term demands, a margin of liquidity is required by banks for demands that can be predicted over the longer-range or that may be unforeseen altogether. These longer-term liquidity needs are generally related to the secular trends of the community or markets that a bank serves. In rapidly expanding areas, loan demand grows faster than deposits accumulate. One function of longer-term liquidity is to provide funds for loan expansion.

In stable communities, on the other hand, deposits may show a steady rise while loan demand remains virtually unchanged. In such cases, the longer view of liquidity requirements may enable the bank to keep more fully invested than it otherwise would. In either case, to gauge the bank's needs for longer-term liquidity, bank management must attempt some long-range economic forecasting on the basis of which it can reasonably estimate loan and deposit levels for perhaps five years ahead. A later discussion will suggest specific ways in which management may attempt to deal with these fundamental uncertainties of the banking business. Economic forecasting is at best an inexact science, however, and conservative bank management will maintain some readily available funds to provide for a margin of error. These funds, too, will be included in the bank's longer-term liquidity requirements.

It should be evident from the foregoing that the management of a bank's liquidity position transcends the use of simple yardsticks provided by balance-sheet ratios. These ratios are convenient measures of overall change, but the position and the need are not always measurable in the same terms. Both the amount of liquidity required and the time at which the demands for funds may be made on the bank must be considered. In consequence, a bank's portfolio of liquid assets will not be uniform either in its makeup at any given moment or in its amount over time.

INSTRUMENTS OF LIQUIDITY

Before exploring the ways in which banks can estimate and provide for their liquidity needs, let us examine briefly some of the instruments of liquidity that are available. These consist, in the first place, of assets in which excess funds can be temporarily invested with the assurance that they either will mature and be paid when the funds are needed or will be readily salable, without material loss, in advance of maturity. In the second place, liquidity instruments include the ways in which banks can borrow or otherwise obtain funds.

Most of the instruments of bank liquidity are available through the money market, which has been defined as "the active market for money and close money substitutes which financial institutions and others rely on to provide the liquidity needed in the usual course of their operations."[10] Money itself, in the form of excess currency and demand deposits due from banks in excess of minimum working balance needs, is a primary form of short-term liquidity. But money is not an earning asset and is therefore not, in any real sense, a money-market instrument.

Federal Funds

Money, in the form of excess balances, may be converted into an earning asset by being loaned usually for one day at a time, as "Federal funds." The most common Federal funds transaction represents a loan of reserve balances by one bank to another.[11] Such loans are often unsecured. Within the same city they may be arranged by an exchange of checks, the borrowing bank's check payable through the clearings on the next business day in exchange for the lending bank's check on its reserve account available on the day of the loan. Between cities (and even within some cities), Federal funds transactions are arranged by telephone, often through correspondent banks or the several funds brokers in New York City, and are effected by transfers of reserve balances through the Federal Reserve wire transfer system. Although loans are typically for overnight, they are frequently renewed.

Another segment of the Federal funds market is the lending of funds to dealers in U.S. government securities. A common arrangement is for dealers requiring short-term financing to sell securities to a bank with an agreement to repurchase them at predetermined prices on the following day or at the maturity of the contract. The bank purchasing the securities may transfer its excess reserves to the reserve account of the dealer's bank, which in turn will credit the dealer's account.

Federal funds are a liquidity instrument to both the selling and buying bank. Federal funds are technically classified as a loan by the selling bank and are a form of borrowing for the buying bank. Because the seller must decide daily whether to renew a transaction, Federal

---

[10]Robert V. Roosa, *Federal Reserve Operations in the Money and Government Securities Markets,* Federal Reserve Bank of New York, July 1956. Cf. Wesley Lindow, *Inside the Money Market* (New York: Random House, 1972).

[11]Any transfer of bank balances that is effected by entries on the books of a Federal Reserve bank in the reserve accounts of a member bank and is available on the same day is a Federal funds transaction. Thus, a corporation large and important enough to command this service may instruct its bank to pay Federal funds to a U.S. government securities dealer against delivery of Government securities to be held in custody. By this device, the corporation is in effect selling Federal funds to the dealer on a secured basis.

funds are perhaps second only to excess reserves in their availability for providing liquidity. Banks experiencing reserve deficiencies that are expected to last only a few days may readily borrow funds. Banks that have borrowed Federal funds in large amounts over long periods of time have in effect borrowed loanable funds from other banks. Total reserves and the lending potential of the banking system do not change. However, by reducing a bank's need to hold excess reserves, the Federal funds market enables it to increase loans and deposits more than it otherwise could.

Until the mid–1960s, Federal funds transactions were mostly limited to larger banks. In recent years, however, over half of all commercial banks have bought or sold Federal funds, at least on occasion. Very small banks now participate in the Federal funds market through their big city correspondents; transactions as low as fifty thousand dollars are not uncommon.[12] Table 7 (page 131) shows that the amount of Federal funds outstanding has been between $13 and $19 billion in the past several years. The recent changes in reserve computation procedures have undoubtedly contributed to the expansion of the market by permitting banks to manage their reserve positions more closely.

Short-term U.S. Government Securities

Short-term U.S. government securities, which have a range of maturities suitable for any liquidity needs, are the most widely used money-market instrument. For short-term and seasonal liquidity, Treasury bills have many advantages. Their availability in weekly auctions and their active secondary market at narrow spreads make them, in some ways, the ideal liquidity instrument. Interest is on a discount basis and is therefore reflected in the market price. Treasury bills are now issued in 91-day, 182-day, and one-year original maturities and, like other short-dated Treasury obligations, can generally be acquired in the market with maturities that can be specifically tailored to a bank's expected need for funds.[13] Intermediate-term U.S. government securities with maturities of two to five years are ideal instruments for longer-term liquidity requirements, such as those for projected increases in net loan demand or longer-range declines in deposits.[14] Bank managers should, of course,

---

[12]Nevis D. Baxter, "Why Federal Funds," *Business Review*, August 1966.

[13]See Roosa, *op. cit.*, pp. 37–41; *Money-Market Instruments* by Morgan Guaranty Trust, 1970, pp. 12–14; and *Handbook of Securities of the United States Government*, The First Boston Corporation, 1970, pp. 39–57, for more thorough descriptions of short-term U.S. government securities and the manner in which they are traded.

[14]The other kinds of marketable U.S. government securities are described in Chapter 10 on Investment Instruments.

remember that pledged U.S. government securities are not a source of liquidity.

Other Marketable Short-term Securities

Short-term U.S. government agency securities; high grade, short-term state and local securities; and railroad equipment trust notes are also used for liquidity purposes. Government agencies with short-term securities include the Federal Intermediate Credit Bank, the Federal National Mortgage Association, the Federal Land Bank, the Federal Home Loan Bank, the Export-Import Bank, and the Government National Mortgage Association. Agency issues are highly marketable, surpassed only by Treasury securities with similar maturities. They have higher yields than Treasury obligations; however, the spread has narrowed as agency issues have become more generally accepted in recent years.

Short-term state and local securities usually have a higher after-tax yield than Treasury and agency securities because their interest is exempt from Federal income taxes. The major types of short-term state and local securities are project notes of local public housing agencies (these are guaranteed by the Federal government); notes issued by states or municipalities in anticipation of taxes, other revenues, or longer-term bond financing; and the early maturing bonds in a serial issue. These securities are usually traded on a yield basis. For the housing project notes, marketability tends to be good; but for the latter two types of issues it varies widely, depending on the issuing unit.

Commercial Paper and Bankers' Acceptances

Commercial paper and bankers' acceptances are frequently available at yields somewhat above those of U.S. government and agency securities of comparable maturities. Both are obligations of private borrowers that are sold through dealers in the money market. Bankers' acceptances are drafts with specific, short-term maturities; they are drawn on and accepted by a banking institution, which in effect substitutes its credit for that of an importer or holder of merchandise. They are sold on a discounted basis and have a good secondary market. Commercial paper is the name given to the short-term unsecured promissory notes of leading industrial firms and finance companies. With the notable exception of the Penn-Central difficulties in 1970, commercial paper has enjoyed an excellent record for safety of principal. Commercial paper is sold on a discounted basis, but some issues have a limited secondary market. Both of these instruments serve many liquidity purposes admirably and deserve careful consideration for part of a bank's liquidity portfolio.

Other Liquid Assets

Any creditworthy loan or investment may be included in a bank's port-folio of liquid assets if its maturity conforms with liquidity needs and if the bank will have no compunction about collecting it at maturity. Among such assets will occasionally be found well-secured notes of nondepositors acquired through so-called money brokers. Such loans are usually secured by the cash value of life insurance or marketable securities. A bank that grants lines of credit to national finance companies can sometimes arrange for those lines to be used during periods of seasonal excess of funds and paid off when the local credit needs are at a peak. If such an arrangement has been made, these loans may be considered part of the bank's liquidity position.

BORROWING AND OTHER ARRANGEMENTS

A bank's ability to borrow or to dispose of assets either temporarily or permanently is a part of its liquidity arrangements. In this sense, a bank's own note discounted with its Reserve bank or correspondent is a prime instrument of liquidity. Two other bank liabilities that are used to provide liquidity—Federal funds and negotiable certificates of deposit—were discussed earlier. Other liabilities that can be used to provide liquidity include Eurodollar balances, short-term promissory notes, and commercial paper issued by bank holding companies. Other arrangements include the sale of loans and securities, and various methods of satisfying loan demands without supplying funds directly.

Direct Borrowing

Short-term borrowing from a Federal Reserve bank or correspondent and the purchase of Federal funds are methods of acquiring funds for relatively short periods of time to restore the bank's reserve balances temporarily depleted by deposit withdrawals to required levels. It is not considered sound commercial bank policy to borrow for long periods, or even very frequently, for the purpose of carrying loans or investments or to meet known and predictable, recurring, seasonal demands for funds. Federal Reserve policy, in this regard, is set forth in the Foreword of Regulation A of the Board of Governors, which states:

> Federal Reserve credit is generally extended on a short-term basis to a member bank to enable it to adjust its asset position when necessary because of developments such as a sudden withdrawal

of deposits or seasonal requirements for credit beyond those which can reasonably be met by the use of the bank's own resources.[15]

The discount officers of a Federal Reserve bank will question a bank's need for borrowing if it remains in debt for more than about sixty days or if it borrows repeatedly in six or seven reserve-computation periods. Correspondent banks may be more lenient, but bank examiners will question the need for substantial or prolonged borrowing for purposes other than short-term reserve adjustment. It is not considered appropriate for banks to borrow merely to take advantage of a spread in rates such as usually exists between the discount rate and the rate on brokers' loan participations acquired from a correspondent bank.

Sometimes, however, a bank's services may be needed to help carry its community through a period of unexpectedly adverse economic circumstances such as crop failures, sharp drops in economic activity caused by natural disasters, strikes in major industries, or other comparable and unpredictable circumstances.[16] Under such conditions, the Federal Reserve System is designed to function as the "lender of last resort" and to supply liquidity to the banks serving the community in need.

Eurodollars

The term *Eurodollar* refers to dollar-denominated deposits held in banks located outside the United States and to dollars that banks abroad acquire with their own or foreign currencies and either employ in the market or lend to customers. Table 7 (page 131) shows that, during recent periods of monetary restraint, Eurodollars have been an important source of liquidity for U.S. banks. In 1969, for example, total commercial bank borrowings of Eurodollars was one of the largest nondeposit sources of liquidity. The Eurodollar market offers a variety of terms, ranging from overnight to one-year deposits at varying rates, generally higher than comparable time-deposit rates in the United States. Access to the Eurodollar market is greatly facilitated if a bank has an overseas branch, and many banks have established branches in London or Nassau (Bahamas) primarily to gain access to that market. Several brokers and dealers have entered this market and made Eurodollars accessible to more banks in the last few years.[17]

---

[15]Board of Governors of the Federal Reserve System, "Advances and Discounts by Federal Reserve Banks," Regulation A.

[16]For example, during the commercial paper crisis in mid-1970, member banks were notified that the Federal Reserve was willing to extend its credit to help banks lend to companies having problems with commercial paper refinancing.

[17]An analysis of Eurodollar transactions and their contribution to bank liquidity is contained in Robert E. Knight, "An Alternative Approach to Liquidity: Part II," *Monthly Review,* Federal Reserve Bank of Kansas City, February 1970, pp. 11–22.

Additional Nondeposit Sources of Liquidity

Other nondeposit sources of liquidity include the sale of capital notes and the issuance of commercial paper through subsidiaries and affiliates. Table 7 shows that the amount of commercial paper issued by bank affiliates rose from roughly $1 billion in mid–1969 to over $7 billion in 1970. This liability source of funds is limited primarily to larger banks using the holding-company structure. Both large and small banks issued negotiable capital notes in denominations as small as one hundred dollars and with maturities as short as two years during the middle and late 1960s. Although the amount of funds obtained in this manner was relatively limited, in 1970 the Federal Reserve began requiring denominations of not less than five hundred dollars and original maturities of more than seven years. Such obligations must be subordinated to deposits and bear on their face the legend, "This obligation is not a deposit and is not insured by the Federal Deposit Insurance Corporation."

Sale of Loans and Securities

The sale (or participation in) loans and securities by banks operating where the demand for credit exceeds the supply of funds has long been an established practice. Originating and selling mortgage loans, for example, has become a business in itself for some banks. They usually continue to service such loans, preserving local customer relationships and acquiring a source of additional income as well. Banks specializing in mortgage origination often finance home construction while holding commitments from savings banks, savings and loan associations, or others to acquire the permanent mortgages. Additional interim financing or liquidity may be obtained through a "warehousing" arrangement with another commercial bank, which will finance the mortgages pending their acquisition by the ultimate investor. Such agreements represent a source of additional funds to the originating bank and a liquidity instrument, or short-term investment, for the warehousing institution.

The sale of blocks of consumer paper, particularly home improvement loans, has also been widely practiced. Such sales are sometimes made without recourse in the case of nonpayment; more often a portion of the proceeds is held as a margin or guarantee funds so that the majority of the risk remains with the originating bank. Agreements to repurchase delinquent items constitute an effective guarantee so that what purports to be a sale of assets may be, in effect, a borrowing arrangement.

The participation in loans with correspondent banks is a method of making loans in excess of the originating bank's legal lending limit and also a method of bringing additional funds into the community. In addition, some large correspondent banks have conserved their loanable funds by allowing some of their smaller correspondents to participate in loans that the larger banks have originated.

A modified technique of selling loans and securities that became popular in the 1960s has been to sell loans or securities to nonbank customers under agreement to repurchase after a stated period of time at a predetermined price or yield. The maturities of the repurchase agreements do not necessarily bear any relation to the maturities of the underlying securities or loans and tend to vary from two months to a year. Since mid–1969, all repurchase agreements except those in U.S. government or agency securities have been subject to the rate maximums under regulation Q.

Frequently, small- and moderate-sized banks have failed to take advantage of the methods described above for obtaining additional funds for their communities. They have simply closed their loan windows rather than take the trouble to make arrangements for placing a portion of the local loans elsewhere. The maintenance of such sources of additional funds may, at times, require the sale of assets that a bank might otherwise hold, but long-range considerations and predictable excess loan demand in the future may well dictate that all-sized banks should keep such channels open even at the cost of temporarily excess liquidity. For example, Table 7 (page 131) shows that loans sold outright provided larger commercial banks with close to $10 billion in early 1970.

Other Methods of Satisfying Loan Demand

During the periods of monetary restraint in 1966 and 1969–70, several large banks developed methods to satisfy loan demands without having to supply funds directly. The methods included the creation of ineligible acceptances and various forms of customer paper guarantees. To a large extent, these marketable credit instruments were created to serve customers who would normally be accommodated at the banks when loanable funds were more readily available. It is estimated that the loan demand serviced in this manner never exceeded $1 billion and that the use of such forms declined rapidly when monetary policy became more expansive.[18] These methods nevertheless represent another potential liquidity instrument for some commercial banks.

---

[18]Detailed descriptions of these methods and their estimated size appears in Robert E. Knight, "An Alternative Approach to Liquidity: Part IV," *Monthly Review,* Federal Reserve Bank of Kansas City, May 1970, pp. 13–18.

9

LIQUIDITY—
POLICIES AND PROCEDURES

At any given time, the liquidity needs of no two banks will be alike, either in relation to the volume of their deposits or with respect to any other balance-sheet ratio. Similarly, the liquidity requirements for a bank will vary over time as funds flow in and out and the actual and potential demand for funds changes from day to day. It is the task of bank management to measure immediate and prospective demands and to anticipate them, to the extent possible, by providing an adequate reservoir of liquidity instruments.

ESTIMATING LIQUIDITY NEEDS

The first basic requirement is to estimate liquidity needs as accurately as possible. The best guides available to a bank are its past experience and its knowledge of community events that may affect demands. As has been previously noted, liquidity needs must be related both to those demands for funds that may be made by depositors and to those that may arise from the community's needs for additional credit. A distinction can be made, therefore, between deposit liquidity and what may be termed *loan liquidity*, the funds held to make additional local loans. In the final analysis, the two must be combined for an estimate of overall liquidity needs.

Liquidity for Deposits

The more essential and probably the larger portion of a bank's liquidity needs at any time will be related directly to the volume and character of its deposit liabilities. Not all deposits require the same degree of liquidity. The classification of deposits (demands, savings, or time) and their sources (individuals, businesses, or public agencies) are not as important as the likelihood that any specific deposit or group of deposits may be withdrawn within a relatively short period of time.

Potential deposit withdrawals may be grouped into (a) those that will surely occur; (b) those that might but are not certain to occur; and (c) those that are unlikely to occur but that, under certain circumstances, could possibly occur. In general, the greater the likelihood of withdrawal, the larger the percentage of liquidity provided should be and the shorter the maturity of the liquid assets held should be.

As an example of withdrawals that will surely occur, one may cite the payroll account that is deposited weekly and nearly immediately checked out or the municipal deposit of tax monies that will inevitably be drawn down over a period of months. Seasonal increases in accounts—an important factor in some banks—are another example of temporary deposits. Deposits that in all probability will be withdrawn within a year may be termed *volatile*. They are often colloquially referred to as hot money and should ordinarily be invested in liquidity instruments with maturities coordinated with the outflows.

The volatility of a bank's deposits can be readily shown in a chart of deposits as of month ends or, more accurately, as of the end of successive reserve-computation periods. A trend line drawn through or near the low points will determine the base or level of nonvolatile deposits and indicate the secular trend of growth (or decline). Fluctuations above this base will represent volatility. At any point in time, the amount of deposits above the base line will be, in effect, the bank's volatile deposits. This concept is illustrated in Chart 13.

Demand deposits, passbook savings, and time deposits are charted separately because it is useful to know the volatility for each and because the margin of safety required may differ substantially from one type of deposit to another. For example, even though certificates of deposit may show limited historical volatility, the danger of high interest rates causing an unexpectedly large outflow of certificates of deposit forces the bank to maintain a substantial margin of safety. The bottom section of Chart 13 shows the combined volatility of all types of deposits. Although separate analysis is essential, and margins of safety may vary widely among the types of deposits, liquidity needs should emphasize the overall movements. For example, there will be lower liquidity needs if fluctua-

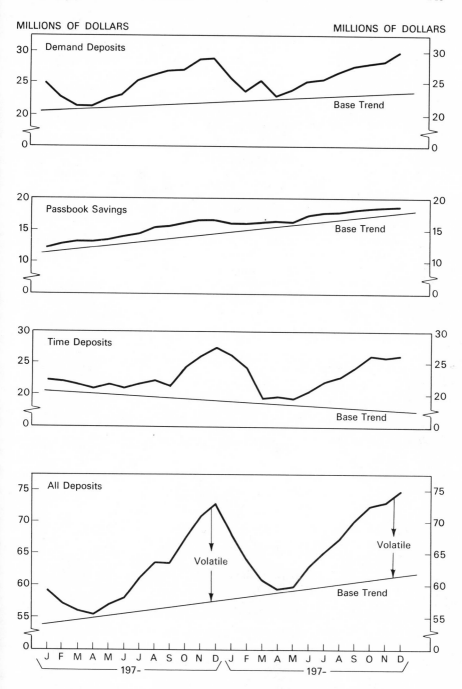

CHART 13 Deposit Volatility

tions in time and demand deposits tend to offset each other, as when the payment of Christmas club accounts is quickly followed by an increase in the demand deposits of local merchants.

The first line of liquidity defense is the liquidity provisions for the volatile portion of overall deposits. Such provisions should be equal to the total of such deposits less the percentage of required reserves held against them, for as deposits decline the release of reserves provides a small part of the requisite liquidity. With respect to country member banks, the liquidity requirements for volatile deposits would be roughly 87 percent of demand deposits and 97 percent of savings and time deposits.[1]

The second line of liquidity defense is related to larger demand deposit accounts, the sudden or unexpected withdrawal of which would make relatively heavy demands on a bank's liquidity position. Management itself should determine what size is relatively large in any particular bank, but as a rule of thumb, demand deposit accounts equal to one-half of 1 percent of total deposits generally may be considered large in this context. When liquidity requirements for the aggregate of large demand deposit accounts are computed, the total of volatile deposits may be deducted from the aggregate of large balances to determine what may be termed *vulnerable* demand deposits. These deposits may be withdrawn unexpectedly and are of sufficient size to require special liquidity consideration. On the assumption that a bank might lose one in five of such accounts over the next few years for any one of a variety of reasons, it is suggested that 20 percent of the vulnerable portion of large demand deposits be held in liquidity instruments.

The third line of liquidity defense is based on the withdrawal vulnerability of large time and savings deposits. These deposits can be vulnerable without having evidenced any previous fluctuations; therefore, a similar 20 percent liquidity reserve is suggested for such deposits. Careful analysis of large time deposits on an individual basis may indicate that a 20 percent requirement is too low in some cases. Bank management will have a fairly clear picture of the prospective use of many large time deposits. The proceeds of a municipal bond issue, for example, may be held in time deposits pending payments on a school construction contract that can be quite accurately timed. Such deposits, like volatile deposits, may require full liquidity protection. It is also

---

[1]The requirements as of May 1972 were 12½ percent for the first $5 million and 13 percent for all other demand deposits for country banks. For reserve city banks, the comparable percentages were 17 and 17½ percent, respectively. The requirements were 3 percent of savings deposits and time deposits under $5 million and 5 percent for time deposits over $5 million for all classes of banks. Source: *Federal Reserve Bulletin,* Vol. 58, No. 5, May 1972, p. A10.

possible, however, to overstate the asset protection needed for some banks. Withdrawals of large time and savings deposits nearly always can be replaced, at some price, by purchasing funds in the money market.

Finally, to meet demands from depositors that might be made in unusual or unforeseen circumstances[2] and to provide that margin of safety that is essential if a conservative banker is to feel secure, a residual liquidity reserve of between 5 and 10 percent of remaining deposits should be held. The percentage should be a function of the bank's willingness and ability to buy liabilities, possibly at a high price, to meet withdrawals.

It should be noted that the liquidity provisions suggested here are related to the normal daily, seasonal, and cyclical swings in deposits plus a margin of safety. The bank can supplement its own liquidity provisions for short periods, of course, by borrowing from its Reserve bank or correspondent. The liquidity to provide for any long-range secular decline in deposits would normally come from the reduction of outstanding loans or the sale of longer-term securities.

Liquidity for Loans

It has been shown that a major portion of the liquidity problem has resulted from rising loan demand rather than from declining deposits and that, to avoid a liquidity squeeze, a bank must maintain a sufficient supply of liquid assets to make the loans that its good customers will require. Such funds, held available to make legitimate local loans, may be termed *loan liquidity*. Part of this demand may be seasonal in character and, like deposit volatility, can be depicted in a chart of month-end loan totals (exclusive of money-market or other loans held for liquidity reasons) such as in Chart 14.

The trend line in Chart 14 is drawn through or near the high points rather than the low points in recognition of the fact that increases in loans make demands on liquidity in the same way as do decreases in deposits. The trend line represents a ceiling, an amount to which loans may be expected to rise periodically or seasonally. Over a period of time, such a chart will reveal cyclical as well as seasonal variations in loan demand. The amount by which loans are below the ceiling, at any given time, represents the amount of short-term liquid assets that a bank should hold to meet these seasonal or cyclical demands for loans.

If loans have been rising more rapidly than deposits and if manage-

---

[2]An example of such an unpredictable circumstance was the withdrawals of both individual and business certificates of deposit during the 1969–70 period when market interest rates exceeded the regulatory maximum rate.

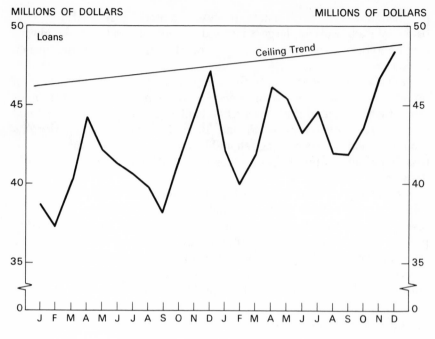

CHART 14   Loan Liquidity Needs

ment expects that they may continue to do so, an additional provision of liquidity may be called for. Future loan expansion is, of course, limited to the funds available to the bank either directly through increased deposits or indirectly through loan participation or the sale of assets. If the bank's loan-to-deposit ratio is already high, it may have to seek other solutions to the problem of high community loan demand, such as active campaigns for new deposits or even a merger with another institution.

Unlike deposit fluctuations, however, the rise in loans is subject to limited control by the bank itself. Management can tighten up its lending policies or even refuse entirely to make some loans. If the loan-to-deposit ratio is not too high and if the bank holds a portfolio of investments that could be converted over time into local loans, then the planning for such a conversion will play a part in the bank's liquidity calculations. By the same token, if local loan demand is relatively static and deposits are continuing to rise, the bank's longer-range need for liquidity will be reduced. In the liquidity calculation shown at the end of this chapter, a space is provided for entering management's best estimate of the net effect of secular changes in loans and deposits. The following discussion of loan and deposit forecasting reviews in more detail the considerations that should go into making such an estimate.

Finally, to provide once more for the unforeseen and unpredictable, a short-term liquidity provision is suggested to meet the unexpected loan demands of good customers who perhaps have not borrowed in recent years. The amount arbitrarily suggested is 20 percent of capital and surplus—enough to make two legal-limit, unsecured loans. A larger sum might be provided by a bank that is very active in commercial lending, because business loan demand is likely to fluctuate more widely over the business cycle than the demand for mortgages or consumer credit.

When deposit and loan figures are charted, unusually sharp increases or decreases may sometimes be evident. These may not represent a change in trend but rather a change in level. For example, if a new, large deposit account is obtained or lost, the level of deposits may be raised or lowered without any effect on the direction or trend of deposit growth as a whole. Similarly, if a bank were to purchase a block of mortgages, perhaps on out-of-town properties, the loan total as charted would show a sharp increase even though nothing had occurred to change the trend of local loan demand. Upward or downward adjustments to the base line for deposits and the ceiling line for loans need not necessarily change their direction; management must continue to exercise its best judgment in interpreting its charts.

Coordinated Forecasting of Loans and Deposits

Over time, the liquidity needs that individual banks experience will be the difference between loan increases and deposit growth. The simplest method for making such an estimate is to assume that history will repeat itself, that seasonal patterns will not vary widely from year to year, and that secular trends will continue. The application of this method of estimating liquidity requirements to several hundred banks over a three-year period has indicated that this is a reasonable assumption much of the time. It is an assumption, however, that needs at all times to be modified by managerial judgment and foresight.[3]

Cyclical Influence. Loan demands tend to rise above the normal trend line in times of high business activity and to fall below expectations

---

[3]The Bank Examinations Department of the Federal Reserve Bank of New York has used a simplified version of this approach in connection with examinations of state member banks. The majority of banks examined could meet the requirements thus calculated; many of those that did not had to resort to borrowing in larger amounts and for longer periods than the examiners considered appropriate.

when the economy as a whole experiences a recession or slack period. The forecasts of loan officers, therefore, need to be tempered by the predictions of the economists. Demand deposits, on the other hand, tend to rise (for all banks) in times of business slack because the Federal Reserve System makes reserves more freely available to encourage credit use and to stimulate an increase in the money supply. In times of high levels of business activity, demand deposits tend to increase more slowly because the Federal Reserve System pursues more restrictive policies.

Time and savings deposits follow trends of their own. Competitive rates of interest play a vital role in determining these trends for the individual bank. A strong local demand for loans has often been the determining factor in persuading bank management to increase the rate of interest paid, within the limitations imposed by law and regulation. But in the economy at large, savings tend to rise in the early stages of a recession and to taper off in boom times, when consumers generally expect a continuation of a high level of income and fear the possibility of further price increases.

The Local Situation.   Deposit forecasting can perhaps rely somewhat more heavily on past experience than can loan forecasting, but both require a current knowledge of the business of the bank's larger customers and a constant awareness of economic developments in the community or markets a bank serves. This knowledge not only is the essential ingredient of operational budgeting but is equally necessary for liquidity budgeting. In large banks, the immediate responsibility for knowing what is going on lies with the area officer, department head, or branch manager—whoever is closest to the market area being served. In relatively small communities, this knowledge should be at the fingertips of the chief operating officer.

The basic techniques of acquiring such knowledge are simple enough. The bank's larger customers may be asked to help forecast their credit needs when bank officers review their annual or interim statements or visit their places of business. Too often, managers of large banks are reluctant to pry into the affairs of their larger depositors, and officers of small banks feel that they are too busy. Both of these are short-sighted attitudes. The expansion plans of business customers, municipal authorities, or local real estate developers are not made overnight. It is the job of the alert bank officer to be aware of what is going on in his community or in the segment of the credit market he is serving so that predictable events will not present him with unexpected problems.

The banker who is not aware of the community's plans for a new school until the bond issue is presented to the voters, who waits until the building permits have been issued before seeking to learn the financing needs of an important local builder, or who remains unaware of a large manufacturer-customer's new product that will require an increased use of credit is simply not performing his job adequately. Many bankers store this kind of knowledge in the back of their heads but do not organize it systematically. They do not add up all they know, as it were, and put it down on paper. As a result, vital decisions may be postponed too long.

Loan forecasting is at best an approximate science, but the approximation will be closer to actuality if it is consciously and conscientiously undertaken. It is suggested, therefore, that comments on past and potential use of credit be made a separate part of the credit files maintained on each large customer. Well-maintained files usually record the date and amount of peak borrowings and a record of the deposit balances maintained. In addition, they should contain the responsible officer's comments on probable credit needs and his prediction of the level of deposit balances likely to be maintained for some period in the future. These comments and predictions will of course be meaningful only if the officer in question has made an effort to find the information he needs by calling on the customer, reviewing his financial position, analyzing his flow of funds, and reviewing his estimate of future business as indicated by unfilled orders, expansion plans, new product development, and so on. The accuracy of the officer's predictions will depend heavily on the caliber and cooperativeness of the borrower's financial officer as well as on the bank officer's ability to ask the right questions. The effort in itself will probably be appreciated by the customers, many of whom look to their banks for just this kind of financial analysis and guidance.

The information in the files should be brought up to date and recapitulated as a formal loan and deposit forecast at least semiannually. The anticipated net demand for funds or net supply of funds can then be related intelligently to the bank's other liquidity needs. Periodically, the projections can be compared with the actual results, and the forecaster's skill can be sharpened through an analysis of past errors. Without such a program for systematically looking ahead, no bank, regardless of how large or small it is, can adequately plan for its liquidity needs or intelligently manage its investment portfolio.

APPROACHES TO MEETING LIQUIDITY NEEDS

Providing for a bank's liquidity needs is often more complex than estimating such needs. In many banks, directors and senior managers have available some estimates of their bank's liquidity needs but do not have adequate policies and procedures for meeting these needs. Several possible approaches are briefly discussed below, and some suggestions are made for choosing the most desirable one.

Loan Conversion

Bankers traditionally believed that the ideal banking assets were short-term, self-liquidating loans or secured demand loans. It was felt that, if such loans were the primary assets of a bank, they could be readily converted into cash when liquidity needs arose. This approach presents two major problems. First, it ignores the liquidity needs for meeting additional loan demands. Second, bankers found that many of the self-liquidating or demand loans could not be easily repaid or converted into cash, particularly in periods of economic stress.

A variation of this approach, propagated by the growing proportion of installment loans, is the idea that most of a bank's liquidity needs could be filled by the principal repayments and interest payments on such loans. This approach overlooks the strong seasonal pattern for both deposits and loans in many banks, and it ignores the potential liquidity needs if the total of outstanding loans grows more rapidly than deposits. In summary, although loan conversion is a source of liquidity, it should be considered in estimating liquidity needs for loans rather than as a valid approach to providing liquidity.

Asset Allocation

Some banks have attempted to provide for their liquidity needs through procedures that are usually referred to as an "allocation of assets" or a "conversion of funds."[4] These plans start with a classification of the liability accounts into various categories of deposits and capital funds. The banker then establishes for his own guidance the percentage of each class of liability he would like to hold in various categories of assets. Liquidity is provided by the assignment of fixed percentages of cash and other liquid assets to each category of liability. Table 8 shows a typical plan.[5]

This approach, particularly if it is rigidly used, has several inadequacies. For example, the analysis presented in the previous section stressed the fact that liquidity needs, even for specific categories of liabilities, vary over time as funds flow into and out of the bank. It is illogical, for instance, to hold the same percentage of the Treasury tax

---

[4]Harold E. Zarker, *The Allocation of Bank Assets* (Boston: Bankers Publishing Company, 1957).

[5]Alvin L. Kuehn, "How Much Liquidity?" *Bankers Monthly*, Vol. 72, No. 7, July 1955, p. 32.

TABLE 8

SAMPLE ALLOCATION OF ASSETS CALCULATIONS
(AMOUNTS IN THOUSANDS OF DOLLARS)

			Bonds				Loans			
Liabilities	Total	Cash & Due from Banks	U.S. Under 1 Year	U.S. Over 1 Year	Other Bonds	Industrial & Commer.	Consumer	Real Est. Mortgages	Commercial Paper	Fixed Assets and Accrued Interest
DEPOSITS										
Treas. tax and loan	1,000	250 25%	750 75%							
State funds	1,000	140 14%	240 24%	120 12%			250 25%		250 25%	
15 largest accts. & 3 largest public funds	9,000	2,070 23%	3,240 36%	2,340 26%	450 5%	900 10%				
All other demand	10,000	1,500 15%	1,400 14%	1,000 10%	800 8%	3,000 30%	2,300 23%			
Savings	6,000	420 7%	660 11%	720 12%	600 10%			3,600 60%		
Savings certificates	600	42 7%	48 8%	30 5%			120 20%	360 60%		
Other liabilities	400		80 20%	320 80%						
CAPITAL										
Capital stock	800									800 100%
Undivided profits, surplus and reserves	1,200					600 50%	300 25%		300 25%	
DESIRED DISTRIBUTION	30,000	4,422	6,418	4,530	1,850	4,500	2,970	3,960	550	800
ACTUAL DISTRIBUTION	30,000	5,000	6,000	5,000	2,500	4,200	3,000	4,000	0	300
DIFFERENCE: OVER (UNDER)		578	(418)	470	650	(300)	30	40	(550)	(500)

Source: Adapted from Alvin L. Kuehn, "How Much Liquidity?" *Bankers Monthly*, Vol. 72, No. 7, July 1955, p. 32.

and loan account in cash and bank balances when it is at a temporary peak following a heavy bond subscription as when it is at a low point following several Treasury calls. Adequate liquidity will be a different percentage of the various liability categories at different times.

Despite this logic, the lure of asset allocation still persists. It seems to have an attractive neatness. For example, in a publication on the subject, the New York State Bankers Association, after accepting the approach to deposit volatility outlined in the preceding section, goes on to allocate the remaining assets.[6]

Beyond the fact that varying degrees of liquidity will be appropriate at different times, there is another basic objection to allocation of even stable or nonvolatile deposits. Given adequate liquidity (and adequate capital), a bank will tend to make the kinds of loans its community needs. It should tend to make all the local loans it safely can and to invest only those funds that cannot be appropriately loaned to local borrowers. It is little more than a statistical exercise to allocate, let us say, 60 percent of savings deposits to residential mortgages in a stable farm community where few new homes have been built in the past decade and where the active demand for credit is for farm machinery purchases and crop loans.

Asset Liquidity Reserves. A much more flexible form of asset allocation is the classification of the assets that are available to the individual bank into so-called reserve categories based primarily on the liquidity of the assets. Emphasis is placed on allocating the assets to meet the diverse nature of the bank's liquidity needs and not on assigning or allocating assets to categories of liabilities.[7]

Writers on the subject of bank liquidity usually divide a bank's liquidity position into *primary reserves, secondary reserves,* and something variously designated *tertiary reserve, secondary reserve II,* or *investment reserve.*[8] The latter, whatever it is called, represents the longer-term liquidity needs discussed above. These categorical separations are perhaps too confining, and the term *investment reserve* may tend to

---

6A *Report of the Committee on Asset Allocation* (New York: New York State Bankers Association, 1960).

7Some banks separately allocate the various reserve accounts to those categories of liabilities for which the bank wishes to determine earnings, costs, and profitability. Because of their arbitrary nature, allocations of assets to liability categories seem to be more psychological than real, but they do no particular harm.

8Roland I. Robinson, *The Management of Bank Funds* (New York: McGraw-Hill Book Company, Inc., 1961) and Roger A. Lyon, *Investment Portfolio Management in the Commercial Bank* (New Brunswick, N. J.: Rutgers University Press, 1960).

obscure the essential difference in purpose between liquidity assets and the investment portfolio, to be discussed later. The separation between shorter- and longer-term liquidity needs and instruments is a fluid and flexible one; what all sections of the liquidity position have in common is that these assets are held to meet estimated needs of funds for other purposes.

Primary reserves are usually defined as cash on hand and amounts due from banks, or as legal reserves plus any additional holdings of noninterest-earning forms of money. They are more readily identifiable than secondary or tertiary reserves but are used to meet reserve requirements and to a large measure are not part of the liquidity position. In the case of deposit withdrawals, primary reserves would provide only 13 percent and 3 percent of the outflows from a country bank's demand and time deposits, respectively (see footnote 1). Primary reserves do not provide any help (indeed, they may be a liquidity drain if additional compensating deposits are required) in meeting liquidity needs arising from loan demands. Furthermore, to maximize income, bank policy should require excess holdings of primary reserves to be held to a minimum. Such policies and procedures are discussed in a subsequent section on managing the money position.

The remaining categories, whatever they are called, represent the true liquidity reserves of both short-term and long-term nature. The traditional approach is that these reserves should meet all the bank's liquidity needs and should consist of interest-earning liquid assets that under all forseeable circumstances can be converted into cash with little or no loss when the needs for which they were provided arise. It is important to remember that pledged securities cannot be converted into cash, unless the deposits they secure are withdrawn.

Liability Management

The final approach to providing for liquidity needs has been accepted by many larger banks in the 1960s. Proponents hold that it is no longer necessary to depend entirely on liquidity reserve assets to meet probable liquidity needs; instead, as such needs arise, they can be met by the management of liabilities. When liquidity is needed, therefore, banks can acquire it by issuing negotiable certificates of deposit, issuing commercial paper, buying Federal funds, or borrowing in the Eurodollar market. These sources were discussed in greater detail in the last section of the preceding chapter.

Astute management of liabilities can significantly help a larger bank with good access to the money markets meet its seasonal liquidity needs and meet its liquidity problems during a cyclical downturn. On the other hand, the contribution of liability management in providing liquid-ity needs during a cyclical boom may be limited and is likely to be very costly. Loan demands tend to run high in such periods, but liability sources tend to become expensive and may be limited by the ceiling on interest rates that banks can pay on deposits.

In the authors' opinion, although liability management may be use-ful (preferably it should be used to reduce the liquidity needs to be met by assets), most banks should rely primarily on the approach, discussed earlier, of using assets to meet most liquidity needs. By holding an ade-quate amount of liquid assets—an approach that may involve some loss of current income during earlier parts of a cyclical expansion—most banks will tend to avoid higher costs and possibly far greater capital losses (from the sale of depreciated bonds) during the later phases of expan-sion. Put in more precise terms, the essence of liquidity management is to equate the probable earlier loss of income with the subsequent higher cost and possible capital losses.[9]

PROVIDING FOR THE LIQUIDITY NEEDS

If a bank's directors and top management accept the idea that assets should be used to provide for most of its basic liquidity needs, the primary considerations become which assets are appropriate and how such assets should be managed. The following paragraphs discuss policies and procedures affecting a bank's primary reserve assets (often called its money position) and its liquidity reserve assets.

Managing the Money Position

A bank's *money position,* as previously defined, is the amount of coin and currency and demand balances due from banks (such balances will be in Federal Reserve banks for member banks) it holds primarily to comply with its legal reserve requirements. The amount of these holdings is affected daily by all the transactions through which payments flow into and out of the bank. Among these are payments for checks presented to the bank, the proceeds of checks and other collection items forwarded by it to other banks, purchases and sales of securities, receipts and dis-bursements of cash, and transfers of balances by mail or telegraph, together with other direct charges to its reserve balances.

Because money yields no income, the well-managed bank, large or small, will attempt to avoid holding any more of it than is necessary.

9G. Walter Woodworth, "Bank Liquidity Management: Theories and Tech-niques," *The Bankers Magazine,* Autumn 1967, p. 78.

For this reason, the basic policy for managing the money position should be to keep excess holdings of money at a minimum. In order to accomplish this objective, the position manager must know at all times approximately what his reserve requirements and holdings of money are. He must, therefore, start each day with a knowledge of the bank's position as of the opening of business and its cumulative average for that portion of the reserve-computation period that has already elapsed. Federal Reserve regulations provide that the average amount of reserves that must be held at the close of each business day for a week starting Thursday shall be computed on the basis of average deposit balances of the week ending prior to the preceding Thursday. A sample form appears in Table 9. Before the new reserve week starts, the Federal Reserve bank lets the member bank know the amount of average reserves it must carry at the Federal Reserve bank. Most states have similar procedures for nonmember banks.

The leeway provided by knowing reserve requirements in advance does not greatly simplify the problem because the balances themselves are subject to change during each day. Having determined the bank's

TABLE 9

BH-216 20M 4-71

TO ACCOUNTING DEPARTMENT
FEDERAL RESERVE BANK
P. O. Box 442
St. Louis, Mo. 63166

REPORT OF DEPOSITS, VAULT CASH AND FEDERAL FUNDS TRANSACTIONS

BANKS IN OUTLYING DISTRICTS OF RESERVE CITIES AND ELSEWHERE

XI - 22

(e) FOR BASE WEEK ENDING: _____ 19__

This Report To Be Mailed On Thursday Of Each Week

Report figures in nearest even thousands as of close of business each day

For non-business days, use figures as of close of last preceding business day

CLOSING BALANCES FOR: DAY	DATE	DUE TO BANKS (a) (Col. 1)	U.S. GOV'T DEMAND DEPOSITS (b) (Col. 2)	OTHER DEMAND DEPOSITS (Col. 3)	CASH ITEMS IN PROCESS OF COLLECTION (Col. 4)	DEMAND BALANCES DUE FROM BANKS (a) (Col. 5)	NET DEMAND DEPOSITS (c) (Col. 6)	SAVINGS DEPOSITS (Col. 7)	OTHER TIME DEPOSITS (Col. 8)	CURRENCY AND COIN (d) (Col. 9)	FEDERAL FUNDS PURCHASED (f) (Col. 10)	FEDERAL FUNDS SOLD (f) (Col. 11)
THURS.		1 829		29 644	2 665	3 186	25 619	9 920	6 220			826
FRI.		1 822		29 572	2 252	3 672	25 440	9 969	6 220			575
SAT.		1 742		31 446	2 033	4 697	26 458	9 975	6 220			560
SUN.		1 742		31 446	2 033	4 697	26 458	9 975	6 220			560
MON.		1 742		31 446	2 033	4 697	26 458	9 975	6 220			560
TUES.		1 703		30 461	2 280	3 263	26 621	9 985	6 220			685
WED.		2 135		31 822	3 504	3 233	27 220	9 997	6 220			554
TOTALS							184 274	69 846	43 540			4 320

(a) Reciprocal interbank demand deposits with banks in the United States, except private banks and American branches of foreign banks, must be reported net.
(b) Includes balances in Treasury Tax and Loan accounts and Series E Bond accounts.
(c) If the total of the amounts reported for any day in Columns 1, 2 and 3 is less than the total of the amounts reported for the same day in Columns 4 and 5, Net Demand Deposits-Column 6 for that day should be reported as NONE.
(d) Includes currency and coin in transit to and from Federal Reserve Bank.
(e) Refer to Schedule of Reserve Periods.
(f) Report only interbank transactions of gross Federal Funds sold and gross Federal Funds purchased for one business day or over week ends and holidays.

I CERTIFY THAT THIS REPORT IS CORRECT:

(Authorized Signature)

requirement at opening time, it is the money-position manager's task to keep track of all important transactions that affect his reserve balance during the day and to take steps to counteract any adverse effects.

The principles of managing the money position are virtually the same in large and small banks; it is the number rather than the nature of the transactions that greatly complicates the task for larger banks in money centers. For the latter, especially for banks serving the New York City money and securities markets, the management of reserve positions is not only a daily but an hourly or virtually continuous task. The rapidity with which funds flow through the money-market banks reflects the payment for most of the nation's security transactions as well as the financing of brokers and dealers. It results form the high degree to which national corporations have consolidated their balances in the money centers as well as how fully they keep them invested. And, finally, the balancing adjustments of all of the country banks and the settlement of the Federal funds markets are made on the books of banks in the money centers.

The basic problems involved in managing a money position can be more readily seen in the analysis of procedures that are adequate to a moderate-sized bank not located in a financial center and having no correspondent balances among its deposits. The basic figures for such a bank are shown in Table 9, which is the form the bank would send to its Federal Reserve bank, and in Table 10, which is a sample of the type of worksheet such a bank might use.[10] These forms are for use by member banks, but similar forms, adjusted to the requirements of state law, can be readily devised for nonmember banks.

A glance at the final column of the work sheet will tell the person responsible for the bank's money position just where he stands at the opening of business each day. This person then needs to calculate the effects of the debits and credits that he knows will be posted to his reserve account during the day. He is then in a position to project his

---

[10]After receiving the form showing a bank's weekly cumulative total deposits and vault cash, its Federal Reserve bank would compute a statement of reserves to be carried at the Reserve bank one week later in the following manner:

Deposit Classification	Amount (000)	Required (%)	Reserves (000)
Net demand—up to $35 million	$ 35,000	12½	$ 4,475
Net demand—remainder	149,274	13	19,406
Savings deposits	69,846	3	2,095
Time—up to $35 million	35,000	3	1,050
Time—remainder	8,540	5	427
Total required reserves			27,453
Less: vault cash			4,320
Net cumulative amount			$23,133
Daily average amount			$ 3,305

TABLE 10

WORKSHEET FOR COMPUTING RESERVE POSITION

Reserve Balances For:		Required Balances with Fed. Res. Bank (1)	Potential Balances with Fed. Res. Bank (2)	Potential Excess or Deficiency (3)	Federal Funds Actions		Other Adjustments Affecting Reserve Position (6)	Closing Balances with Fed. Res. Bank (7)	Actual Excess or Deficiency (8)
Day	Date				Federal Funds Purchased (4)	Federal Funds Sold (5)			
(brought forward)				*+20					*+20
Thur.		3,305	3,480	+175				3,480	+175
Fri.		3,305	3,260	-45				3,260	-45
Cum.		6,610	6,740	+150				6,740	+150
Sat.		3,305	3,260	-45				3,260	-45
Sun.		3,305	3,260	-45				3,260	-45
Cum.		13,220	13,260	+60				13,260	+60
Mon.		3,305	2,860	-445				2,860	-445
Cum.		16,525	16,120	-385				16,120	-385
Tues.		3,305	3,280	-25	300			3,580	+275
Cum.		19,830	19,400	-410	300			19,700	-110
Wed.		3,305	3,410	+105				3,410	+105
Cum.		23,135	22,810	-305		—	—	23,110	#-5
Avg.		3,305	3,259	-44	43	—	—	3,301	—

*Allowable excess or deficiency in reserve balances brought forward
#Allowable excess or deficiency in reserve balances to be carried forward

current and cumulative average balance as of the close of business the same day. On the basis of this projection, he can make a decision regarding what actions, if any, will be necessary to keep his position in reasonable balance. A suggested form for making these calculations appears in Table 11. For small banks with only moderate deposit fluctuations, not much more is needed. For larger banks seeking to keep excess reserves to the barest minimum, a closer scrutiny of daily transactions will be necessary.

The bulk of the credits and debits affecting the reserve accounts of a bank not located in the money centers are usually evident in the clearing figures each morning (checks presented to it and checks forwarded by it for collection) or are the result of transactions, such as securities purchases and sales, that it has itself originated. In sharp contrast is the situation of banks that operate in the money centers or that carry substantial amounts of due-to-bank balances. During the course of each day, the latter are subject to immediate and unpredictable demands in the form of interbank transfers and other payments arranged in Federal funds by their depositors.

Nevertheless, even for a country bank, the unpredictable can loom large in the management of its reserve position. The volatility of large deposit accounts can cause management of the money position to go awry as the result of unexpectedly large withdrawals or even large deposits that cannot be put to use. Alert money managers will therefore attempt to keep a close watch over the larger depositors and will take notice of the transactions that may affect the reserve position not only on a particular day but later in the reserve-computation period as well. Large deposits and withdrawals can be scanned daily for clues to future deposit swings, and an attempt can be made to get advance notice of future transactions from the financial officers of important corporate customers. At the same time, a calendar of maturing certificates of deposit and securities and large loan repayments should be maintained and taken into consideration in the daily adjustments of the reserve position. The money-position manager should also receive a brief daily memorandum of the sources of funds available to him and a list of correspondent balances and liquidity instruments.

With the broadening of the Federal funds market, even relatively small banks can invest most of their volatile deposits. Excess reserves will still probably tend to accumulate somewhat in country member banks, particularly at times when the Federal Reserve System is making credit freely available. There are several reasons for this. In the first place, Federal funds transactions of less than one hundred thousand dollars

TABLE 11

MONEY POSITION
TUESDAY—(AMOUNTS IN $000)

	Current	Cumulative
Accumulated actual excess or deficiency		(−) 385
Required reserves tonight	3,305	
Reserve balances collected (our books)	2,860	
Potential reserve position	(−) 445	
Known transactions affecting reserves today:		
Credits:		
Yesterday's immediate cash letter	1,181	
Deferred items available today	885	
Security sales available today	615	
Currency and coin in transit	100	
Credit in local clearings	—	
Other	—	
Total credits	2,781	
Debits:		
Remittances charged today	2,206	
Securities purchased charged today	—	
Notes due today	—	
Tax and loan call	100	
Currency and coin orders	—	
Debits in local clearings	55	
Other	—	
Total debits	2,361	
Net credits minus debits	(+) 420	
Potential excess or deficit tonight	(−) 25	(−) 410
Adjusted today:		
Credits:		
Transfers from bank account	—	
Borrowing from Federal Reserve	—	
Federal funds bought	300	
Securities sold for "cash"	—	
Total credits	300	
Debits:		
Transfers from reserve account	—	
Federal funds sold	—	
Total debits	—	
Net adjustments	(+) 300	
Adjusted excess or deficiency	(+) 275	(−) 110

are generally discouraged.[11] Second, banks are limited to selling Federal funds by the size of their reserve accounts. They are expected not to incur substantial reserve deficiencies even for one day. Finally, the amount to be earned on the full investment of the excess reserves of these smaller banks is hardly enough to make the effort worthwhile when all the costs are taken into consideration.

At times when Federal funds are freely available, it may be easier to maintain an over-invested position (where reserve requirements exceed reserves held before transactions in Federal funds) and buy funds for one or two days to balance out to the requirements over the period than to accumulate an excess and try to sell it. Smaller banks are able, in effect, to keep themselves fully invested by using this strategy. Many larger money-market banks profitably maintain an over-invested position when Federal funds rates are below those at which they can lend or invest for short periods.

One final factor should be noted. Under the regulations of the Board of Governors of the Federal Reserve System, a member bank not only has an entire reserve-computation period in which to average reserves but also is permitted to carry forward to the following reserve-computation period any excess or deficiency in its reserve balance in an amount not to exceed 2 percent of the bank's required reserves. However, a deficiency thus carried forward has to be made up in the successive period and may not be carried forward to a third without penalty.

Managing the Liquidity Position

Sound policy dictates that the liquidity position should consist primarily of assets that are of highest quality and short maturity and that can be readily sold without adverse effects on any of the bank's customers. The assets, as well as liabilities and other possible liquidity arrangements, that are generally used to fulfill this position were described in the preceding chapter. The purpose here is to describe briefly the primary means of attaining the highest return while insuring an adequate liquidity position.

The basic procedure to follow in managing the liquidity position is that of matching the assets with the time period for which the liquidity is desired. Assets used to meet volatile demand deposit fluctuations and seasonal loan demands will appropriately be different from assets used

---

[11]However, in periods of very tight money, amounts as low as ten thousand dollars are not turned away. Some banks have devised streamlined procedures for handling these small amounts in volume.

to meet possible residual outflows of savings deposits and secular increases in loans.

Seasonal loan demands should basically be covered by assets that either mature very close to the time the demands materialize or can be readily sold with a high probability of no loss at that time. The matching assets can be any of the liquid assets described in the preceding chapter and should be selected on the basis of the highest available after-tax yield. The other category of liquid assets must be highly marketable and should, therefore, be limited to Treasury bills and possibly some agency obligations maturing within a year. The basic concept is that, if the yield curve for Treasury bills has a positive slope (which is the normal situation), the yield of a longer-term bill for the period held (remember that one year is the maximum maturity) will usually be higher than the yield to maturity for a bill with a maturity that matches the holding period.

An example should help clarify this concept. Suppose a bank feels that it will need one hundred thousand dollars to meet seasonal loan demands in roughly three months. Should it use 91-day bills yielding 4.5 percent or 182-day bills yielding 5.0 percent? Using the formula for the yield for the estimated holding period,[12] the bank should find that the yield over 91 days for the 182-day bill will be 5.5 percent if interest rates remain the same. Further, the bank should find that, unless the rate on 91-day bills rises above 5.5 percent,[13] the bank will be better off buying the 182-day bills. Thus, unless the bank believes that the rates on 91-day bills will increase from 4.5 to above 5.5 percent in the next three months, the 182-day bill will have a higher return.

The liquidity needs for potential cyclical or secular increases in loans, on the other hand, might be held in longer-term liquidity instruments. The major forms of assets acceptable for this purpose are U.S. government securities, Federal agency securities, and higher quality, marketable

---

[12]The formula for determining the yield for the period held is:

$$Yh = Yo + \frac{Tr\,(Yo\text{-}Ym)}{Th}$$

where Yh is the yield for the period held, Yo is the original yield, Ym is the market yield when sold, Tr is the remaining time to maturity, and Th is the time held (in units consistent with Tr).

[13]The break-even market yield, Yb, is determined by:

$$Yb = Yo + \frac{Th\,(Yc\text{-}Yo)}{Tr}$$

where Yc is the market yield for a security maturing at the end of the holding period and the other symbols are the same as those in footnote 12.

state and local securities.[14] Under most circumstances, these securities will have maturities of one to three years at the time they are bought. Short-term securities are appropriate if the bank feels there is a high probability that rates will rise over the next year or so. The potential price fluctuations for securities maturing in much over three years disqualifies such securities for even longer-term liquidity needs.[15] Acceptable securities with maturities exceeding three years should be considered part of the investment portfolio. If banks use the philosophy of spaced maturity (described in Chapter 13) in managing their investment portfolios, acceptable securities can be reclassified as liquid assets when their maturities fall below four years.

SAMPLE LIQUIDITY COMPUTATIONS

The figures shown in Table 12 are those of a small bank in a resort community at a time when deposits are just rising from the seasonal low point and when loans are still at the seasonal peak. This bank—quite appropriately, considering its size and location—does not depend on liability management as a source of liquidity. Although this bank's classification of liquidity needs and holdings into short- and longer-term categories may be sufficient, larger banks should be more explicit in matching their assets (and potential liabilities) with the purpose for which the liquidity is desired.

Table 12 shows a modest deficiency in short-term liquidity, but at a time when deposits can be expected to rise and loans to fall. The bank's longer-term liquidity requirements have been well provided for. It should be emphasized as strongly as possible, moreover, that a calculation such as this is at best a close approximation and a guide to policy, not a determinant to it. Bank management, in the light of all it knows about the local situation, may well be satisfied with the liquidity position revealed by the table.

14The marketability of state and local bonds varies widely. For example, see George H. Hempel, *Measures of Municipal Bond Quality* (Ann Arbor: University of Michigan Press, 1967), pp. 15–44, and "Liquidity and Muni Bonds," *Monthly Review*, Federal Reserve Bank of San Francisco, January 1968, pp. 10–12.

15For example, the price of five-year Treasury notes declined over 8 percent from February 1969, to February 1970, and roughly 4 percent from November 1969, to February 1970. Source: Salomon Brothers, "Bank Market Roundups," 1969–70.

TABLE 12

LIQUIDITY POSITION
JULY 1

	Estimates Affecting Liquidity ($000)	Liquidity Requirements (%)	Amount of Liquidity Needed ($000) Short-term	Longer-term
Deposit liquidity:				
Demand deposits				
Volatile	430	87	375	
Vulnerable				
Large	1,174			
-Volatile	430	744	20	149
Residual				
Total	5,193			
-Large	1,170	4,023	10	402
Time deposits				
Volatile		0	97	—	
Large		60	20	12
Special		100	100	50	50
Residual				
Total	4,831			
-Above	160	4,671	5	234
Loan liquidity:				
Seasonal loan demand		0	100	—	
Unexpected demand		116	100	116	
Net secular loan increase		200	100	50	150
Aggregate estimated needs			591	997

Liquidity instruments held:	Amounts ($000) Under 1 Year	1–3 Years
Federal banks and correspondent balances	304	
Acceptances, commercial paper, and loan participations	—	
High-grade securities	100	1,200
Firm commitments from others to purchase assets	—	
Totals	404	1,200
Less borrowings	—	
Net liquidity provided	404	1,200
Excess (+) or Deficit (−)	(−)187	(+)203

IO

LENDING—
CONCEPTS AND TYPES

Lending is an essential function of commercial banking. Through lending, bank management strives to satisfy the legitimate credit needs of the community or credit markets that the bank serves or intends to serve. Furthermore, bank loans contribute materially to bank profitability by providing a higher return than most other bank assets and by being a key element in the creation and maintenance of depositor relationships.

There are significant differences in approach between the acquisition of bank loans and the acquisition of securities for liquidity or investment. The purchase of securities is generally conducted impersonally—objective measures such as relative interest rate, credit quality, marketability, and maturity are the major criteria. Bank lending, on the other hand, often tends to be influenced by more subtle and subjective factors, such as an evaluation of the borrower's character, the history of the borrower's relationships with the bank, and his possible influence on prospective new business. These differences emphasize the need to understand the basic concepts and types of lending and to have well-formulated loan policies and practices.

This chapter will examine the importance of lending to bank management's total objectives, outline the basic criteria that bank management should use in evaluating bank loans, and identify the basic characteristics of the various types of bank loans. The following chapter will discuss the formulation of sound lending policies and will explore some of the necessary procedures for granting and servicing loans.

CONTRIBUTION TO BANKING OBJECTIVES

It has long been recognized that one of the fundamental obligations of a commercial bank is to try to serve the credit needs of its community or service area. Which of these credit needs are legitimate is a matter to be discussed later. For the moment, legitimate credit may be conceived of as any use of bank credit that will further the stability or growth of the community or the economic well-being of its citizens.

The credit needs of the community will be served whether commercial banks serve them or not. The American financial scene has numerous competitive institutions and government agencies serving credit needs that, originally at least, commercial banks either failed to recognize or were reluctant to provide for. Bankers may complain about this "unfair competition," but the fact remains that commercial banks did not make consumer loans in volume until long after the finance companies had shown the way. Commercial banks generally were not prepared to make the volume or kind of mortgage loans for which the public turned to the savings and loan associations in such large numbers. Even Federally insured mortgage loans were looked upon with suspicion in the late 1930s by all but a few farsighted bankers.

Not all credit needs can be appropriately filled by commercial banks. Some are not eligible for bank credit because of their capital or long-term nature. The banks, however, should at least be aware of such needs. Through their relationships with the market, other institutional investors, and their correspondent banks in the money centers, banks can facilitate the flow of longer-term or capital funds into their communities and help to meet any extra need for short-term funds.

Although most commercial banks take their highest risks in their loan portfolio, bank loans tend to be the most profitable bank asset. This assertion has been substantiated by the Functional Cost Analysis program recently offered by the Federal Reserve banks. From 1966 through 1969, the gross yield on all loans and each of the major categories of loans—commercial and agricultural loans, installment loans, and real estate mortgage loans—nearly always exceeded the gross yield on investments. The one exception was in 1969, when the gross yield on investments exceeded the gross yield on real estate mortgages, and even in that year the return on new mortgages was probably higher than that on new investments. Furthermore, although the assets with the highest gross rates of return generally tended to have the highest operating costs, the net yields on all loans and most of the major categories of loans tended to be higher than the net yields on investments.

Aside from their profitability, bank loans are an important means of creating and maintaining depositor relationships, particularly with business firms. Most banks lend only to firms that keep deposit balances at the bank, and most firms maintain deposits primarily at banks that they believe are willing to fill their borrowing needs. Similar relationships are becoming more commonplace for state and local governments and individual customers.

Two types of risks are typically greater for bank loans than for most other banking assets. First is the credit risk—that is, the possibility that promised payments will not be made. Generally, a bank has to take on a certain degree of credit risk. The reward—higher return and contribution to banking objectives—is usually high enough to compensate the bank for taking this type of risk. A second type of risk is the liquidity pressure often associated with bank loans. The demand for bank loans is typically highest in boom periods, when tight monetary policies cause security prices and the rate of deposit growth to decline. In addition, it is impractical to sell most bank loans because of their personal nature and their deposit relationships. In summary, in order to service the credit needs of its community profitably, a bank must be willing to assume a somewhat higher average risk on loans than on other bank assets.

CRITERIA FOR EVALUATING LOANS

Several criteria form the general basis for evaluating all types of bank loans. Most important are the suitability of arrangements made for the repayment of the loan and the validity of the purpose for which it is granted. A third essential criterion, safety or ultimate collectability, is inherent in the other two but involves the additional technical consideration of protection against unforeseen circumstances.

Soundness, in the view presented here, is not necessarily limited to safety but also includes consideration of the critical needs of the community. A perfectly collectable loan may be made for a speculative or economically unsound purpose. Making such loans in number, however, is not sound banking, especially if it results in the rejection (for lack of funds) of perhaps riskier loans that would contribute more to the economic development of the community and the longer-run growth of the bank itself. Sound lending, it should be remembered, is an art, not a science.

The point is not that banks should ignore risk or sacrifice reasonable safety. A loan that is clearly unsafe should not be made. However, absolute safety is neither the only nor even the best measure of soundness, and competent and imaginative lending officers can often make safe loans in borderline credit situations.

Payment

Chapter 1 showed how bank lending bridges the gap, or time lag, between production and consumption. In this connection, it has often been said that credit is the lifeblood of the economy. If this is true, then credit that ceases to flow through the economy and becomes stagnant (as a substitute for permanent capital, for example) can be said to represent a hardening of the economic arteries.

One of the basic criteria for evaluating bank loans, therefore, should be that the money loaned should normally flow back to the bank as the transaction being financed is consummated or liquidated. The terms of repayment, in other words, should be related to the form and nature of the transaction being financed, and a definite repayment program should be established for every loan, no matter how well secured.

Another way of stating this principle is to say that a sound bank loan should be collectable from planned self-liquidation of the borrower's assets or from the anticipated income or profits of the borrower rather than from the forced liquidation of any collateral that may be pledged. Whenever a bank has to foreclose and sell collateral, it thereby demonstrates that the extension of credit was unsound in the first place, even if the bank incurs no loss. The borrower usually does lose, and the community may suffer as well. A community loss becomes abundantly clear if many banks are forced to liquidate numerous loans; disposal of the collateral depresses the market sharply, thus effectively destroying existing values in the entire community. In essence, the collapse of real estate values in the mid–1930s was the direct result of unsound mortgage lending in the 1920s—lending that was unsound precisely because it was based on collateral values rather than on realistic payment schedules.

The proper function of collateral is to minimize the risk of loss to the bank if for unforeseeable reasons the income or profits of the borrower fail to materialize in sufficient quantity for repayment of the loan. This protective function will be elaborated upon later in this chapter. In most cases, capacity to pay, if properly measured, is better security than is collateral.

The terms on which various kinds of loans are made will not be uniform because they will be made to finance transactions taking place over differing periods of time. The rate of repayment and the final payment date should be estimated at the time the loan is granted, and a repayment schedule should be established on that basis. Any deviation from a repayment schedule so established will be an automatic signal that something has gone wrong with the original estimates and that the loan may be in need of immediate attention. Even more important, such a signal will indicate a change in the flow of funds through the loan portfolio that will affect the bank's liquidity position.

Some ninety-day notes are put on the bank's books with little thought to the length of time for which the funds will really be needed. This type of note has long since lost favor with the informed student of banking; however, it is still widely used by many banks, largely as a matter of habit. The same may be said of many demand (the bank can demand repayment at any time) loans that rely heavily on collateral values. Experienced bankers know that such demand loans are often the slowest and longest-term loans in their portfolios. The above instruments are generally appropriate for financing very short-term financial transactions in highly liquid assets. In other situations, the bank should make arrangements for periodic reductions in the loan at the time it is made.

Another aspect of repayment in need of careful review is the traditional requirement of an annual "cleanup" or period of time during which the borrower is completely off the bank's books. To require a cleanup from borrowers who have a long-term or semipermanent need for working capital (such as finance companies or dairy farmers) is to delude oneself about the nature of the loan and to encourage borrowers to switch loans from one bank to another for no other reason than for compliance with an unrealistic tradition. Some bankers argue that the cleanup gives them an opportunity to review the credit before taking it on again. Outstanding loans should be periodically reviewed also, and a bank may be in a better position to work with a weak borrower who is more steadily dependent upon it. If it holds firm against the policy of "throwing good money after bad," it will have essentially the same opportunity to review the credit standing of the borrower when it renews a note as when it originally accepts it.

The principle of relating repayments to the nature of the transaction justifies not only making some longer-term loans but even sometimes keeping a borrower on the books without material reduction for considerable periods of time. A customer whose business is expanding rapidly, for example, may need to use his profits to expand his physical plant and may at the same time need additional short-term credit to carry the higher inventory and receivables resulting from his increased but profitable volume. In such cases, the bank's credit is related to the increased flow of transactions through the business of the borrower and can be considered sound, even though, for a period, the loan is not being repaid.[1]

In summary, it should be a basic premise of a bank's lending policy that the means and timing of repayment be considered when a loan is granted and that loans be made only when a borrower agrees in advance to a repayment program related to a realistic appraisal of his ability to repay. The actual period may range from a few weeks (or even days) to twenty years or longer (as in mortgage lending), and the longer term will ordinarily require more stringent credit scrutiny or the pledge of collateral. The essential thing for both the bank and the borrower is that there be a payment program.

Purpose

The validity of the purpose for which the proceeds of a loan are to be used is a less obvious criterion for evaluating loans than the prospects of its repayment, but it is nevertheless an essential ingredient of soundness in the broader sense. The purpose of most business loans either is explicitly stated or can be deduced from a comparison of the borrower's financial statements. The fact that the purpose of some forms of individual loans is often not asked for or recorded evidences a misunderstanding on the part of both the bank and the borrower concerning the appropriate role of a bank as a supplier of liquid funds to the community. Recent surveys have indicated that the modern businessman is seeking sound financial advice as well as credit from his banker. He obviously cannot expect to receive very sound advice if he keeps his banker in the dark about his affairs. Individuals may not be looking for advice to quite the same extent, but it is clear that banker cannot know whether the money he lends will produce income or profits to repay the loan and cannot relate the repayment program to the nature of the transaction unless he knows what it is. Purpose and payment are intimately interwoven.

Purpose becomes even more important when credit is scarce. The major focus of monetary policy is to restrict the creation of new credit at times when the economy is fully extended; the expectation is that the commercial banking system, forced to ration credit, will choose to use its limited resources to finance productive rather than speculative activity. In addition, commercial banks have a vested self-interest in the balanced economic growth of their communities; when their lending resources are

---

[1]Under such circumstances, a bank will frequently grant new advances although requiring continued repayment on the old, thus preserving the form of continued amortization.

limited, they should—as a matter of policy if not a matter of course—seek to employ those resources in ways that will contribute most to economic growth.

Protection

It could be claimed with considerable justification that, if a loan is made for a sound purpose and the repayments are realistically scheduled to flow from the liquidation of the transaction being financed, little more is required to make it a good loan. Life is uncertain, however, as Robert Burns observed many years ago. "The best laid schemes o' mice an' men gang aft a-gley." Because of a bank's responsibility to its depositors as well as its stockholders, bank management must take every possible precaution so that, if the borrower's affairs "gang a-gley," the bank will not be the loser.

The principal bulwarks against unforeseeable contingencies are the creditworthiness of the borrower (and of endorsers and guarantors) and the value of the collateral pledged to secure a loan. To the extent that complete creditworthiness may be questioned, collateral assumes added importance—at times perhaps too much.

A borrower is worthy of credit if he can produce unimpeachable evidence of his ability and willingness to repay his loans as agreed. Creditworthiness or credit standing is based to a large extent on character and reputation and, for sizable loans, on the financial condition of the borrower as shown by his financial statement and his earning record. A detailed description of financial statement analysis is beyond the scope of this book; however, it may be noted that a bank's appraisal of its customers' creditworthiness is not unlike the bank supervisor's appraisal of the soundness of the bank itself. Essential to both is the relationship of the borrower's net worth to his obligations and to the risk inherent in the business. The customer's net worth, like the bank's capital, serves to assure the lender that the borrower will be able to meet his obligations. Earning capacity is a vital ingredient of both creditworthiness and supervisory confidence, as is liquidity—the relationship of current assets to current liabilities. And character, which along with capital and capacity is one of the "three C's of credit," is as important in the evaluation of the creditworthiness of a commercial enterprise as is the supervisor's appraisal of management in a commercial bank.

To be assured of creditworthiness, it is essential that the bank's lending officers be provided with adequate tools to appraise credits effectively. To achieve this end, the bank should insist on financial statements and earnings records from all important borrowers, no matter how sterling their character may appear or how often the principals in the business play golf with one of the bank's managers or directors. Moreover, the statements should be complete and sufficiently detailed to permit effective analysis. Where sizable amounts are involved, the figures should be audited by a reputable accounting firm.

It is also important that bank management insist on a continuing close analysis of the financial position of the borrower. Periodic reviews of outstanding loans in various size or class categories should be required. Early observation of unfavorable trends will enable the bank to take effective protective measures or render often vital financial guidance that may make the difference not only between repayment or default but also between the success or failure of the borrower. The larger the loan and the greater the risk factor, the closer the bank's contacts with the borrower should be.

Some bankers try to obtain a lien on some asset of the borrower to support a loan whenever possible. There is nothing wrong with this practice, if it does not lead to overreliance on security to the neglect of the more important credit considerations discussed above. For business loans, the real significance of collateral or other protective arrangements lies in the fact that such devices enable bank management to make economically desirable loans or to work out weak credit situations when such action would not be entirely safe without security. Collateral agreements tend to give the bank residual control over some of the key assets of the borrowing firm. Many loans to small or new enterprises or to businesses that are expanding rapidly could not be justified on the basis of creditworthiness alone. Longer-term loans to the most creditworthy of borrowers also require additional protection because of the greater risk involved in the time factor itself. Collateral protection for business loans may be arranged in many different ways, depending on the nature of the business and the particular circumstances in each case. In many instances, it may take the form of a direct pledge of assets, such as liens on fixed assets or the pledge of inventory or receivables.

In the contracts for most longer-term business loans, many banks also demand protective covenants requiring the borrower, for example, to maintain certain minimum balance sheet ratios or to agree not to pledge certain assets for another purpose as long as the loan is outstanding. Many loan agreements also contain provisions limiting dividend payments or withdrawals by the principals, and some set ceilings on the salary payments to senior officers. In connection with loans to small or closely held corporations, it is usually desirable to obtain the endorsements of the principals and their wives in order to tie in the real net worth of the corporation as support for the loan. Statements of such businesses frequently reveal substantial amounts due to the principals.

When such debt is formally subordinated to the bank loan, it serves, in effect, as additional capital.

Experienced lending officers agree that there are few occasions when unsecured loans to individuals for more than nominal amounts can be justified unless the individual is engaged in business or unless the loan is directly related to a specific, short-term transaction and is written for an equally short term. No matter how wealthy the individual, no matter how good his statement, he should be required to secure his obligations. A firm rule in this regard will prevent the necessity of making many difficult decisions in borderline cases.

This discussion of the criteria for bank loans, a subject that lies at the very heart of commercial banking functions, has been far from exhaustive. Nevertheless, it should be clear that a bank's lending policies and practices will be sound if its directors and top management lay down firm guidelines that specify appropriate purposes for which the bank's credit may be used, relate the bank's repayment requirements to those purposes, and make certain that the bank obtains sufficient protection against unforeseen risks.

TYPES OF LOANS

Although the basic contributions of and criteria for bank lending discussed above apply generally to all types of bank loans, different shades of emphasis are appropriate for different types of loans. The most basic differentiation is between wholesale and retail banking. The wholesale side of banking is concerned with the provision of lending, deposit, and ancillary services to business organizations, and retail banking concentrates on the provision of lending and deposit services to individuals, even to persons of modest means. Some of the differences in policies and procedures appropriate for these two types of operations are discussed in the following chapter; however, a more detailed differentiation among the types of loans is usually required for the development of loan policies and procedures.

Chart 15 shows the percentage distribution of the major types of loans for all commercial banks in selected years from 1923 through 1971. The following discussion emphasizes the three major types of loans made by most commercial banks—commercial (business and farm) loans, short- and intermediate-term consumer loans, and mortgage (real estate) loans. Some of the other types or special forms of bank loans will be briefly discussed; no attempt will be made to examine separately any of the numerous specialized fields of lending found in banks that serve particular industries.

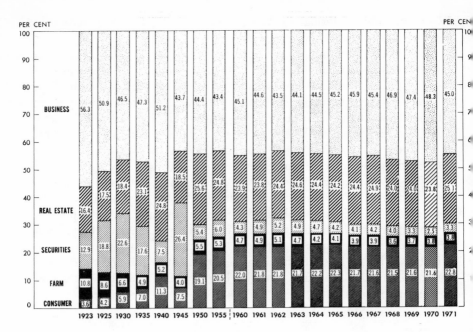

CHART 15 Percentage Distribution of Loans, by Type of Loan, All Commercial Banks, 1923 to 1971 (Sources: 1923–1949: R.W. Goldsmith, *A Study of Savings in the U.S.*; 1950 to 1971: Federal Deposit Insurance Corporation, *Annual Reports*.)

Commercial Loans

Traditionally and practically, the foremost obligation of a commercial bank is to supply the credit needs of business enterprises, including farm operations, in its community. Loans that accomplish this general purpose, whatever form they take, are essentially commercial loans. Chart 15 shows that commercial loans have averaged about half of all loans made by commercial banks from 1923 through 1971. In terms of purpose and payment, commercial loans range from short-term, self-liquidating loans to finance the manufacture, storage, or shipment of commodities, through loans to supply working capital over varying periods of time, to loans to finance the acquisition of capital assets.[2] Some of the basic character-

---

[2]Space does not permit more than a cursory discussion of commercial lending. More comprehensive coverage of this subject is contained in B.H. Beckhart, ed., *Business Loans of American Commercial Banks* (New York: The Ronald Press Company, 1959); Hubert V. Prochnow and Roy A. Foulke, *Practical Bank Credit* (New York: Harper & Row, 1963); the sections on credit policy and commercial credit in *The Bankers' Handbook* (Homewood: Dow Jones-Irwin, Inc., 1966); and *Commercial Loan Analysis* (Washington: The American Bankers Association, 1971).

istics of the three major categories of commercial loans—seasonal loans, working capital loans, and term loans—are discussed in the following paragraphs.

Seasonal Loans. The first category consists of short-term advances that furnish working capital in excess of normal needs. In its pure form, the seasonal loan is taken out only for seasonal needs and is repaid when inventory and receivables are partially converted into cash at the end of the seasonal upsurge. It is, then, a self-liquidating loan, its repayment dependent on the conversion of other current assets into cash. Seasonal loans have traditionally been the backbone of commercial banks' asset structure; they are the traditional commercial loans conceived of as eligible paper under the Federal Reserve Act.

Although secured seasonal loans have become more prevalent in the late 1960s and early 1970s, the majority of seasonal loans made by commercial banks are not secured.[3] Because of the self-liquidating feature, most seasonal loans present few serious problems beyond the need for careful credit analysis. Principal emphasis should be placed on the probability of conversion into cash of an amount of current assets suitable for the prospective loan and any other maturing liabilities.

Ordinarily, banks actively seek seasonal loans. Rates and terms as favorable as possible are offered as inducements to prospective borrowers and depositors. Some seasonal loans are transaction loans, made to finance a specific seasonal need, but most are made against a previously approved line of credit. These lines of credit can present some special problems if the bank is not careful. A line of credit is not a legal commitment to lend, but a bank would suffer great embarrassment if it could not supply funds virtually on demand under an established line. If lines are too freely granted or are granted with too little concern for the borrower's actual needs, they may remain unused until, in a period of credit stringency, their sudden activation may put considerable pressure on the bank's own liquidity position.

Longer-term Working Capital Loans. Many business enterprises need working capital for periods longer than a season. Although the amount of credit needed may fluctuate seasonally, its employment in some amount tends to be prolonged or virtually continuous. The working capital loan is generally riskier for the bank, because it is usually repaid out of earnings or refinancing. It can be repaid from current assets only

---

[3]The increase in secured seasonal loans probably coincides with a decrease in the liquidity position of many firms. For some financially weaker companies, secured seasonal loans are the only form of credit that the banker can appropriately offer. Accounts receivable are the most common form of security for seasonal loans.

when the borrower's need for current assets exhibits a cyclical or secular decrease. Hence, the receipt of repayment funds for the working capital loan is usually less certain than for the seasonal loan.

Working capital loans are a legitimate credit need for many businesses. Any business that must carry a relatively large and varied inventory throughout the year, or a business that sells in volume on credit, is a likely candidate for working capital loans. Most banks can fill this type of financing need, but they should be aware of its dangerous characteristics and establish credit terms accordingly.

In reviewing working capital loans, bank officers should be concerned not only with the current asset position of the borrower but also with his profitability and net worth. Unless the borrowing firm shows a substantial equity position in a profitable business, the bank should usually require additional protection in the form of pledged receivables or inventory. Because a longer period of time is involved, it is often prudent to require the borrower to maintain certain agreed upon balance-sheet ratios or to limit dividend and salary payments.

Working capital loans may take several forms. Some are single transaction loans for a specific purpose. Two problems with such an arrangement are that it may not permit seasonal flexibility and that maturity agreements are often inadequate. Some rather widely used maturity agreements, such as demand notes and ninety-day renewable notes, clearly do not conform to the previously espoused principles of purpose and payment.[4] Other working capital loans are in effect made when a customer fails to clear up his line of credit over a seasonal period. This arrangement is acceptable only if the bank and the borrowing firm both recognize—in the interest charges, credit analysis, and so on—that the loan is for longer-term working capital purposes and agree on periodic review of the line of credit and some plan for repayment.

A specialized arrangement used for both seasonal loans and longer-term working capital loans is called revolving credit. The bank commits itself to lend up to a stated amount over a period of up to several years.

---

[4] If a clearly defined source of repayment is not established at the time the loan is made or is recognized not to exist, the loan must be considered permanent. Some bankers believe banks can legitimately supply permanent funds to business. For example, Victor J. Reizman (in "A Theory for Permanent Lending," *Journal of Commercial Bank Lending*, October 1970, pp. 32–37) points out that a bank would be favorably inclined to make a seasonal loan to one company requiring it in the summer and to another company whose seasonal needs are high in the winter; however, many banks would balk if these two companies were to merge and require loans all year because the working capital needs occur all year. Reizman questions whether the customer is less valuable or safe to the bank because of the merger.

The outstanding loan ordinarily rises and falls within the commitment, and the borrower may in fact be out of debt for extended periods. Under a revolving credit plan, the borrower pays a small commitment fee on the unused portion of his line in addition to the agreed upon rate of interest on the amounts used. This fee compensates the bank for holding money available and assures the borrower that he may use the funds when he needs them. A closer look at the borrower's financial condition, a discussion of purpose and payment, and often certain restrictive provisions should be a part of the revolving credit agreement.

A final arrangement is a combination of line of credit and amortized term loan to provide for the seasonal and longer-term working capital needs of the borrowing firm. This arrangement will be clearer after the following discussion of term loans.

Term Loans. *Term loans* are usually defined for statistical purposes as loans with an original maturity of more than one year. Functionally, a term loan is one that, regardless of its specific maturity, will be repaid out of the net cash income of the business over a considerable period of time. Nearly all term loans are amortized over the life of the loan and have quite explicit repayment dates. The proceeds of term loans are typically used to acquire capital assets, such as plant and equipment, to enlarge or replenish working capital, or to clean up a short-term debt.

Term loans generally are repaid in three to ten years. Some banks enter into combined loans with insurance companies and pension funds when the borrowing firm can appropriately repay the loan only over longer periods. These banks typically make a loan equal to the repayments in the first five to ten years, and the other financial institution lends the amount that will be repaid after that period.

Because of the long exposure to risk, bankers are usually very careful in analyzing applications for term loans. A longer term means a greater chance for economic, cyclical, or management changes that may impair the quality of the loan. In evaluating the granting of term loans, bankers are concerned not only with the net worth and profitability of the borrower but also with the management situation and the firm's cash flow projections. Cash flow is usually a better measure of the borrower's ability to repay a term loan than are profit projections. Although projected net cash inflows from operations are generally larger than projected net profits (because of noncash expenses, such as depreciation), it is important to remember that loan repayments and scheduled expansion in plant and equipment, which do not affect profits, do reduce available cash flows.

Term lending has assumed increasing importance in recent years.

In 1970 and 1971, term loans by large commercial banks averaged $32 billion, roughly 40 percent of the commercial loans at such banks.[5] Most small banks also make term loans, although in some cases they may not be specifically designated as such. Term loans may be the primary source for financing the plant and equipment needs of creditworthy firms that are too small to borrow in the capital markets.

Large enterprises traditionally have financed their capital needs primarily by borrowing in the capital markets or directly from institutional investors. Many needs for capital financing are still filled in this manner. Frequently, however, the amount of a particular acquisition will not be large enough to justify a market flotation, or the cash flow will be sufficiently large to enable the borrower to repay all or part of the obligation in a shorter period of time than would be acceptable to an institutional investor.[6]

Despite some doubts that have been raised about the appropriateness of commercial bank term lending, the term loan represents a clear case of a bank meeting the credit need of a customer by relating purpose to payment. For protection, in addition to the collateral usually obtained and the provisions for regular amortization, term loans typically contain convenants establishing minimum working capital levels and minimum net worth-to-debt ratios and limiting dividends or withdrawals from the business during the term of the loan. Such agreements provide a continuing control over the obligor that is not always attainable through the corporate securities that term loans have replaced in bank portfolios.

Short- and Intermediate-term Consumer Loans

Short- and intermediate-term consumer lending by commercial banks has come of age since the end of World War II. Chart 15 (on page 176) shows that after the war, such consumer loans rose from slightly less than 8 percent of all commercial bank loans to an average in recent years of above 20 percent of total loans. Banks, which used to look upon consumer lending with suspicion, now regard consumer credit needs as an important element of the community's total demand for credit. Indeed, despite their late start, commercial banks have become the dominant financial institutions in consumer lending.[7]

---

[5]Based on the loans of 160 weekly reporting banks contained in *Federal Reserve Bulletins*, 1970–71.

[6]Rate differentials or anticipated rate changes also play a role in the decision of a large borrower to use his bank or to go to the market.

[7]In 1970 and 1971, commercial banks were supplying roughly half of all installment consumer loans made by financial institutions and a substantially higher proportion of noninstallment consumer loans. Source: *Federal Reserve Bulletins*.

In broad usage, short- and intermediate-term consumer loans include both installment and noninstallment credit. The latter consists of charge accounts (including credit cards) granted by merchants, service credit, and single-payment loans granted by banks to individuals. Installment credit, which accounts for a much larger amount of consumer lending, consists primarily of loans made to meet previously incurred or extraordinary expenses (the typical personal loan) and loans to finance the purchase of specific goods or services (the "buy now, pay later" concept). Bank check credit plans are classified as personal loans, but bank credit cards outstanding are classified as loans to finance the purchase of goods or services.[8]

Almost all personal installment loans to individuals are made by direct negotiation between the bank and the borrower. Installment sales credit may be handled either directly or indirectly. In the latter case, installment sales contracts are purchased by the bank from the seller of the goods or services. Indirect lending is almost necessary for banks seeking a large volume of consumer loans. Many banks do both direct and indirect business, although some bankers find an inherent conflict of interest between, for example, direct automobile financing and their relationships with the dealers from whom they purchase paper.[9]

Consumer Credit Principles. Whether a bank lends directly or indirectly, the credit principles of consumer lending are essentially uniform. The net worth of the individual borrower is generally difficult, if not impossible, to obtain. The essential ingredients of sound consumer credit are the borrower's ability and willingness to pay. These ingredients are roughly measurable in terms of the borrower's character and the amount and stability of his income. Character and reputation are usually synonymous, and the applicant's previous record for repayment, at the bank or elsewhere, is usually the best credit guide. Volume lending in the field of consumer credit is likely to be unduly risky if the bank does not have access to a credit bureau in which all or most of the local consumer lenders, including merchants, participate and pool their knowledge of the credit records of consumers. Without such a central record, duplicate and excess borrowings are an ever-present danger.

Application forms for consumer loans are generally fairly simple, asking the borrower to state his income, its source, the purpose of the loan, and his other debts. It is essential to verify all such statements, because a borrower who misrepresents any of these vital facts is probably a poor risk.

---

[8]Classifications used by the Board of Governors in *Federal Reserve Bulletins.*

[9]Dealers derive a part of their profit from the differential between the finance charges they assess and the lower rates at which banks discount their paper.

As in any other form of lending, the relationship of purpose to payment is of great importance. The purpose should be reasonable in light of the borrower's capacity to repay. Although consumer lenders usually take a broader view of capacity than an officer trained in the commercial lending tradition, and although it is not necessary to make a moral judgment as to whether the applicant ought to spend the money for a particular purpose, loans to finance extravagances are seldom good risks. In other words, banks err in financing Cadillacs for borrowers who need transportation but can at best afford secondhand Chevrolets. Although it is sometimes appropriate to refinance outstanding debts, requests for funds for this purpose are likely to be a sign of overextension.

It can be firmly stated that the longer the terms of the loan, the greater the risk. Too often, terms are set by competition (especially in indirect lending), but sound credit principles disallow undue lengthening of terms. Otherwise, delinquencies will mount, collection costs will eat up profits, and losses will be substantial.

Special Considerations with Indirect Lending. Sound principles for indirect lending require, in the first place, careful selection of dealers who exhibit both moral and financial responsibility. A second vital principle is that an obligor actually exist for all paper purchased. This can usually be assured by mailing forms directly to the obligor and by requiring that all payments be made directly to the bank. Finally, bank managers should place at least a portion of the credit risk on the dealer's shoulders. They can accomplish this by purchasing the paper with full or partial recourse (the usual procedure in the purchase of service or appliance sales paper), by agreeing that the dealer will repurchase returned assets at a fixed price or by establishing dealers' reserves. The latter is the most common procedure for automobile financing. The customers' notes are purchased from the dealer on a nonrecourse basis at a discount that is often less than that charged by the dealer to the obligor. All or part of the differential is held by the bank as a reserve against which delinquent loans may be charged. The collection of delinquent loans, including the repossession of the chattel, is thus the dealer's responsibility. At the end of a stated period, the amount by which the reserve exceeds an agreed upon percentage of outstanding loans is returned to the dealer.

In situations where inventory financing (usually on a "floor plan" basis) is required, the bank's primary protection is its collateral claim, which is no better than the dealer's moral responsibility and the bank's periodic, thorough, and surprise checking of the chattels. Sales out of trust are an all-too-common occurrence. In some used car and appliance financing, a bank may find itself pitted against some of the shrewdest and least-principled business operators on the modern scene, and losses can be sudden and substantial if the bank relaxes for a moment. Another important requirement in such inventory financing is curtailment, the reduction of the loans secured by merchandise remaining unsold for long periods. Competitive pressures have often caused banks to relax what they know are sound policies—for example, requirements for monthly payments on unsold cars or other chattels.

Bank Credit Cards and Check Credit Plans. These two variations of traditional consumer credit have grown rapidly in recent years. Bank credit cards were introduced by Franklin National Bank in 1951. It was the mid–1960s, however, before bank credit cards began to approach their present widespread usage. The stepped-up growth in bank credit cards was caused by such factors as the increased availability of high-speed computers, the profitability of some early plans, and the desire of many consumers to be part of the limited-cash-and-check society.

The potential profitability of bank credit cards derives from two sources: (1) the discount at which the bank purchases sales slips from the merchant, ranging from a high of about 6 percent to a low of 2 or 3 percent on large volume; and (2) the interest charged the card user who does not pay his bills within a specified time. This charge is usually at the rate of 1½ percent per month on the unpaid balance.

By the early 1970s, bank credit cards have achieved wide usage by consumers and wide acceptance by merchants. The major problem is that many bank credit cards remain unprofitable. Credit and fraud losses have been high because of unsolicited mailings, difficulties in control, and the tendency for dealers to give banks the dealer's weaker credit customers. In addition, competition for dealers has kept quality and discounts low, many consumers have used their credit cards more for convenience than for installment buying, and credit cards have been less successful than many other bank services in attracting supplementary business.

The unprofitability of bank credit cards represents a definite challenge to bank management. Unsolicited mailings are now illegal, and many banks require pictures on the credit card and/or personal pickup of the credit card. Arrangements with merchants—for example, release limits, discounts, and responsibilities—are being closely scrutinized. Finally, the problem of inactive cardholders and merchants must be closely studied.

The development of check credit plans has closely paralleled that of credit card plans since 1955, the year the first check credit plan was introduced. Although there is considerable diversity in the check credit plans in operation, they all have one characteristic in common—check credit customers are extended a prearranged line of credit that can be activated at their discretion. Repayment is usually at a scheduled monthly rate, and there is generally no charge for early repayment. The size of the line of credit is typically based on a few characteristics related to an individual's ability to pay—income, home ownership, family, other indebtedness, and so on. Because the primary dangers of this form of credit are that the borrower may borrow from many sources and that credit principle of purpose is violated, the credit lines all generally have maximum limits of one to five thousand dollars. Some form of periodic review should be required. The principal advantages of check credit plans include the relatively high interest rates usually charged and the lower costs of bookkeeping and credit review.

Mortage Loans

Mortgage loans are a specialized form of consumer and commercial lending. They are nearly always secured by real estate, and the majority are long term. Chart 15 shows that mortgage loans have remained slightly less than one-fourth of all commercial bank loans since 1955.

The true purpose of a mortgage loan is to finance the acquisition or substantial improvement of real property. Real estate can also be pledged to secure obligations incurred for other purposes. In such cases, however, the real purposes, rather than the form of collateral, should determine the terms of repayment and dictate any other protective features that may be called for.

Mortgage loans in commercial banks are typically first liens on residential or business properties.[10] Residential mortgages are generally considered more desirable, because dwellings, unless of unusual size or design, have a broader market than business properties, which are often limited to specialized uses. Construction mortgages are short-term loans that may lead to long-term commitments. Commercial mortgages are often term loans in disguise, in which case they should be treated as such.

Residential Mortgage Lending. Commercial banks can make both conventional mortgages and F.H.A. insured and V.A. guaranteed mortgages. Most banks prefer the higher yields and smaller amount of paperwork for conventional mortgages to the greater safety of insured or guaranteed mortgages. Since the early 1930s, residential mortgages have been amortized monthly over the life of the mortgage. Most commercial banks prefer original maturities of twenty to twenty-five years on conventional mortgages.

---

[10]National banks may not lend on unimproved property, nor may they directly acquire second mortgages (Section 24, Federal Reserve Act).

Commercial banks should carefully consider the basic characteristics of residential mortgages before deciding how aggressively they will try to attract such loans. Under present conditions, the interest charge is usually fixed over the life of the mortgage. If the level of interest rates declines, fixed charges are generally advantageous to the bank (although some borrowers may renegotiate); but rising interest rates usually turn fixed mortgage rates into a handicap.

Conventional residential mortgages can be sold only with some difficulty. Insured or guaranteed mortgages, however, are fairly marketable.[11] Most banks, however, do not originate mortgage loans in sufficient volume to be concerned with secondary markets. They look to monthly amortization and prepayments for such liquidity as may be found in the mortgage portfolio.

For the evaluation of residential mortgages, the principal consideration should be the borrower's ability to repay the loan in conformity with the payment schedule. A bank should never make a mortgage loan without knowledge of the mortgagor's income and financial obligations. Obvious as this may seem, such information is lacking in too many mortgage files. Even if it does appear on the mortgage application, there is rarely any follow-up to determine whether the ability to repay is being maintained. The good experience of the past thirty years, during which real estate prices have increased steadily, is no excuse for carelessness in mortgage lending.

Because of the uncertainties of an individual's long-term future, considerable attention is devoted to evaluating the real estate that serves as collateral for conventional mortgages. The basic principles are that the amount of the loan should be limited to a reasonable percentage of the true value of the property and that the repayment rate should allow the mortgagor's equity to remain constant or increase during the life of the loan. Value is established by an appraisal. Conservatism will call for some discounting of peak prices, which may reflect an inflated demand. Values will vary in each community, however, because they are strongly affected by growth prospects. Past trends as well as future prospects need to be taken into consideration, and a concept of "fair value" must be developed to fit each bank's particular circumstances. Competition in appraisals, sometimes indulged in, is obviously a dangerous practice.

---

[11]Three Federal agencies have contributed to the increased marketability of mortgages. These are the Federal National Mortgage Association, the Federal Home Loan Mortgage Corporation, and the Government National Mortgage Association. The basic technique they follow is to purchase (or at times sell) mortgages with funds obtained from a bond issue secured by blocks of mortgages to public investors. A detailed description is contained in "The Secondary Mortgage Market," *Economic Review*, Federal Reserve Bank of Cleveland, July 1971, pp. 14–32.

The condition of a property is as important as its age. Therefore, another vital element in the protective arrangements that should exist to safeguard mortgage lending is the requirement of adequate maintenance. All mortgaged properties should be periodically reappraised; if deficiencies in maintenance are revealed, the bank should make every effort, including the offer of financing, to encourage the mortgagor to make necessary repairs. If a bank has been reasonably selective about the character of its mortgagors, the borrower will recognize that adequate maintenance will be as great a benefit to him as to the bank.

Construction Mortgage Financing. The origination of mortgage loans through the financing of building construction is a specialized field deserving comment. All banks occasionally finance the construction of a home or business building for a valued customer with the expectation that they will acquire and hold the mortgage on the completed premises. Such loans require special attention because of the ever-present possibility that construction costs may exceed the original estimates, leaving the bank more deeply committed than it had planned to be.

The bulk of construction financing, however, is done by banks that sell the permanent mortgages to other institutions. The origination and sale of mortgages is a banking business with its own risks and specialized techniques. However, either directly or in participation with correspondent banks, it can be a very profitable form of essentially short-term lending.[12] If the originating bank retains the servicing of the mortgages, this type of financing not only is a source of additional revenue but also provides valuable customer contacts. The origination and sale of mortgage loans is also one way in which banks in rapidly growing areas can serve their communities beyond the limits of their own resources.

Commercial Mortgage Lending. In true commercial mortgage lending, the primary consideration is the relationship of the income derived from the property to the cost of maintaining it, paying taxes, and servicing the loan. In some cases, the income may be derived from an operating business, although such loans are likely to be true business loans. More often, the income from the property is the product of a lease or leases to tenants, with whom the bank does not deal directly (except as they may be customers for other banking services).

A complete description and appraisal of the property should, of course, be on file, but the cost or replacement value of a commercial

---

[12]James F. Schneider, *Construction Loans for Your Short-Term Portfolio,* Thesis for Graduate School of Banking, Rutgers University (A.B.A. Library).

property is distinctly secondary to its yield as an investment, which effectively establishes its resale value. It is also important that the bank know the amount of the income from the property and be assured of the continuing availability of that income for servicing the mortgage. The bank should, therefore, not only obtain assignment of the leases but also know the credit standing of the lessees.

SPECIAL FORMS OF BANK LOANS

Banks make other types of loans in addition to the three major types. Many of these are specialized subgroups of the major types. The same general credit principles are appropriate; however, because of the specialized nature of these loans, particular considerations and specifically trained loan personnel may be required. Several of the many special forms are briefly described below.

Loans to finance companies and, in some situations, to other types of firms that have unusually large amounts of debt in their financial structure, should be analyzed as a long-term commitment. Finance companies rotate their debt, cleaning up loans on each line of credit periodically. Although such rotation is reassuring to the banker, as it indicates that other banks also have confidence in the borrower and allows some flexibility if the banker wants to get out of a given situation, the continuous character of the debt is unchanged. The banks involved certainly cannot all get out of the same loan at the same time.

Factoring is a specialized form of lending in which the bank purchases the borrower's accounts receivable, with or without recourse. It was not until 1963 that the Comptroller of the Currency ruled that factoring was a legitimate banking activity. Some banks decided to start their own factoring operations, but most banks that have entered factoring have done so by acquiring commercial finance companies engaged in factoring.[13] The banker performs the credit investigation and protects himself by accepting only those accounts that are receivable from good credit risks.

Leasing is a specialized form of lending that has been started by a sizable number of banks in recent years. The bank retains title to the property leased, but the individual or business lessor is able to use the services from the leased asset. The credit principles applied in leasing should be similar to those applied to term loans. The profitability of

---

[13]Fuller M. Rothschild, "Banks in Factoring—Past, Present and Future," *Journal of Commercial Bank Lending*, October 1969, p. 31.

leasing derives from the bank's ability to depreciate the leased chattel for tax purposes. Barring legal complications, leasing seems to be a natural expansion of bank lending; however, the expertise required in leasing may slow its acceptance.[14]

---

[14]Douglas C. Kay, "Leasing for Your Bank," *Journal of Commercial Bank Lending*, June 1970, p. 31.

II

LENDING—
POLICIES AND PROCEDURES

Lending is the essence of commercial banking; consequently, the formulation and implementation of sound lending policies are among the most important responsibilities of bank directors and management. Well-conceived lending policies and careful lending practices are essential if a bank is to perform its credit-creating function effectively and minimize the risk inherent in any extension of credit.

A bank needs policies specifying how much of what kinds of loans will be made to whom and under what circumstances. Lending policies should in every case be set down in writing, because only then can they be clearly and uniformly understood by the officers who grant loans and the directors who approve them. Moreover, the very act of expressing a policy in words to which all agree will sharpen the issues and make the end product more effective. Once established, even the best of policies needs periodic review in light of ever-changing conditions in the community.

Putting sound lending policies into practice calls for the establishment and supervision of an effective organization and the adoption of appropriate procedures. This chapter will discuss the key factors determining sound lending policies and will explore some of the necessary procedures involved in granting and servicing loans.

DETERMINING THE SIZE OF THE LOAN PORTFOLIO

Chart 10 (on page 123) shows the loan-to-deposit ratio for all insured banks in three size groupings of banks in selected years from 1946 through 1971. Some banks use such ratios to determine the size of their loan portfolio, but their approach seems far too rigid. Basic to decisions about the size of the loan portfolio are an assessment of the legitimate credit needs of the community or credit markets that the bank serves or intends to serve and an appraisal of the bank's ability to meet that demand. In some communities, the demand for credit is virtually insatiable. In more fully developed and stable communities, management may have to search out opportunities to make sound loans. In any event, the limiting factor should be the community's needs and the bank's ability to meet those needs rather than any arbitrary set of ratios representing preconceived ideas of appropriate or average statistical relationships.[1]

Assessing Credit Needs

Some banks determine the credit needs of their community simply by having a bank officer sit at a desk in the bank's lobby and wait for potential borrowers to come in. Up to a point, this is an effective method and is probably typical of many of the country's smaller banks. Borrowers do come in and, if encouraged by constructive consideration of their requests for credit, will bring their friends. The needs for credit can then be assessed by the actual demand. However, because of lending officers' prejudices or predilections, too frequently some segment of the borrowing public feels that it is somewhat less than welcome in a particular bank and promptly searches out competitive sources of credit. For example, the managers of some banks in residential communities may (and too often do) feel that they can amply satisfy all local credit needs without making consumer loans. In many cases, bank examination data have shown their reasoning to be faulty. In communities where banks with abnormally low loan-to-deposit ratios are found, government agencies and other financial institutions are likely to be supplying a major portion of the credit.

---

[1] The disparity in loan-to-deposit ratios among the three size groupings of banks in Chart 10 and the fact that in mid–1971 loan-to-deposit ratios by state ranged from 53.5 percent in West Virginia to 83.7 percent in New York (loan-to-deposit ratios were less than 60 percent in all states and above 70 percent in 13 states) demonstrate considerable differences in credit needs and in the ability to meet these needs. Source: Federal Deposit Insurance Corporation.

To know something about the credit market of a community, it is necessary to go outside the bank, in thought at least, and find out who is borrowing where. The outside look need not be a formal market research project,[2] particularly in smaller communities where the officers and directors have an intimate knowledge of most of the economic activity. For larger banks in large communities, a formal market survey is highly desirable, if only as a periodic check on the knowledge of directors and top management. Information about the credit needs of the bank's actual and potential customers for the present and the foreseeable future is essential not only for the establishment of lending policies but for the determination of liquidity needs and investment policies as well.

Ability to Meet Loan Demand. If a bank has adequate capital (see Chapter 5) and acceptable liquidity (see Chapters 8 and 9), it should make all the sound local loans it can. If its own resources are not sufficient to meet the community's legitimate needs, it should exert every effort to participate with correspondent banks or other financial institutions in local lending or to place such loans directly with them while retaining, if possible, the servicing of the loans and the direct contacts with customers.

In the past, some banking experts have been concerned about the diversification of a bank's loan portfolio and have counseled against a complete concentration in local credits, particularly in communities economically dependent on a single industry. If such diversification can be obtained only at the expense of the legitimate credit needs of the community in question, a principal function of commercial banking is negated. The answer lies not in denying local credit needs but in the diversification of the banking structure itself, through more extensive branch or holding company banking.

If a bank has adequate liquidity and capital protection, it can and should lend to the limits imposed by the volume of its relatively stable deposits. Its ability and willingness to lend are the most important factors in its creation and maintenance of strong depositor relationships with both larger business customers and the small business or individual borrowers. Just as the making of loans creates deposits in the banking system as a whole, the making of loans by an individual bank creates depositor relationships, spurs economic activity in the community, and in the long run results in higher deposit levels for the bank itself.

Of course, a bank may not always be able to meet all the credit

---

2Market research will be discussed at greater length in Chapter 16, Marketing Policies.

needs of its community. If it cannot, it restricts or allocates bank credit according to policies, specifying the types of bank loans that can be made and the terms of acceptable loans, such as the rate charged, compensating balances required, and repayment plans allowed.[3]

POLICIES SPECIFYING TYPES OF BANK LOANS

A bank's lending policies are, in effect, screening devices by which the directors and bank managers seek to limit the bank's loans to the type and character that they think appropriate, particularly when loan demand is pressing hard against a bank's available funds. From a policy viewpoint, the character of a loan (see the discussion of the criteria for evaluating loans in the preceding chapter) should take precedence over its form. In other words, it is more important that loans be sound than that they be mortgage loans, business loans, consumer credit, and so on. The form of lending should reflect the demands of the community.

Here again, simple statistical relationships, although widely used as rough guidelines, should not be determinative. A bank in a rapidly growing residential community normally will and should have a higher proportion of mortgage loans than a bank in a stable industrial area. The latter, by the same token, normally will and should have a higher proportion of commercial loans and perhaps of consumer credit.[4] It is desirable for the directors and top management to establish ceilings on the various forms of lending, but they should do so primarily to distribute available bank credit in proportion to the community's needs so that one form of demand will not be slighted because another is too liberally supplied.

Some writers on this subject would relate the character of the loan portfolio to the kind of deposits held by the bank. They would recommend, for example, that mortgage loans and term loans be made only

---

[3]Bank policy should primarily limit the bank's lending commitments rather than its loans currently outstanding. For a sample commitment-contingent liability form and some potential sources of comparable commitment percentages, see Peter A. Reilly, "Does Your Bank Know What Its Total Lending Commitments Are?" *Banking,* July 1971, pp. 22–23.

[4]It is important that the bank be flexible about such relationships. The authors know of suburban banks in unit-banking states that have a high proportion of commercial loans to smaller businesses. (For a written example, see "Aggressive Commercial Lending Policy Helps Double Bank's Size," *Banking,* June 1971, pp. 22–24.) Furthermore, widespread branching systems and bank holding companies are often heavily involved in all types of loans.

out of the more stable or longer-term savings deposits. In the discussion of liquidity needs in Chapter 8, it was shown that some portion of demand deposits is just as stable as any deposit can be. It is important for liquidity reasons that longer-term loans not exceed stable deposits, but it makes no real difference whether such deposits are demand or time.

There are several additional, special considerations that may play a part in determining the types of loans that some banks are willing to make. Whether a bank, particularly a medium- or smaller-size bank, should accept business loans (or leases) with maturities in excess of three to five years is a problem that vexes many Boards of Directors. If the bank has adequate staff to evaluate the payment, purpose, and protection for such loans, and if the bank is willing to allow the interest rate on such loans to vary[5] with general interest rates, usually it should fill its community's credit needs for this form of borrowing. The regular cash flows from such loans or leases more than offset the longer time to final maturity.

Business loans to two types of firms may present some special problems. The preceding chapter indicated that lines of credit to finance companies typically represent long-term loan commitments by the bank. A bank cannot turn these loans on and off in response to credit ease or tightness. Also, many loans to finance companies are rather impersonal. Although compensating balances tend to be high, they are seen as a part of the interest charge and will be withdrawn immediately if the company cancels the line of credit. Unless the bank's Board of Directors feel that lines of credit to a finance company are clearly part of the credit needs of the community that they want the bank to serve, they should compare lines of credit to finance companies with alternative long-term investments.

Lending to small concerns on any but a short-term seasonal basis also often presents special problems. Many of these companies are closely held corporations that, as a matter of tax policy, show minimum profits and operate with a nominal net worth. Salaries paid to the principal stockholders are often larger than net profits, and the real net worth is reflected either in loans made to the company by its principals or in the net worth of the principals themselves. Banks should try to serve the legitimate credit needs of such small concerns (this is an essential banking function and generally leads to profitable customer loyalty if the firm grows); however, sound policy requires that debt to stockholders

---

[5]See the following discussion of fixed versus variable rates. A bank is taking significant additional risks if the interest rates on such loans are fixed.

be subordinated formally to bank debt and that the endorsement or guarantee of the principals (and their wives) be obtained by the bank as additional protection. If quality of management is a vital consideration in the extension of credit, banks may also require the assignment of life insurance on the principals.

Whether to confine a bank's consumer lending to direct loans or to purchase loans from automobile and appliance dealers is another matter that perplexes some bank directors. The major virtue of indirect lending is the volume it generates. Because of the keen competition for dealer business, a bank usually has to accept the average run of a dealer's credit risks, even though it formally reserves the right to be selective. Financing the dealer's inventory, another necessary step, entails its own risks and expensive procedures. As a result of all these factors, the rate of return from indirect financing is generally lower than that from direct lending. However, it is possible for large volume to be generated and the business to be profitable if carefully handled; witness the success of some major finance companies specializing in this field.

Lending directly to the bank's own customers is, by contrast, a safer and less expensive means of extending consumer credit. Mistakes involve no more than a single borrower here and there, and most of the applicants for loans will be already known to the bank. Direct lending promotes customer relationships and brings in other business. Many banks that can obtain a satisfactory volume of direct consumer loans have learned that for these reasons they can offer lower rates to selected borrowers and enjoy a higher rate of return.[6]

Mortgage loans outside a bank's primary market area should be evaluated as an investment. Policies regarding mortgage loans within a bank's primary market are more difficult to formulate. Nearly all banks will make mortgage loans to valued customers. However, the long term and fixed return on most mortgage loans, as well as the lack of compensatory balances or service requirements from most borrowers, discourage a sizable number of banks from seeking other mortgages. One of the primary remedies for this reluctance is the variable-rate mortgage, discussed later in this chapter.

Construction lending presents a different sort of problem. The loans are short term, but there are several types of risk that must be understood and assessed. Banks that do not have the expertise to evaluate construction loans carefully should probably avoid them. On the other

---

[6]Figures furnished to the authors by a large suburban bank clearly justify its own policy decision to withdraw from dealer financing and concentrate heavily on advertising for direct loans, which, it had concluded, were considerably more profitable.

hand, if suitable managerial expertise is available and credit needs for such financing exist in the bank's community, this type of lending provides a useful service and is often very profitable.[7]

POLICIES AFFECTING LOAN TERMS

A bank's terms of lending are determined by policies establishing the desirable levels of interest rates, compensating balances, repayments, and collateral. Each of these policy areas is discussed in the following paragraphs.

Interest Rates

The range of rates that a bank may charge on various kinds of loans will be largely determined by forces beyond its control, that is, the level of rates in the market and the forces of competition. Within these limits, the individual bank retains a significant degree of flexibility for establishing interest rate policies that will help to determine the volume and character of the bank's loan portfolio and to bring about changes therein over time. Toward this desirable end, a knowledge of the broad implications of interest rates is essential.

The general level of rates at any given time results from the interplay between the demand for and the supply of funds in the market. There is a tendency for demand to increase when business activity rises and to fall when business activity slackens. The supply of funds, on the other hand, is determined by the rate of savings and the credit policy of the Federal Reserve System. By providing reserves to the banking system, the Federal Reserve makes possible the creation of credit that aids not only the commercial banks but, through them, other lenders as well. When funds are plentiful, market rates generally decline. Banks are forced to seek loans more aggressively, often by lowering their rates to induce marginal borrowers to come into the market. When funds are scarce, banks raise their rates, and some potential borrowers may defer the use of credit or seek it elsewhere. By and large, rates are more likely to determine where a borrower obtains his funds than whether he borrows. High rates will not long deter the borrower who can use the funds

---

[7]The high rates on construction loans appear to result more from the belief of many lenders that construction loans are very risky than from actual losses. For an analysis of the risk factors involved and the yields and losses on construction loans, see Peter A. Schulkin, "Construction Lending at Large Commercial Banks," *New England Economic Review*, July/August 1970, pp. 2–11.

profitably, nor will low rates induce borrowing that cannot be put to productive use.

Although the level of rates depends on the forces of supply and demand, the cost of lending constitutes a floor beneath this level. The rates that banks charge must be sufficiently high to cover (1) the cost of the funds loaned; (2) the cost of making and servicing different kinds of loans (including a proportionate share of the overhead expenses of the bank); (3) a cost factor representing the probable losses that may be incurred over time; and (4) a reasonable margin of profit. It is important that bank management be aware of these costs. Differences in the second and third categories of these costs, in particular, go far to explain why (at any given time) rates on different kinds of loans may vary widely. Banks quite naturally tend to set lower rates on loans that cost less to process and that entail less risk—larger, shorter-term, or unsecured loans, for example. Processing cost per dollar of loan decreases as the size of the loan increases and as less collateral is required. Collection cost and potential losses diminish as the term of the loan shortens and the responsibility of the borrower increases. And it is the most creditworthy borrower who is most likely to be granted a large or unsecured loan.

Above this theoretical floor, bank lending rates are established in a highly complex and competitive market that includes a variety of other lenders, many of whom are specialists in particular kinds of credit instruments. For example, when large corporations need capital financing, they may arrange term loans with their banks or private placements with insurance companies, or they may go to the public capital markets. Their choice will be influenced partly by rate and partly by the various terms imposed by different lenders. For short-term financing, the same corporations (if their credit standing is high) may choose between banks and the commercial paper market. The purchaser of a home who seeks mortgage financing may choose among a commercial bank, a savings bank, a savings and loan association, a life insurance company, and a private lender. Finance companies and credit unions compete with commercial banks for consumer loans, as do various government agencies for farm loans. There is, in short, no lack of competition in most of the broad segments of bank lending.

Despite the prevalence of competition, however, direct rate competition among banks serving the same market is rare. In fact, the more competitive a bank's situation, the greater the likelihood that its lending rates will conform closely with those of its immediate competitors. Such a bank cannot long charge higher rates for the same kinds of loans without losing many of its best customers. If it offers lower rates, it is likely to receive more applications than it can accommodate.

Most banks, therefore, offer a so-called prime rate of interest to their better quality, larger commercial customers. The prime rate is usually the same at all medium- and larger-sized banks throughout the country. The prime rate generally reflects rate competition, usually with a slight lag, with commercial paper as well as the overall supply and demand for bank credit. Changes in the prime rate typically originate in New York City banks and quickly spread throughout the country. Present commercial banking philosophy is to try to make more frequent, smaller changes in the prime rate in order to make it more responsive to changing money-market conditions. If this philosophy continues, there will probably be more "split-level" prime rates and more prime rate changes originating outside of New York City. In late 1971, several large banks instituted "floating" prime rates that automatically changed in response to changes in other money-market rates.[8]

The primary cause of rate differentials within a competitive lending market is differences in the quality of supporting services or the conditions of the lending arrangements. Rate differentials can also be deliberately maintained either to persuade some borrowers to seek credit elsewhere or to attract certain specific borrowers or types of loans. It is in the light of the general uniformity of rates for comparable kinds of loans that interest rate differentials operate as an impersonal, semiautomatic control mechanism governing the use of bank credit.

For example, when credit is scarce, large banks serving the national market may deliberately maintain the prime rate above the rates available in the market in the hope that some of their larger borrowers will sell commercial paper or seek acceptance financing and thus relieve the direct pressure of loan demand on the banks. Under similar circumstances, if banks find term loan demand too heavy, they may set higher rates on such loans, hoping to persuade some of their potential customers to sell securities in the capital market. Conversely, posting lower-than-average rates can serve to attract business that a bank considers especially desirable. Thus, if a bank offers lower rates than do the finance companies on consumer loans that meet specific high standards, it tends to attract the cream of this business in its community. To attract desirable mortgage customers, some banks establish competitively attractive rates for mortgages of shorter-than-average term or above-average protective equity.

The rates established by the individual bank on loans in clearly

---

[8]For a more thorough discussion of the prime rate and recent shifts in the philosophy of changing the prime rate, see "The Conflict of Interest Rates," *Banking*, August 1969, pp. 29–30; "The Chase Manhattan's Split-Level Prime Rate," *The Bankers Magazine*, Spring 1967, pp. 42–44; M.A. Shapiro and Company, Inc., "A Look at the Prime Rate," *Bank Stock Quarterly*, June 1971, pp. 11–14; and C. Colburn Hardy, "How Banks Are Reacting to Floating Prime Rate Concept," *Banking*, December 1971, pp. 22–23.

distinguishable categories will play a substantial part in determining the quality and character of that bank's loan portfolio. The very process of defining the categories and setting the rates is an instructive exercise in policy formation. It compels the directors or senior management to carefully consider the bank's long-run portfolio objectives and makes management more keenly aware of the bank's competitive position, with respect to both rates and cost. In addition, if rates are set according to an established policy and impartially administered, there will be little difficulty in convincing customers that they are fair. Borrowers seldom complain about high rates *per se*. They do complain if they think they have been arbitrarily charged more than someone else for the same kind of loan.

Within the competitive framework described above and with the floor of lending costs always in the background, the spectrum of lending rates ranges from the prime rate on the low side to what the competitive market will pay on the high side. Usury laws in most states establish ceilings for rates on all types of consumer loans but not on loans to corporations. In recent periods of monetary tightness, this difference encouraged banks to lend relatively more to corporations, which were paying rates substantially above the usury maximums.

Effects of the Truth-in-Lending Law. This new law, which went into effect in mid–1969, is basically a disclosure law. It requires the commercial bank or other consumer lender to state plainly the terms of the contract in language that is uniform and concise. It also grants the customer the right to sue his creditor for failure to comply with the requirements of the law. For this reason, Boards of Directors should make certain that their bank includes compliance with the Truth-in-Lending Law in its lending policy. The major impact of the Truth-in-Lending Law, in addition to the cost of the additional paperwork, may be to make consumers more aware of what is involved in borrowing money or buying on time. Such awareness should be favorable to banks, which generally offer the lowest rates on consumer loans.[9]

Fixed versus Variable Interest Rates. Traditionally, most commercial banks have varied the rates on outstanding seasonal commercial loans and lines of credit in accord with changes in the prime rate or some other measure of the general level of interest rates. On the other hand, the

---

[9]For a detailed description of the Truth-in-Lending act and its potential impact, see Hugh Chairnoff, "What Truth in Lending is All About," *Business Review,* Federal Reserve Bank of Philadelphia, June 1969, pp. 18–23. Bank directors should read Herbert Bratter, "Some Pointers for Directors on Truth in Lending," *Banking,* June 1969, pp. 42 and 98.

rates on consumer installment loans, mortgage loans, and many commercial term loans have typically been fixed, at the rate agreed on when the loan was made, for the life of the loan. The limited maturity of most consumer installment loans may explain the acceptability of fixed rates on these loans. However, many banks have begun to question fixed rates on longer-maturity loans, such as mortgage loans and commercial term loans. Some banks have already shifted to variable rates on one or both types of loans.[10] This questioning and changing of policy has been encouraged by the rapid increase in interest rates in the middle and late 1960s.

The basic argument for fixed rates is that planning for the bank and the borrower will be simplified because both know what the interest payment will be. Furthermore, proponents argue that over long periods of time the interest return with fixed rates would be similar to the overall return if the banks were to use variable rates. The basic argument for variable rates is that the cost of a sizable proportion of a bank's funds is affected by the general level of interest rates. Thus, the bank's profits and sometimes its cash inflows may be unduly hurt in periods of rising interest rates, if it is unable to bid competitively for funds. On the other hand, profits and possibly cash inflows may increase unduly when interest rates fall. It is generally felt that profits and fund inflows will be more stable (possibly at a somewhat higher level) with variable interest rates.

The authors tend to favor charging variable interest rates for both commercial term loans and consumer mortgage loans. The preferable method for doing this would seem to be to make changes in the periodic payments for commercial term loans and changes in maturity (in effect, the proportion of the monthly payment for principal would vary) for mortgage loans. In addition to the logical arguments favoring variable rates, both simulated and real-life experience so far provide favorable support for the use of variable rates.[11] Such problems as misinterpretation, apprehension and downright anger on the part of bank customers

---

[10]For a discussion of the impact and use of variable rates on mortgages by commercial banks, see "Variable Rates on Mortgages: Their Impact and Use," *New England Economic Review*, Federal Reserve Bank Of Boston, March/April 1970, pp. 3–20.

[11]Simulations under several types of economic conditions have come out favorable for variable rates on commercial term loans (for example, in "A Profitability Model Comparing Variable and Fixed Rate Loan Policies," an unpublished study by Robert Hayes, over longer periods of time the variable-rate policy resulted in 10 percent higher profit to the bank). In three of four simulated economic situations —in sharply rising, widely fluctuating, and mildly fluctuating rate markets but not in a sharply falling rate market—and in several real-life experiences, variable rates on mortgages seemed preferable to fixed rates (see "In Simulation and Real Life Variable Rates Really Work," *Savings and Loan News*, January 1971, pp. 21–26).

when rates increase can be overcome if the banking community is willing to put forth the effort.

Income participation clauses are rate-varying techniques that deserve special mention. Loans incorporating these clauses give the commercial bank a stated basic rate of return plus the right to some percentage of future revenues from the loan-financed assets or the right to buy stock from the company at a fixed price (warrants). Income participations and warrants are normally referred to as equity participations or equity kickers, but these terms are misnomers, because the lenders have no legal position of control or ownership. Some banks have used income participation clauses with commercial term loans and with loans on income properties, such as apartment houses. Although the authors believe that such clauses make economic sense, legislative threats to make all the interest on such loans nondeductible for the computation of income taxes and to outlaw income participations and warrants as forms of equity (which banks are legally prohibited from holding) will probably keep banks from using this technique very widely.[12]

Compensating Balances

The terms on a given loan are influenced not only by the rate charged but also by the size of the balance that the commercial bank requires the borrower to maintain. In essence, the matter of compensating balances arises out of a quite natural relationship between banks and their customers. Individuals and companies find it necessary to maintain deposit accounts for operating purposes at levels presumably related to the scale of their operations. Once this relationship is established, normal practice would be to channel loan requests to the bank in which deposits are maintained. Under ordinary circumstances, the size of an appropriate loan would seem to be roughly related to the amount of the bank deposits customarily maintained.

Under many conditions, this natural relationship appears to be valid. The demand deposits of a business are usually required to average 5 to 10 percent of the business's unused line of credit and 10 to 20 percent of its actual loan outstanding. Although such proportions might cause a borrowing business to maintain slightly higher-than-normal demand deposit balances, there usually is a good deal of flexibility in the arrangement, and the cost of the money required to maintain the required balance probably would not be very substantial. In the case of consumer

---

[12]For a discussion of income participation clauses and other methods of participation in the success of an enterprise, such as warrants or bank-owned Small Business Investment Companies, see Harold S. Taylor, "The Equity Kicker: Accord and Discord," *The Bankers Magazine,* Autumn 1969, pp. 33–36.

installment loans or mortgage loans, many banks give preferential treatment to their own depositors, but few banks explicitly require deposit balances.[13]

In periods when monetary policy is restrictive, the requirements for maintaining compensating balances usually become more stringent and are administered more rigidly. Deposit balances of a business are usually required to average 10 to 15 percent of the unused line of credit and 20 to 25 percent of the outstanding loans. Such an increase in the compensating balance requirement typically raises the effective cost to the borrower.[14] For example, if the required compensating balance is 25 percent and a firm that typically has maintained a $10,000 deposit balance needs $100,000, the firm must borrow $120,000 to get the $100,000. A stated interest rate of 8 percent (on $120,000) would lead to interest costs of $9,600, or an effective annual rate of 9.6 percent on the $100,000 available.[15] The impact of this arithmetic, of course, will be more severe on borrowers who would normally have relatively low bank balances, such as finance companies, and less severe on companies that need to maintain more sizable cash balances to conduct their normal business. Nevertheless, the loan applicant who has maintained good working balances with his bank year in and year out whether or not he needed to borrow will seldom be denied legitimate credit of at least four or five times his average balance, no matter how tight money becomes.

Some bankers claim that compensating balances also serve to keep in the bank money that can be loaned to others. This contention is questionable. When the customer in the preceding example needs $100,000, he will simply arrange to borrow $120,000, which will give him enough to increase his compensating balance by the required amount. The bank

---

[13]An interesting innovation that has been tried at a few banks is the use of time deposits as part or all of the compensating balance. The basic idea is that the lower servicing costs and lower reserve requirements for time deposits allow a bank to pay interest on compensating balances and still earn a higher profit. See Omer L. Carey, "The Case for the Compensating Time Deposit," *The Bankers Magazine*, Spring 1967, pp. 55–60.

[14]This is the desired effect. Recent studies have shown that nonprice items such as compensating balances, maturity, and credit standards are all used in the credit rationing process. For example, see Duane G. Harris, "Rationing Credit to Business: More than Interest Rates," *Business Review*, Federal Reserve Bank of Philadelphia, August 1970, pp. 3–20.

[15]In Douglas A. Hayes, *Bank Lending Policies: Domestic and International* (Ann Arbor: University of Michigan Business Studies, XVIII, No. 4, 1971), it is pointed out that such examples tend to overstate the effective rate because most banks use average annual balances as the compensating balances, allowing deposits to drop very low in periods of greater need for funds as long as this low level is offset by high deposits in periods of lesser financial need in the same year.

will have no more funds to lend than it would have had if it had loaned the $100,000 without the balance requirement.

Repayment and Collateral

The basic factors underlying repayment and collateral policies were discussed in the preceding chapter. It is prudent policy to require that all loan requests include realistic, stated repayment plans. The cleanup period for lines of credit should also be explicitly stated. The maturity and form of repayment that are acceptable will vary from bank to bank, depending on the credit needs of the bank's community and the ability of the bank to meet these needs.[16] Collateral requirements should remain relatively constant. A realistic collateral policy should serve to improve credit worthiness enough to enable bank management to make economically desirable loans and should not be used to restrict credit.

GRANTING AND SERVICING LOANS

The manner in which loans are made, reviewed, and collected also involves important policy decisions. The directors and top management must determine the organizational structure of the lending function, delegate appropriate authority to the lending officers, and establish procedures for the review of important loan applications and outstanding loans.

Organization

Although the basic responsibility for lending policy rests with the entire Board of Directors, it is customary for the Board to delegate special responsibility for supervising the lending function to a Directors' Loan Committee or, in smaller banks, to the Executive Committee. The lending officers are required to report to the committee the loans granted, and the committee must assure itself that the loans have been made in accordance with the law and the bank's own lending policies. In larger banks, there is usually also a Senior Officers' Loan Committee, which directly supervises the work of the lending officers and reviews policy matters on a continuing basis. The Officers' Loan Committee serves as the principal liaison between the lending function as a whole and the Board of Directors. In small banks, the chief executive officer is the principal lending officer and exercises the functions of the Officers' Loan Committee.

---

[16]Examples of varying repayment terms appear in Harris, *op. cit.*, pp. 3–20, and Julian L. Clark and John B. Pipkin II, "Making Bank Loan Policy Effective," *The Bankers Magazine,* Winter 1968, pp. 28–34.

As banks increase in size, the lending function becomes more specialized. The various forms of lending require quite different techniques, and each involves a large body of specialized knowledge not likely to be possessed, to an optimum degree at least, by any one individual. In larger banks, therefore, the lending function is usually organized into departments such as the mortgage department, the consumer credit department, and so on. The largest banks, serving businesses across the nation, organize their commercial lending officers into area groups or industry groups as well. This specialization enables a bank to render the maximum service to the borrowers whose line of business or area problems are thoroughly familiar to the lending officers serving them. This specialization is one of the principal advantages of larger banking organizations. One reason why many small banks have not adequately served all the credit needs of their communities is the simple fact that they are not large enough to afford specialists even in such a common field as consumer lending.[17]

Lending Authority

It is poor policy under any circumstances for the directors themselves to grant loans, although they frequently do so, especially in smaller banks. In the first place, most bank directors lack the technical knowledge to make loans on any other basis than the amount of the security or their personal knowledge of the character of the applicant. These may be safe enough loans, but they are not likely to be all the loans that the community legitimately needs. Second, directors are likely to be influenced by subjective considerations that have no rightful place in sound lending, whether they be considerations of friendship, the social position of the applicant, or unadulterated self-interest. It is virtually impossible for directors who are active in the business, social, or political life of the community not to be influenced in some degree by their outside affiliations, no matter how diligently they strive to remain impartial and objective.

The task of directors and top management is to determine what types of loans the bank should or should not make and to review the loans granted by the officers to assure themselves that the loans are consistent with established policy. The authority to lend should be delegated to active officers—who, ideally, should not be permitted to engage in outside business activities that might in any way conflict with their banking responsibilities. Lending officers should, of course, be free to consult with

---

[17]Consumer lending officers, more often than not, have been recruited from the ranks of finance companies, because the whole philosophy of consumer lending differs so sharply from the commercial lending in which bank officers have been trained.

top management, particularly when policy is not entirely clear or unusually large amounts are involved.

The maximum amount that a bank may lend to any borrower is established by law. For national banks, it is 10 percent of capital and surplus on an unsecured basis.[18] Higher percentages are often allowed for secured loans. At least one officer or group of officers should have authority to grant loans up to the legal limit in every bank. The authorities of the other officers are also generally expressed in terms of maximum dollar amounts, secured and unsecured. These authorities should be established by the Board of Directors, made a matter of record, and periodically reviewed.

If lending policies have been clearly stated and are thoroughly understood, rather liberal lending authority should be granted to the officers. Prospective borrowers like to feel that they are dealing with the bank officer who makes the final decision. One of the common complaints about branch banking is that branch managers must refer loans to the head office. The resulting delay is not the only problem; a borrower whose loan is declined may be left with the feeling that he might have been more persuasive if he had had the opportunity to negotiate directly with a more responsible officer. Overly strict limitations on the authority of junior officers not only creates poor customer relations but also hampers the development of those officers. There is no better way of training loan officers than to permit them to exercise their own judgement and, if they make mistakes, to let them work their way out of the ensuing difficulties. Certainly, every branch manager worthy of his hire should have the authority to grant on his sole responsibility loans at least as large as the legal limit of a unit bank of comparable size. In many progressive branch organizations, even larger authority is granted.

Credit Review

In order to make sound lending decisions, lending officers must have the benefit of all the pertinent information that may be available about the borrower and his affairs. The assembly and analysis of this information is the task of the credit department. In small banks, the lending officers themselves usually perform the credit review, but such an arrangement is far from ideal. Even the best lending officers are likely at times to become overenthusiastic about the prospects of their good customers or to take for granted facts that should be carefully checked and verified. It is for this reason that larger banks establish credit departments separate from the lending function. The job of such credit depart-

---

[18]Section 5200, United States Revised Statutes (U.S.C., Title 12, sec. 84). Most state laws have similar provisions.

ments is to investigate actual and potential borrowers, analyze their financial statements, and make objective recommendations with respect to specific lines of credit or loan applications. In the largest banks, the credit department is a sizable organization in itself, staffed with experts at analyzing the various types of industry to which the bank caters.

The credit review function needs to be performed even in the smallest banks. In larger banks, the credit department should be important enough to justify using an experienced officer as the full-time department head. In banks too small to require a full-time credit officer, the credit review function should be assigned to the comptroller-auditor. It is a vital function, and the directors of even small banks should make certain that it is adequately performed.

At the heart of the credit review function is the credit file, the bank's written record of its investigation of each important borrower and its business with him. Bank supervisors have for years been urging even the smallest banking institutions to establish and maintain at least simplified forms of credit files. These should contain, as a minimum, an analysis of the borrower's statement and earnings record, a brief history of the borrower's business and his relationship with the bank, and the loan officer's notations regarding the purpose of each loan granted and the repayment program agreed upon. The file is also the natural place to keep copies of correspondence concerning the borrower and records of credit inquiries and interviews both in the bank and at the customer's place of business.

These are the rudiments of credit analysis and review, a broad subject, the technical aspects of which lie beyond the purview of this discussion of policy. The task of policy is to require that the credit review function be effectively performed. Credit analysis, however, is not a decision-making process. It is consultative or advisory. It should contribute a careful and factual analysis of all the available information so that a lending officer can make his own decisions intelligently. Occasionally, the latter's more intimate knowledge of the borrower's operations or his faith in the management of a particular enterprise may outweigh, in his judgment, the credit analyst's danger signals. If so, the lending officer should make the loan on his own responsibility, a fact that should be fully recorded in the files. A summary of the file should accompany each important loan when it is submitted to the directors for approval, whether it be a new loan or previously granted credit up for review.[19]

---

[19]The two primary causes of the credit problems of some banks in the early 1970s were lending on too little knowledge and excessive reliance on credit analysis by other banks. "The Quality of Credit is Strained," *Business Week,* June 26, 1971, pp. 70–74.

A further sound policy, not exercised enough, is to require a review of refused loan applications for substantial amounts. Particularly important in branch banking organizations operating over fairly extensive areas is that senior management and the directors assure themselves that branch managers or loan department heads are not turning down legitimate requests for credit merely to protect their records of safe lending. If senior management and directors wish to encourage imaginative lending that is sound in the broadest sense, they must encourage their lending officers to develop sound loans from some weak looking applications and must expect and be tolerant of occasional mistakes.

Loan Collection

The essential corollary to an aggressive, forceful lending policy is a vigorous collection policy. No loan should be put on the books without agreement on a repayment plan. Large loans should not be renewed without review by the Officers' Loan Committee in large banks or by the directors in smaller institutions. Any failure to comply with original repayment terms should be promptly followed up, the reason for the delinquency ascertained, and corrective or protective action insisted upon.

The directors or the Loan Committee should receive reports of all delinquent borrowers. The proportion of loans on which payments are delinquent is a good measure of the soundness of lending policies and collection techniques. With respect to small loans, such as those in the consumer credit department, the delinquency reports may appropriately be in the form of aggregate amounts by class of loan and, where indirect financing is involved, by individual dealer account. Consumer loans are generally considered delinquent when a scheduled monthly payment remains unpaid for thirty days or more, although the operating officers will institute special collection procedures when payments are only a few days overdue. Notes ninety days or more past due are seriously delinquent and are usually classified "loss" by bank examiners.

The American Bankers Association and some state bankers' associations and local credit bureaus regularly publish average rates of delinquency on consumer loans for various localities and different classes of loans.[20] Comparison of the individual bank's figures with these published statistics will give the directors a clear indication of the relative success of their own bank's operations. In the rate of delinquencies, any increase —either absolute or in comparison with other banks—is a danger signal that may indicate that credit policies or collection techniques need

---

[20]American Bankers Association, Installment Credit Committee, "Delinquency Rates on Bank Installment Loans" (monthly bulletin).

tightening.[21] Individual dealers whose paper shows an abnormally high rate of delinquency should be carefully investigated and perhaps dropped.

In the case of delinquencies in large loans, such as many commercial loans, the directors should promptly receive a detailed account of the cause of the delinquency and the corrective steps taken by the lending officers. Prompt action to protect the bank when borrowers first begin to get into difficulty often makes the difference between success or failure of a progressive lending policy.

In some cases, of course, the inability of the borrower to make a scheduled payment may be readily explainable. The loan may still be perfectly sound. Under such circumstances, it is better to revise the payment schedule formally to meet the new circumstances rather than to let the delinquency run on, even though the reasons for it are recognized. In other words, sound collection policy requires that any changes made in agreed upon repayment schedules be by agreement, not unilateral.

LOAN DEVELOPMENT

A discussion of lending policies and procedures would be incomplete without some comment on the spirit in which banks approach lending. In loan negotiations, many banks still appear to be on the defensive, protecting themselves against the onslaughts of potential borrowers behind barricades of minimum ratios and standardized lending procedures. Other banks seem to regard lending as a challenging opportunity and go out seeking loans, some perhaps a little too aggressively. The authors' viewpoint concerning bank policy has been that local lending is the primary function of a commercial bank and that a bank should make all the sound local loans it can. If this viewpoint is valid, no well-run bank can take a passive attitude toward lending.

In recent years, demands for all kinds of loans have sometimes pressed hard against the funds that many banks have had available for lending. Loan-to-deposit ratios have been rising steadily, and few banks have felt the need to go out and look for loans. Yet now, as in the past, the outstandingly successful banks in all parts of the country are those that have found the means to make more loans than their neighbors and to make some loans that their neighbors would not make at all. Even today, there are still many banks with relatively low ratios of loan to deposits. These may be the result, at least in part, of the banks' failure to seek out and service all the potentially worthy users of credit in their communities.

---

[21]On the other hand, if a bank's delinquency rates are consistently below average, its credit policies may be too strict; it could be turning away some acceptable business.

The essence of loan development lies in a willingness first to examine carefully every request for credit and try conscientiously to make it "bankable" and second to search actively for opportunities to promote the growth of the community and the individual businesses therein with sound credit. The two go hand in hand, and the bank that has an established reputation for constructive lending will not have to do as much searching. Nevertheless, a major objective of visits by bank officers to their customers' places of business, be they farms or factories, should be to find additional productive purposes for the customers' use of credit.

Those banks that have done an outstanding job of loan development are usually managed by outstanding and imaginative men. It is doubtful whether directors can establish loan development as a policy objective without full confidence in the high quality of the bank's operating management. But even in the most conservatively managed bank, there is room if not for broad loan promotion, at least for a limited amount of promotional lending. The directors and senior management could well afford to set aside a sum equal to a modest percentage of the bank's capital and surplus as a revolving fund from which to make loans that they consider to be marginal credits. Such lending, if successful, can contribute materially to the growth and welfare of the community. As the president of a relatively small bank that has aggressively followed such a policy points out:

> Every one of our town's industries grew up here from small-scale beginnings. Not one of them was "attracted" from elsewhere. Our bank financed each one in its early stages, sometimes employing considerable ingenuity to find ways of keeping the loans bankable. For example, today's largest local employer started with one assistant in a basement garage. He financed his entire business expansion, above that permitted by plowed-back profits, on credit obtained from this bank.[22]

Opportunities for promotional lending do not present themselves regularly. Each one is different, but experienced lending officers will recognize promising situations when they arise. They offer banks a challenging opportunity not to deny credit automatically but rather assess ideas imaginatively and, within reasonable and previously established limits, to take considered risks. Many of an aggressive bank's most valuable and loyal customers will be those who initially were something of a credit gamble—a greater-than-average risk, deliberately taken.

---

[22]James A. Maurice, "Total Service Concept of a Small-Town Big Bank," *Burroughs Clearing House,* 46, January 1962, pp. 37, 82. Mr. Maurice was president of the Monticello State Bank of Monticello, Iowa.

I2

INVESTMENT PORTFOLIO —
INSTRUMENTS
AND BASIC CONSIDERATIONS

This book has stressed that the primary obligation of a commercial bank is to serve the credit needs of its community. It has emphasized also the need for protective liquidity and has advocated the provision of sufficient additional liquid assets to meet any foreseeable local demand for loans. Banks in some areas or at some times, however, will have provided adequate liquidity and granted all the sound local loans they can and still have excess funds to invest. Funds not needed for lending or liquidity protection in the foreseeable future and those not available for lending because they must by law be used to secure public deposits constitute the source of a bank's investment portfolio, as distinguished from its liquidity reserves and its loan account.

In communities where the demand for credit is high, the investment portfolio may consist almost entirely of pledged securities. If the demand for credit is moderate, which is likely where the community is relatively stable and has little immediate growth potential, the bank's portfolio is usually larger and more flexible. In any event, the problem of how best to invest funds that will not or cannot be used for lending poses policy considerations of notable complexity. This chapter examines the primary types of instruments that commercial banks may use in their investment portfolios and the basic considerations that tend to affect portfolio decisions. Specific investment portfolio policies are discussed in the following chapter.

INSTRUMENTS USED IN BANK
INVESTMENT PORTFOLIOS

As the term is used here, *investment instruments* are not necessarily confined to investment securities. They include any earning asset acquired outside the credit market from any source other than the customers typically served by the bank. Thus, F.H.A. insured mortgages on properties outside the bank's normal territories are, in this sense, investments. The acquisition of local municipal securities, on the other hand, may be governed by considerations of customer relations and local lending rather than strictly related to the problem of investing surplus funds.

U.S. Government Securities

The risk-free nature of U.S. government securities and the highly efficient market for such securities explain the importance of U.S. government securities to the commercial banking system. Income from all U.S. government securities is subject to Federal income taxes but is exempt from state and local income taxes. Marketable U.S. government securities may be used as security for deposits of public moneys and for loans from Federal reserve banks.

There are four basic types of marketable U.S. government securities—bills, certificates of indebtedness, notes, and bonds. The characteristics of Treasury bills and certificates of indebtedness were discussed in Chapter 10, "Bank Liquidity." The primary difference between notes and bonds is in their maturity. Treasury notes are issued with a maturity of not less than one year or more than seven years. These notes are available in minimum denominations of one thousand dollars in either registered or bearer form. Interest is paid on the registered notes semiannually and on the bearer notes when the appropriate coupon is surrendered. Treasury bonds can be issued with any maturity, but their maturities have generally been in excess of ten years at date of issuance. Bonds are available in either registered or bearer form and pay interest semiannually. Treasury bonds cover a wide range of maturities; maturity selections by buyers are based on portfolio requirements and the willingness to assume the risk of market fluctuations. Until early 1971, the coupon rate of interest on all Treasury bonds was limited to 4¼ percent. When interest rates were high, as they were in most of the 1960s, no new Treasury bonds were sold. In early 1971, Congress enacted legislation that premitted the Treasury to issue up to $10 billion of Treasury bonds with no limit on the coupon rate of interest.

Agency Obligations

The amount of outstanding securities that are not a direct obligation of the Treasury but that, in one way or another, involve Federal sponsorship or guaranty has increased rapidly in recent years. Yields on securities of Federal agencies are generally somewhat higher than the yield on U.S. government securities of similar maturity. Although agency securities are not direct obligations of the Federal government, they are regarded in the investment community as being of credit quality nearly equal to that of U.S. government securities. In 1971, they became eligible for purchase by the Federal Reserve System in its open market operations. It is generally felt that the U.S. government would not allow a default on any of these bonds. Agency issues are therefore treated as nonrisk assets and usually may be carried separately from risk assets in a bank's statement of condition. Although all agency securities are subject to Federal income taxes, most agency securities are exempt from state and local income taxes. In addition, agency securities may be used as collateral to secure the fiduciary, trust, and public funds of the United States government and many state and local governments.

State and Local Government Bonds

The increasing demand of state and local governments for funds has resulted in a rapidly growing market for state and local securities. The interest payments on this type of indebtness are exempt from Federal income taxes and generally from income taxes imposed within the state of issue.

Intermediate- and longer-term state and local bonds can be divided into three broad categories. Housing Authority Bonds are issued by local housing agencies to build and administer low-rent housing projects. Although the bonds are issued under the auspices of local housing agencies, the Housing Act of 1949 provided that "the full faith and credit of the United States is pledged to the payment of all amounts agreed to be paid by the local agencies."

A bond is called a general obligation if all the property in a community can be assessed and taxed at a level that will produce the revenues necessary to pay the debt. The primary tangible tax base is real estate, on which the taxing authorities possess a lien equivalent to a first mortgage. Sales taxes, income taxes, and governmental subsidies are also important state and local revenue sources. The pledge of "full faith and credit" by a state or local unit usually includes a promise to levy taxes at whatever level debt service payments require.

Revenue bonds are payable solely from the earnings of a designated public project or undertaking. This type of bond includes all obligations not payable from or guaranteed by the general taxing power of the state or local government. The revenue supporting these bonds may come from (1) specifically dedicated taxes, such as those on cigarettes, gasoline, and beer; (2) tolls for roads, bridges, airports, or marine port facilities; (3) revenues from publicly owned utilities; or (4) rent payments on buildings or office space.

Because Housing Authority bonds are guaranteed by the Federal government, they are virtually riskless. The credit risks inherent in other types of state and local debt are related to the ability and willingness of the governmental unit either to pay its obligations or to revise its capitalization. With general obligation bonds, the ability to pay is mainly contingent on the economic background of a community, the diversity of industry, the stability of employment, and so on. The ability to pay revenue bonds can generally be ascertained by a comparison of operating income with debt service requirements.[1] Revision of capitalization is the issuance of additional debt with a credit position and a claim on taxing power or earnings equal to or superior to the existing bonds. Issues of revenue bonds usually specify the extent to which additional debt may be undertaken. There is usually no such protection for general obligation bonds.

Two other characteristics of state and local debt are particularly pertinent for commercial banks. First, nearly all general obligations have serial maturities. A bank could, therefore, buy one issue with maturities in several years. Second, banks own nearly half the outstanding state and local debt. This strong ownership position tends to widen price fluctuations in periods when many banks are buying or selling these securities.

Corporate Bonds

The corporate bond is an obligation (usually long term) of a private corporation. Although a municipal body may generally be assumed to have a continuing existence, a private corporation is subject to the vicissitudes of a market economy. The credit risk assumed by purchasers of corporate bonds is therefore a quite serious consideration; the failure of the enterprise may result in permanent and total loss.

---

[1]For a more complete analysis of the credit risks of general obligation and revenue bonds, see George H. Hempel, *Measuring Municipal Bond Quality* (Ann Arbor: University of Michigan Press, 1967), and George H. Hempel, *Postwar Quality of State and Local Debt* (New York: National Bureau of Economic Research, 1971).

Banks generally do not purchase corporate bonds, because there have been only brief interludes in recent history when the tax-equivalent yield on state and local bonds did not exceed the yield on corporate bonds of equal quality. The market for corporate bonds is primarily composed of institutions subject to minimal or no Federal income taxation.

Other Bank Portfolio Instruments

Another bank portfolio instrument is the mortgage guaranteed or insured by the Federal government. F.H.A.-insured and V.A.-guaranteed mortgages may be purchased by commercial banks from several Federal agencies as well as other banks or nonbank financial intermediaries. The government-sponsored Federal National Mortgage Association and Government National Mortgage Association have contributed to the development of a national, secondary mortgage market by purchasing and making purchase commitments where and when investment funds are in short supply and by selling when and where investment funds are available. Even with the efforts of these agencies, however, the liquidity of guaranteed or insured mortgages may be severely limited in periods of restrictive monetary conditions.

BASIC CONSIDERATIONS AFFECTING PORTFOLIO DECISIONS

The primary aim of bank portfolio policy is to obtain the maximum income with the minimum exposure to risk. Maximizing income, of course, does not mean simply purchasing instruments with the highest yields currently available. Income has to be computed over the longer run. Nor can risk ever be entirely eliminated; taking reasonable risks is part of the commercial bank's daily routine.

Both the amount of income and the degree of risk in any investment will be directly affected by (1) the probability of default; (2) the general level of interest rates at the time of purchase; (3) its maturity; and (4) its marketability. Each investment decision requires a balancing of income potential against risk in the light of these factors and the particular circumstances existing or foreseen at the time.

Tax considerations also play a vital role in portfolio policy. It is the after-tax income potential of an investment that is of signal importance. For banks in the 48 percent bracket, tax reduction may well be one of the primary objectives of portfolio management.

Pledging considerations must also be recognized. Under existing conditions, commercial banks have to pledge qualified securities as backing for Federal and most state and local government deposits.

Quality

Both income and risk are directly affected by the credit standing of the issuers whose obligations a bank acquires. Generally speaking, the lower the credit rating, the higher the yield. At the same time, the risk of market loss is greater on lower-quality bonds, because they usually fluctuate more widely in price.

Obligations of the United States government, of course, enjoy the very highest credit standing. They are virtually riskless and are so considered in several of the capital adequacy formulas previously reviewed. Like the obligations of corporations, those of the various states and their political subdivisions vary widely in credit worthiness. Many state and local obligations have credit worthiness equal to or greater than most of the bank's best loan customers. On the other hand, some state and local obligations are of questionable quality.

The credit standing of state and local governments and corporate obligors whose securities are actively traded in the market is rated by several well-known services.[2] The ratings receive wide attention. They are referred to by the Comptroller of the Currency in his "Investment Regulations" as presumptive evidence of investment quality,[3] and they are generally accepted as a rough measure of quality differences among various securities. Nevertheless, these ratings should be recognized as guides and not as a substitute for the individual knowledge and judgment of the informed investor who maintains his own credit files and makes his own careful analyses.

Chart 16 shows the yields on fully taxable United States government securities, corporate securities of high and medium grade, and high-grade municipal securities over an eleven-year period. Because of their exemption from Federal income taxes, yields on municipal securities are of course lower than those on obligations of the United States government and on high-grade corporate issues. Tax considerations aside, Chart 16 shows graphically the premium placed by the market on the unquestioned credit of the United States government as compared with the best of corporate bonds. Similarly, the difference in yields between corporate securities of high and medium grade reflects the value the market places on credit worthiness.

---

[2]The best known of these rating services are Moody's Investors Service and Standard & Poor's Corporation. They now charge a fee to rate state and local issues.

[3]Comptroller of the Currency, *Digest of Opinions*, Par. 310.

PERCENT   PERCENT

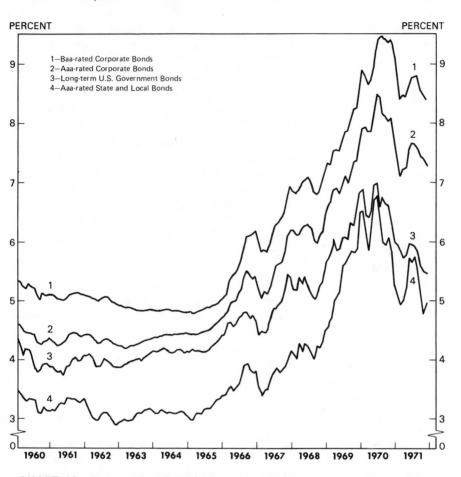

CHART 16 Average Monthly Yields on Selected Long-term Securities, 1960–71 (Source: *Federal Reserve Bulletins,* Federal Reserve Board, 1960–72.)

Most banks are permitted by law to purchase any readily market-able debt obligation that qualifies as an investment security under regulations promulgated by the Comptroller of the Currency. The Comptroller has defined *investment securities* as, among other things, not "distinctly or predominantly speculative."[4] As a matter of policy, commercial banks should take investment portfolio risks that complement the risks taken in their loan portfolio. Most banks' principal source of income, as well as risk exposure, is their loan account. These banks should have a high-

---

[4]Comptroller of the Currency, *Digest of Opinions,* Par. 100, Section 3 (c).

quality and lower-income investment portfolio. Banks with limited risk loan portfolios may take somewhat greater risks to achieve higher income from their investment portfolios.

Closely related to credit considerations are the principles of diversification of risk, both geographic and by industry, that have been of concern to writers on investment policy in the past. The examination report forms of the Federal supervisory authorities contain elaborate schedules for analyses of corporate securities by class and quality as well as by maturity. In nine cases out of ten, these schedules are left blank today because few banks hold any such securities. As a result, these concerns have become somewhat academic.

Geographical distribution still has significance for holdings of state and local securities. Some authorities specifically counsel against the acquisition of local municipal bonds for reasons other than those of community and customer relations because the loan account already represents a concentration of assets subject to adverse developments in the local economy.[5] Some investment in local municipal securities can be justified as serving community needs, particularly issues too small for general distribution. The advantages of diversification must be balanced against the bank's relatively thorough knowledge of local conditions. In any case, geographical diversification should generally be sought only in municipal obligations of reasonably strong credit standing or in municipalities that the bank has thoroughly investigated.

Interest Rates

A glance at Chart 16 shows how interest rates for securities of similar quality and maturity have varied over time. Income from portfolio assets will be clearly influenced, therefore, by the level of rates existing in the market at the time of purchase. Market levels also affect risk because prices are most likely to decline when they are abnormally high. Conversely, when securities are acquired at relatively low prices (high returns), the chances of market depreciation are much smaller.[6]

The rates in the market at any given time reflect, in the first instance, the current equilibrium between the forces of supply and demand. The supply and demand conditions also mirror the market's expectations of

---

[5]Roland I. Robinson, *The Management of Bank Funds* (New York: McGraw-Hill, 1962), p. 119. "Possibly the leading principle of diversification that a bank needs to follow is that of not duplicating its loan account."

[6]William C. Freund and Murray G. Lee, *Investment Fundamentals* (Council on Banking Education, Washington: American Bankers Association, undated) Chapter 3, "Bond Prices and Yields." This booklet describes in simple language the technical aspects of price-yield relationships underlying this discussion.

changes in interest rates. Short-maturity obligations reflect almost entirely the current and short-term prospective strength of the supply and demand for funds; however, longer-term rates are substantially colored by market guesses about probable future conditions. Among these, the rate of inflation has recently loomed large.

Many market analysts separate longer-term rates of return into two segments. The first segment is a projection of what the "real" rate of return (excluding inflation) historically has been on bond investments. The second segment is a risk factor representing the expected rate of inflation. For example, historically the "real" return on high-grade corporate securities has been about 3½ percent; if inflation is expected to average 5 percent annually, investors will demand an 8½ percent rate of return.

Short-term securities and marketable paper are part of the floating supply of money and near-money substitutes, although the supply of longer-term market instruments is more closely related to the flow of savings into investment channels. Therefore, while the level of rates may move up and down, the relationships among rates for different maturities are also constantly shifting as changes take place in the supply of money and the flow of savings.

One can graphically portray the maturity pattern of rates (often called the term structure of interest rates) in the market at any given time by plotting the yields of outstanding securities of equal credit standing for different maturities. The yields on United States government obligations are usually plotted, and the resultant yield curve presents a visual image of investor preferences and expectations.[7] The shape of the yield curve is closely related to the state of the economy and to the counter-cyclical operations of monetary and fiscal policy. When business activity is high, the demand for money is strong, and the Federal Reserve System is likely to be restricting the creation of new credit. The growing demand and shrinking supply of money are generally reflected in the sharp advance of short-term interest rates. Longer-term rates, reflecting expectations of a return to more normal market conditions over a period of time, do not ordinarily increase as rapidly or as far. When short-term rates are rising, the shape of the yield curve tends to become flat, with short-term rates equaling the long. If short rates rise above the long, as they have upon occasion, the curve is said to be descending.

When business conditions are slack, the demand for money tends to decline. At the same time, the Federal Reserve attempts to increase the availability of credit through open market purchases of securities, channeling funds directly into the commercial banking system. An over-

---

[7]Such a yield curve is published monthly in the *Treasury Bulletin*.

abundance of funds sharply depresses short-term rates; the decline in longer rates lags behind. In periods of business recession, therefore, the yield curve is usually ascending or sloping upward.[8]

Chart 17 shows the yield curves for U.S. government securities on December 16, 1968; May 28, 1970; and May 7, 1971. They illustrate dramatically how much the level of interest rates can shift in a relatively short period. In late 1968, the economy was expanding, but monetary policy was still relatively nonrestrictive. The yield curve at that time was essentially flat, with short-term rates slightly above long-term rates. By May 1970, high demands for borrowing, a faster rate of inflation, and tight monetary policy had raised the entire yield curve. The decline in the yield curve as of May 1971 reflected increased liquidity, decreased demands for borrowing (particularly in short-term maturities), and an easing in monetary policy.

Changes in the level of interest rates are a vital concern of portfolio management. They are of special significance in relation to maturity, which will be discussed in greater detail below. It would naturally seem desirable for banks to acquire securities when prices are low and rates high and to sell when the opposite conditions prevail. However, it is usually when rates are high that banks have the least funds available and are experiencing the heaviest demand for loans. When banks have a surplus of funds, rates tend to be low.

When the yield curve is sharply ascending, the temptation is strong for commercial banks to confuse their liquidity positions with their portfolios and to lengthen maturities in search of higher return. In the process, they may commit themselves to too low a rate for too long a time. A subsequent rise in rates will cause these purchases to decline in market value; when the banks need the funds for lending, they are faced with

---

[8]Concerning the relationship between short- and long-term interest rates, there are two widely held theories that are often combined for the interpretation of yield curves. The liquidity-preference theory holds that the risks of holding long-term maturities are greater than those of holding short-term maturities and that the community of bondholders prefers to avoid risk; therefore, the yield curve normally will be positively sloped, with long-term rates higher than short-term rates. The expectations theory holds that long-term rates are an average of a series of expected short-term rates; the yield curve normally will be flat, because the holder of a long-term security will earn, on the average over a specified time, the same amount as a holder of a series of short-term securities. Over the course of a business cycle, a shift may occur in the level of the entire yield curve as well as in the relation between long- and short-term rates. At cyclical troughs, both liquidity and expectational factors act to produce a positively sloped yield curve, indicating that short-term rates are expected to increase faster than long-term rates in the future. At cyclical peaks, liquidity factors act to produce a positively sloped yield curve, and expectational factors act to produce a negatively sloped yield curve. The slope of the curve in this instance will depend on the relative strength of the two forces. Source: Federal Reserve Bank of St. Louis.

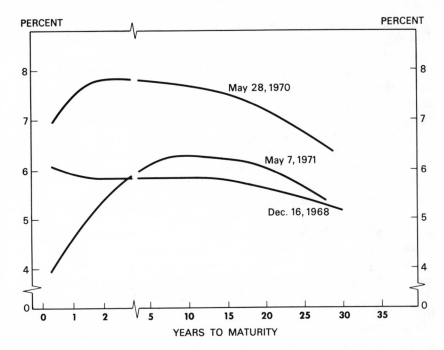

CHART 17 Yields on Various Maturities of U.S. Government Securities (Source: Federal Reserve Bank of St. Louis.)

the prospect of selling securities at a loss. If the banks cannot afford to absorb these losses, they become "locked in" to unnecessarily low yields.

It should be noted that this error of judgment is not a mistake in portfolio policy but in the management of the liquidity position. The poor record of some banks in this regard during the recessions and credit crunches since World War II emphasizes the thesis that the liquidity position should be kept clearly separated from the portfolio in the minds of bank policy makers and investment officers.

The portfolio is a more or less permanent revolving fund, the size of which will change only with the slow accretion of stable deposits or with fundamental modifications of the local demand for credit. Its management consists largely of making adjustments to changing interest rate levels in ways that will increase after-tax profits without substantially increasing risk.

Maturity

If a bank acquires a creditworthy security for its portfolio with the expectation of holding it to maturity, it commits itself to receiving a stated yield for a given period of time. The longer that time period, the more uncertain the conditions not only at the time when the obligation falls due but also during the intervening period. This uncertainty is comprised of two factors: a credit factor and an interest rate or income factor.

When an investment involves credit risks, there is always the possibility that the credit standing of the obligor will vary over time. The longer the time, the greater the possibility of change. Because banks usually acquire the securities of obligors with high credit standing, the possibility of deterioration is greater than the chance of improvement. Investors were once willing to purchase railroad first-mortgage bonds with maturities of one hundred years, but subsequent events have amply demonstrated the danger of such long commitments.

Even if credit risk is not an important factor, there is always uncertainty about the prospective level of interest rates both at the time when the obligation falls due, allowing the funds to become available for reinvestment, and (of even greater concern) during the period when the security is held. The longer the maturity, the greater the odds that income (and market value) over the long run will be affected (favorably or adversely) by changes in the level of rates. In other words, investing in a thirty-year bond yielding 6 percent is tantamount to making the decision that the average return on one-year funds will not exceed 6 percent over the next thirty years.[9] The longer the time to maturity, the clearer the investment manager's crystal ball must be.

There is, however, no fixed relationship between maturity and either risk or income. There may be occasions when less risk will be entailed in longer maturities than short ones, as when yields are abnormally high; on other occasions, short maturities are the instruments of caution despite their abnormally low yields. In any event, the difference is never simply between short and long; it is the question, "how short?" or "how long?" that requires the policy maker's searching decisions. Nor is maturity a factor that can be measured in isolation. It must be considered in close conjunction with the level of rates at any given time and with the prospects of changes in that level over the life of the investment.

Full understanding of the implications of maturity for investment policy requires some knowledge of certain basic, technical facts.[10] One particularly important consideration is that, although short-term rates

---

[9]The possibility exists, of course, of selling the bond in the interim, but the profit or loss realized will reflect the degree of variance from the expected yield.

[10]Techniques and technical considerations have generally been deliberately omitted from this discussion when possible. Some knowledge of them, however, is necessary to provide a basic understanding for those involved in formulating policy. For a more detailed discussion of the techniques and technical considerations relating to bond investment, see *Inside the Yield Book,* a collection of memoranda to portfolio managers from Sidney Homer and Martin Leibowitz of Salomon Brothers, 1970–72.

vary more widely than long-term rates (as noted previously), the effect of a given rate change on price is magnified as maturity is extended. Table 13 illustrates the point.

The effect on price is further enhanced if the bonds have optional call dates in advance of final maturity, as is the case with many U.S. government issues. Such securities trade on a yield-to-maturity basis when current yields exceed the coupon rate but sell on a yield-to-call basis when current yields are lower than the coupon. The change in the method of yield computation when the price shifts from below par to above par (or *vice versa*) magnifies the range of price fluctuation considerably. Thus, when bank managers are extending maturities at a time when bond prices are relatively low, they may find it advantageous to purchase, at a discount from par, bonds with optional call dates.

These technical considerations may mostly be left to the technicians (investment officers, dealers, correspondent banks, and advisory services). What the policy maker really needs to know is that the prices of securities rise when interest rates fall and decline when rates rise and that the price swings resulting from any given change in rate will widen as maturity is extended.

Marketability

The primary sources of a bank's funds are deposits and capital. In recent years, deposits have provided between 80 and 90 percent of the loanable or investable funds of the banking system. These funds are in large part payable on demand or within relatively short periods. As such, they are subject to fluctuations over time. Although a bank usually establishes liquidity reserves designed specifically to meet these fluctuations and to meet changes in loan demands, the marketability of so-called residual investments cannot be ignored. In periods of severe stress, addi-

TABLE 13

RELATIVE PRICE CHANGES FOR BONDS OF DIFFERENT MATURITIES
REFLECTING A YIELD CHANGE FROM 5 PERCENT TO 7 PERCENT
(6% COUPONS)

Maturities	Point Change	% Change
One year	1.91	1.5
Two years	3.72	3.7
Five years	8.54	8.2
Ten years	14.90	13.8
Twenty years	23.23	20.6
Thirty years	27.56	23.9

tional funds might be needed. For banks that pursue aggressive investment policies (see the following chapter), marketability considerations are of major importance. Banks with such policies must be able to sell most of their portfolio when they desire to do so.

U.S. government securities have the highest marketability of any type of security. The riskless character of the asset and the broad market enable the holder to convert the security to cash with a minimum of loss. The depth of this market is indicated by the fact that trading in government securities vastly exceeds the total sales volume on the New York Stock Exchange.

Securities of U.S. government agencies are traded in the same market as the direct obligations of the Federal government. The market for government agency bonds has rapidly improved as their high credit quality has been recognized and as the supply of such securities outstanding has grown. The greatest constraint in the secondary market is the limited supply of outstanding issues. In early 1972, marketable securities of U.S. government agencies and sponsored corporations totaled approximately $48 billion, as compared to the $262 billion outstanding marketable debt of the Federal government. Sometimes it is difficult to acquire offerings of a given issue in any significant size at a price close to the quoted market. But it is nearly always possible to obtain reasonably competitive bids when one desires to sell.

The marketability of state and local bonds is a function of quality, maturity, the quantity of bonds being offered and outstanding, and the market's familiarity with the name. Although many banks hold local issues of municipal securities to develop business within the community, it should be recognized that marketability outside the immediate area may be low. For this reason, some reasonable proportion of the bond account should be held in nationally known issues capable of attracting buyers under any market conditions.

The marketability of corporate bonds also varies widely. Most of the owners of corporate bonds hold them in long-term investment accounts. Although the bonds in those accounts generally are of above-average quality, are issued by well-known companies, and are widely held by a reasonably large number of investors, they are not actively traded, and sizable blocks cannot be sold except at substantial discounts.

Despite recent improvements, the safest assumption to make about mortgages is that they are not readily marketable.

Taxes

The impact of Federal income tax laws and regulations on portfolio policy is another highly technical aspect of investment management with which bank directors can be expected to have little more than general familiarity. However, some background knowledge of tax consequences is essential to the broad formulation of portfolio policy.

The Federal income tax laws affect portfolio management in two important ways. In the first place, the income from obligations of states and political subdivisions (including public housing authorities) is entirely exempt from Federal income taxes. This fact naturally makes such securities attractive to investors who, like commercial banks, are subject to the income tax. This very attractiveness, however, tends to be reflected in higher prices and lower yields for such securities, as shown in Chart 16. The differential, however, seldom reflects the entire tax advantage. The degree by which it does so will vary with market conditions. In the 1960s, tax-exempt obligations sold at yields roughly 20 to 40 percent below yields of fully taxable obligations of reasonably comparable quality and maturity. Larger banks, which usually pay income taxes at the rate of 48 percent on their marginal income, nearly always benefit from the purchase of tax-exempt issues. For such banks, one can make a rough comparison between tax-exempt yields and the yields of taxable bonds by doubling the quoted yield on a municipal obligation. Thus, a 4 percent yield on a tax-exempt security is roughly equivalent to an 8 percent yield on a fully taxable U.S. government bond. For small banks, which are subject to a lower marginal tax rate, tax-exempt securities will only occasionally be attractive. Such banks should, however, be alert to these occasional market opportunities.

The second characteristic of the Federal income tax laws that strongly affects the management of investment portfolios is the tax treatment of capital gains and losses. Commercial banks, unlike any other businesses, have to treat both short- and long-term capital gains as ordinary income for tax purposes. Similarly, both short- and long-term capital losses can be used for the reduction of taxable, ordinary income. The implications of this tax treatment of capital gains and losses for management policies are discussed in the next chapter.

Pledging

Commercial banks have to pledge securities to back the deposits of the Federal government and its agencies and those of state and local governmental units.[11] The types of securities that are acceptable and the amount required in relation to the public deposits vary widely from state to state. Commercial bank managers have two primary concerns

---

[11]In the authors' opinion, pledging is a very inefficient method of securing public deposits. They believe FDIC insurance coverage of all public deposits is a preferable alternative.

about pledging. First, they must make sure that they hold enough pledgeable securities for the amount of existing and expected public deposits. Second, in pledging individual securities, they have to consider the possibility that they may decide to sell a pledged security. A security often becomes considerably less marketable when pledged, because substitution of another security may require several weeks.[12] Generally, the bank pledges securities that it does not plan to sell. The bank that does not plan to sell any of its portfolio securities should be able to pledge most of them. The portfolio manager of an aggressive bank that does plan to sell some of its portfolio holdings should go through individual pledgeable and long-term issues and pledge only those securities that he believes are least likely to be sold.

---

[12]To an increasing extent, pledge agreements include the right to free substitution, which materially alleviates this problem.

13

INVESTMENT PORTFOLIO—
POLICIES AND PROCEDURES

Within the framework of the basic considerations discussed in the previous chapter, it is the responsibility of the Board of Directors and senior management to develop investment portfolio policies and procedures that will establish the guidelines within which the investment portfolio will be managed. Specific policies and procedures will differ among banks because of differences in size, location, condition, and managerial capabilities. Nevertheless, there are basic ingredients of such policies that should lead to the sound, flexible, and profitable operation of the investment account.

A bank's investment portfolio, like ancient Rome, is not built in a day. Its composition is the result of many separate actions taken over considerable periods of time. Investment policies and procedures consist of coordinating these actions in a plan to accomplish specific objectives within carefully determined limitations.

DETERMINING INVESTMENT POLICIES

The investment policies of a bank should establish the general criteria and objectives underlying the buying and selling of securities for other than liquidity purposes. They should (1) be in writing; (2) establish limits of size, risk, maturity, and marketability; (3) relate to the bank's individual situation and the type of markets or community that the bank serves; (4) take into account the needs of the bank for pledging securities to secure public deposits; (5) establish guidelines with respect to trading securities; and (6) specify the authorities delegated to the investment officers within the framework of the policy itself.

They should be in writing so that everyone involved can agree on the basic objectives. Written policies provide an essential continuity of approach to changing markets and a basis for evaluating the results. All policies, of course, should be reviewed periodically in the light of changing circumstances.

Written policies should start off with a clear statement of objectives. In the broadest sense, the investment objectives of all banks are alike— to maximize income consistent with the maintenance of high standards of quality; to keep the bank's funds fully employed; to minimize tax liability; and to provide adequate securities for pledging. The specifics, however, will vary from bank to bank and it is useful to state these objectives clearly in writing, preferably by resolution of the Board of Directors, to provide continuing and thorough understanding of them.

Identifying the Portfolio

The first specific is to identify the portfolio itself as distinguished from the liquidity position. Common parlance, and many writers, refer to the "investment account" as being the sum of all the marketable securities owned by a bank. Similarly, it is common practice for bank management to provide the directors only with a list of the bank's security holdings showing book value and market prices. This list is generally subdivided into U.S. government securities, state and local securities, and other securities. The range of maturities is generally shown as well. Few banks, however, make the attempt to identify those securities that are held specifically for liquidity purposes and those that are held for long-term investment.

Length of maturity alone will not be the distinguishing feature, because under certain circumstances (in anticipation of rising rates, for example) a portion of the investment portfolio may be held temporarily in short-term issues. The real distinction is the purpose for which the securities are held. Liquidity assets are held to meet potential demands for funds. The investment portfolio, by contrast, represents the investment of funds for income. The first step, therefore, in determining portfolio policy is to consider the two sets of assets separately.

The Size of the Portfolio

The size of the portfolio will be determined by (1) the amount of available funds not required for the provision of liquidity and to meet the legitimate loan demands of the community and (2) the amount of securities required for pledging. The first is the residual of the bank's liquidity calculations as discussed in Chapter 9 and the demand for loanable funds and the bank's lending policies that are discussed in Chapter 11. The second will vary with the laws of the state in which the bank is located and with the aggressiveness with which the bank seeks public deposits.[1]

The Federal government and most states require that nearly all categories of public deposits be fully secured by specified securities.[2] The type of securities that are acceptable for pledging varies greatly with the type of public deposit. For example, U.S. government securities are the only collateral acceptable to secure some public deposits. Others can be secured by either U.S. government securities or state and local securities, usually of the same state or municipality depositing the funds. Clearly, bank managements must know their specific pledging requirements to determine their portfolio needs.

Limiting Risk

The amount of risk appropriate for the investment portfolio will depend primarily on three considerations. The first of these is the amount of risk the bank has assumed in its loan portfolio. In all likelihood, a bank that has aggressively met the loan demand of a thriving community will have only a small amount of funds left over for investment. These funds should be invested very conservatively. If, however, a bank is serving a stable community in which loan demands are not strong, it can afford to take somewhat greater risk in its portfolio. It is axiomatic, however, that the lower the quality or rating of a bond, the more management should know about the obligor. Many bonds, particularly those of small and not-well-known municipalities, sell at higher/ yields (lower prices) than the general market and consequently represent fine investment opportunities for those bank managements that know the situation intimately.

The second consideration in risk taking is, therefore, a realistic evaluation of the expertise of the investment officer or of the sources of information available to him. Many medium- and smaller-sized banks do not have sufficient knowledge and experience to properly evaluate unusual investment opportunities. They do well to confine themselves, as

---

[1]Some banks actively solicit state and municipal deposits on which interest payments are a tax-reducing expense. The deposits are then invested in tax-exempt securities that are used to secure the deposits. The differential, on a fully tax equivalent basis, can be a source of considerable profit. This technique is discussed more fully below.

[2]For a detailed study of security for public deposits, see Charles F. Haywood, *The Pledging of Bank Assets* (Chicago: Association of Reserve City Bankers, 1967).

a matter of policy, to securities that enjoy a high rating and a broad market. Correspondent banks and competent investment advisory services can, however, supply some of the expertise required to take advantage of favorable market circumstances to produce higher yields at some risk. A balanced approach for a moderate-sized bank would be to entertain such opportunities but to limit the amount of funds that could be invested in securities below an established quality level.

For some banks, considerations of capital adequacy may be a factor in limiting the risks they wish to take in their investment portfolios. If maximizing yields by switching out of U.S. government securities into state and municipal or corporate securities will bring requests for additional capital from the bank examiners, a careful calculation must be made as to the cost of additional capital in relation to the additional earnings potential. If management believes the cost of raising new capital exceeds the benefits from a higher-risk portfolio, the bank should reconsider its switching decision. If management believes the after-tax benefits from a higher risk portfolio exceed the cost of raising new capital, serious consideration should be given to the sale of additional capital (subordinated debt capital might be appropriate in this situation; see Chapter 17.)

Maturity

We have seen, in Chapter 12, that the risk of price fluctuation increases with maturity. This risk is twofold—the quality of a given security may change and the level of interest rates may change. These changes may be either adverse or favorable. If the quality of a bond improves, its price will rise over time. If the level of interest rates declines, the value of the investment will increase.

But how can the policy maker know what will really happen? He cannot. His job is to establish a balanced policy that will work out well on the average (if he is lucky!). There are two basic ways to do this. The first is to limit maturities to the hopefully foreseeable future and to space maturities within that limitation in order to achieve at least average results. The second is to offset, or average out, long maturities with very short maturities, the so-called barbell approach.

Maximum Maturities. No one can truly foresee the future course of investment history, and, therefore, the risks of the future can be reduced by limiting the time span of investment decisions. For this reason, many banks limit the maximum maturity of their investments to ten or fifteen years. They sacrifice little income in doing so—the income advantage in extending maturities beyond fifteen years is minimal, because the yield curve tends to flatten out around this point in future time.

Commercial bank experience with longer-term bonds has not been very happy during most of the post-World War II period because of the rising trend of long-term interest rates. Many banks still find themselves with substantial depreciation on holdings of such bonds acquired ten to fifteen years ago. On the other hand, one should not lose sight of the full sweep of history and the long periods in the past during which the secular trend of interest rates was downward. Should the policy makers become convinced that this particular phase of history was in the process of repeating itself, there would be ample justification for extending maturities beyond fifteen years.

If management decides to limit maximum maturities to ten to fifteen years, there still remains the question of what maturities to hold within that policy limitation. From the previous discussion of the relation of maturity to yield, it would appear that the ideal course of action would be to hold short-term securities when interest rates are likely to rise and to lengthen maturities when rates are expected to decline. Under the flexible monetary policy followed by the Federal Reserve since 1951, this is tantamount to shortening maturities when business conditions (and the demand for credit) are expected to strengthen and to lengthening maturities when the first signs of a business recession appear on the horizon.

There are several problems in the application of this theoretical ideal. First, even in cyclical periods such as the 1950s, bank portfolio managers found themselves under pressure to improve earnings that encouraged the purchase of longer maturities when interest rates were relatively low. When interest rates were high (and expected to decline), banks tended to have limited amounts to invest in any maturity. Second, business cycles do not always act as the textbooks seem to say they should. For example, the 1960s might be described as ten years of growth without recession but with two credit crunches. It is evident that portfolio management is closely integrated with economic forecasting, which is considered by some to be a dubious art at best.

Because of the manifest uncertainties in such an ideal approach to maturity distribution, banks have frequently been counseled to solve the problem by spacing maturities more or less evenly within the maximum range established by policy.[3] In this way, the bank will assure itself

---

[3]Roland I. Robinson, *The Management of Bank Funds* (New York: McGraw-Hill, 1962), p. 370. "Once an account has been put on a spaced basis and as long as there are neither additions nor withdrawals from this investment account, the proceeds from the securities which mature each year can be reinvested in securities of the longest maturity admitted to the account. Since time itself tends to shorten the maturity of the account, this reinvestment tends to keep the average maturity of the account constant."

of at least average yields, or a little better. It will not be gambling on changes in the level of interest rates or the state of the economy.

If not followed in too doctrinaire a fashion, the policy of spaced maturities is probably the best one for most banks of moderate size. Even those banks, however, should not blindly reinvest the proceeds of maturing securities in the longest permitted maturity at times when interest rates appear to be rising. Nor should they wait for bonds to mature before selling them and reinvesting in longer maturities when interest rates appear to be falling.

The "Barbell" Approach. Another way to play the averages in investment policy is to keep a part of the portfolio very short (mostly under one year) and invest the rest of the funds available in very long maturities at the highest possible yields. The yield on the short portion of the account will fluctuate with business conditions and the state of the credit markets and tend to counteract the income results from the long-term portion of the investment account. If rates in general rise, the long-term bonds will produce less than one might have hoped and will show substantial depreciation. But as the short-term securities come due and the proceeds are reinvested at rising yields, the total income from the portfolio will rise. Conversely, if rates decline, the yield from the short-term securities may fall, but the rates of income (and potential profits) on the long-term bonds will offset the income loss.

The operation of such a "barbell" maturity portfolio requires a somewhat higher degree of sophistication than a policy of spaced maturities. The barbell approach will be most successful if management can correctly interpret the changing economic scene and switch out of long maturities into short maturities when it believes that interest rates will rise, or if it has the courage to take its profits near the top of the market and go short despite the evident loss of immediate income.

The barbell approach to maturity distribution has the added advantage of providing a greater degree of liquidity to the investment portfolio, should it be needed. During the credit crunch of 1969–70, many municipalities withdrew their deposits to invest in higher-yielding money-market instruments. To meet these withdrawals, banks had to sell the securities pledged to secure such deposits. A bank could liquidate the short end of its barbell portfolio with minimum losses. Banks forced to sell intermediate- or longer-term bonds were not so fortunate.

Marketability

One of the facts of the bond market is that marketability costs income. If a bank expects to trade its investment portfolio in the manner described later in this chapter, it will do well to confine its investments to well-known, marketable issues, even at some sacrifice of yield. If, however, a bank has carefully gauged its liquidity needs and is convinced that it will not have to sell bonds out of its investment portfolio before their maturity, yield can be appreciably increased at a sacrifice of marketability.

Small issues of little-known obligors, which are often of high credit standing, can provide higher than average yields. "Odd lots," amounts under twenty-five thousand dollars, that are of little interest to the large investor can often be picked up at substantially lower prices (higher yields) than large blocks of the same security. What is cheap to buy, however, is expensive to sell. A bank should sacrifice marketability for income only in the case of bonds that it is perfectly willing to hold to maturity. Some portion of the investment account might be set aside to take advantage of nonmarketable opportunities, but it should not be so large a portion that a bank gives up the flexibility that is essential to the long-run maximization of income.

Community Needs

Many banks are too small, or do not have the available resources, to satisfy the needs of their local municipalities for credit. This does not mean, however, that they should ignore these needs. If they want to stand well with the local authorities (and benefit from related deposit relationships), they will take an active interest in local bond issues. By calling on their correspondent banks, or by establishing close working relationships with municipal bond dealers, they are able to put in bids in their own name for amounts considerably in excess of their portfolio needs. It is the function of the local bank to attempt to arouse interest in local bond and note issues and to solicit partners to bid aggressively for such securities. If the First Hometown Bank of Anywhere puts in the highest bid (or even the second highest), the local officials are duly impressed even if they know that 99 percent of the issue is spoken for by others. It should be the policy of every bank, therefore, to make arrangements with correspondent banks and other dealers so that it can bid effectively for the securities of its local municipalities and school districts.

Securities for Pledging

The pledging of securities to secure public deposits is an anachronism that goes back to the days when the king had prior claims in preference to his subjects on any available assets. The pledge requirements of various public bodies vary widely. There have been recent efforts in various jurisdictions to simplify them and to substitute a general bank guarantee for at least a part of the requirements for the specific pledge of securities.[4] The process of pledging itself is a cumbersome one, both for the bank and the public body, entailing a great deal of record-keeping and unnecessary delay, both of which can be very expensive.

But where a pledge of specific securities is still required, a bank has only the choice of either securing public deposits or not accepting them. In formulating investment policy, therefore, it is incumbent on management to determine how aggressively it will seek public deposits of various kinds and how to provide the necessary collateral.

Government securities are acceptable in nearly all cases. It would usually be profitable to accept the demand deposits of public bodies and to secure them with U.S. government securities. It would seldom be profitable, however, to pay market rates for public time deposits and to secure them with U.S. government securities, because the yield on such securities is generally lower than market rates for bank time deposits. One cannot, therefore, consider the question of public deposits without taking into account the tax considerations involved in owning (and pledging) state and municipal or tax-exempt bonds.

POSSIBLE INVESTMENT STRATEGIES

The tax consideration involved in owning (and pledging) tax-exempt securities leads to a strategy that may be called the *municipal bank*. The principle is that a bank should seek enough state and municipal deposits to fund the holdings of tax-exempt securities that it needs to minimize its tax liability whether or not the securities have to be pledged to secure the deposits.

The first step in establishing the municipal bank is to estimate the bank's net taxable income from ordinary operations for the ensuing year. Let us assume that this figure is $600,000 and that transfers to reserves for bad debts and other estimated losses are expected to amount to $100,000. Let us assume further that the bank's effective tax rate is 40 percent. Its prospective earnings picture will look like this:

Net taxable income	$600,000
Less losses and transfers to reserves	100,000
Income subject to tax	500,000
Less tax at 40%	200,000
Net after-tax income	$300,000

---

[4]The laws of the states of Connecticut, New Jersey, and some others have recently been revised in this respect.

Now let this bank actively solicit $4 million in public time deposits at the going rate of 5 percent, or an additional cost of $200,000 per annum. Let it invest the proceeds (less 5 percent reserve requirements), or $3,800,000, in tax-exempt securities yielding 4 percent, or $152,000 per annum. Its earnings picture would now look like this:

Net taxable income	$600,000
Less additional interest	200,000
Revised taxable income	400,000
Less losses and transfers to reserves	100,000
Net taxable income	300,000
Taxes at 40% rate	120,000
Net	180,000
Plus additional tax exempt income	152,000
Net income after taxes	$332,000

The solicitation and investment of these deposits in tax-exempt securities will be seen to have added more than 10 percent to the after-tax income of the bank.

The arithmetic of these calculations will vary from bank to bank and from time to time depending on the level of market rates and the particular situation of each individual bank with respect to its taxable income and effective tax rate. The same calculations, moreover, are pertinent whether or not public deposits are available to fund the desired amount of tax-exempt securities. The municipal bank concept, however, is especially pertinent with respect to those deposits that require security. Such funds are only available to purchase the pledged securities, and there is an inherent logic that hopefully will not be lost on the Internal Revenue Service in using deposits of public bodies to purchase and hold their obligations.

The profitability of the municipal bank will be increased to the extent that the bank acquires demand as well as time deposits of its municipal customers. Given a substantial demand deposit account, a bank can afford to bid more aggressively for time deposits of that municipality to cement the relationship. It can also afford to bid somewhat higher prices for the short-term obligations of its good deposit customers, especially if it needs them for pledging. Because of its obvious profitability, municipal finance has become an increasingly competitive business. It is an area that no bank that is paying more than a nominal amount of income taxes should neglect.

Trading or Switching Securities

Most small banks buy securities for their investment portfolio and put them away until they mature. This is not the way to maximize income consistent with safety. There are times to buy and times to sell (and buy something else), and even the smallest bank can take advantage of the broad cyclical movements in the securities markets.

One can make a valid distinction between *trading* and *switching*. *Trading* is a day-to-day operation that requires easy access to the markets and an expertise not available to most banks. *Switching* involves the mobility of a portfolio in relation to changes in economic conditions and related changes in rate levels. A bank that is alert to switching activities will be in the market far less frequently than a bank that has the capacity to trade actively, but its purchases and sales can, nonetheless, add appreciably to its income over time.

It should be noted here that the accounting rules applicable to banks make a distinction between trading profits (and losses) and portfolio profits and losses. A trading bank will establish a trading account, and the profits and losses resulting from its trades will be shown as a part of its operating earnings. To operate a trading account, a bank must take depreciation as well as actual earnings into its operating results. It must "mark to market," that is, treat depreciation as an actual loss, with respect to those securities that it has designated as its trading account. Gains and losses on portfolio transactions, on the other hand, are shown "below the line," that is, not as operating earnings but as unusual transactions. Thus, banks report operating earnings that include trading account results and then their "net profits," taking portfolio gains or losses into consideration.

It is the authors' view that securities held for liquidity should be treated for accounting purposes as a trading account whether they are actively traded or not. For the most part, they will be of short maturity and their value as liquidity instruments will be their market value. Those banks that are able to trade their liquidity portfolios because of their own knowledge or because of access to expert advice will probably add appreciably to their income over time.

Intelligent management of the portfolio also provides *switching* opportunities for increased income and/or profits. These increases are beneficial to the stockholders whether they are reported as earnings "above the line" or as the result of securities transactions "below the line."

· Most portfolio switching will be in response to changing economic and credit conditions. As indicated in the discussion of maturity, it will be advantageous to switch into longer maturities when interest rates are expected to fall because of slack economic conditions and to switch into short maturities (even at some sacrifice of current income) when economic activity and the demand for credit are rising. Another way of putting this is that a bank should shorten maturities when it takes profits (when yields are low and prices high) and that it should lengthen maturities when it takes losses (when yields are high and prices low).

Banks are always happy to take profits, but many banks are reluctant to take losses. Taking losses, however, can be profitable at times if a bank has net taxable income against which to offset them. Let us assume, for example, that a bank owns some 20-year municipal bonds that it bought at par ($1,000) several years earlier when rates were lower. Because of the rise in the level of interest rates, these bonds are now selling at $800. For each $1 million of such bonds that the bank sells, it will take a loss of $200,000 that, if it is in the 50 percent tax bracket, will be a net loss of only $100,000. Let the bank then reinvest the proceeds in bonds of comparable quality and maturity at the same price of $800. It will have a built-in appreciation to maturity of $200,000, or, after 50 percent taxes, $100,000. This is at least a break-even proposition.

But in the year of the sale, the bank will have realized a tax saving of $100,000 and will, therefore, have this additional amount to invest at the higher yields available when it takes its losses, and the return on this additional investment resulting from the tax saving will appreciably increase its income over the next twenty years.

If, in the process of taking such losses, a bank can switch into higher yields or into securities with a greater potential for appreciation, it can often recover its loss in a period of three to five years while adding to total income over the life of the new bonds purchased.

Aside from the reluctance to show losses even though they can be demonstrated to be profitable, the benefits of this switching are limited by the availability of taxable income against which to offset the loss. In this connection, however, it should be borne in mind that banks, like other corporations, have the privilege of carrying losses forward for five years. This year's losses can be offset not only against this year's taxable income but also against that of the ensuing four years.

The accounting profession has ruled that for reporting purposes, it would be an acceptable accounting practice to amortize losses or gains on securities transactions over the life of the securities purchased as replacements. This concept recognizes the fact that the initial loss is recoverable from the increased income over time. The supervisory authorities and the Securities Exchange Commission have not yet allowed this accounting method for the banks and holding companies under their jurisdiction. If allowed, this accounting method would go a long way toward alleviating the reluctance of bank directors to show large losses in any one year even though such losses may be in the best interests of the bank in the long run.

INVESTMENT AUTHORITY AND CONTROL

A bank's investment policy should delegate specific authority to designated officers to purchase or sell securities up to certain amounts, just as a bank's loan policy should permit the bank's lending officer to commit the bank for stated amounts. Opportunities for profitable switching or trading that may be evident to the investment officer or called to his attention by a correspondent bank, a dealer, or an investment advisory service, do not last long in the market. If decisions must be referred to an Investment Committee or even to a chief executive officer who may be away from the bank at the moment, profitable opportunities will be irretrievably lost. A sound policy, therefore, will set trading limits based on the size of the bank and the investment officer's knowledge and experience, within which he should have full discretion. It is relatively simple to compare the results of trading, say every six months, with what would have resulted had no purchases or sales been made. Such a comparison should be a clear indication of the investment officer's acumen.

PART IV

OTHER
BANK POLICY AREAS

14
AUDIT AND CONTROL

It is unfortunate that bank directors and supervisors have to concern themselves with the possibility of losses resulting from the dishonest acts of bank officers and employees. Yet such losses are a real and ever present danger because in banking, people handle money. Bank officers and employees are human beings subject to all the pressures and temptations of a society that emphasizes the things money can buy. Unlike other people subject to similar pressures, bank employees are daily faced with the physical availability of money in large quantities. In the United States, the problem is made even more serious by the multitude of small banks, any one of which may be seriously embarrassed, if not ruined, by a major defalcation.[1]

A less publicized but no less effective pilferer is the inefficiency that inevitably creeps in when banking operations are left without adequate supervision or review. Even minor inefficiencies, such as needlessly handling paper or copying figures that could be reproduced by carbon paper, can result in slow but steady drains on a bank's resources. Over a period of time, these losses probably exceed the more dramatic losses from dishonest acts. Errors, too, can be an important source of loss of money, time, and prestige. All these kinds of losses, the risk of which

---

[1]Most of the banks closed since 1945 have been victims of employee dishonesty. Source: Federal Deposit Insurance Corporation.

is inherent in banking, can be reduced by the formulation and administration of a soundly conceived program of control and audit that covers not only financial transactions and book entries but operating procedures as well.[2]

ASSESSMENT OF THE RISK

The record of bank defalcations in the United States is a sorry one and shows no indication of diminishing. Table 15 shows that the American Bankers Association reported 1,768 cases involving amounts of $10,000 or more for the years 1958 through 1970. Although the total of over $166 million is not large in relation to the total resources of all banks, a single defalcation can loom shockingly large in a particular institution.

Most dishonest acts in banking are unpremediated. They take place when money, which is readily available, appears to be the only solution to a problem brought on by the pressures to which some individual bank officer or employee may become subject. Such pressures may be social or psychological (the desire to be a good fellow or to live up to the style of the Joneses), or they may be simply accidental—for instance, illness in the family or the need to correct some personal mistake or involvement. In most cases, the individual initially convinces himself that he is "borrowing" the money and only gradually becomes more deeply enmeshed as he finds he cannot pay it back. The longer such a crime goes undetected, the more brazen and cynical the individual is likely to become.

Few individuals are not subject to financial pressures of one kind or another in the course of their lives. A bank examiner, on entering the cage of a girl teller, once factiously inquired, "And how much are you short?" The young lady burst into tears and confessed that she had "borrowed" ten cents for bus fare the night before. This rather pathetic incident is but one end of a scale that leads to the respected bank presi-

---

[2]One succinct statement of the objectives of audit and control is:

Commercial banks should have a budgetary control system to control their operations. Bank income must be derived from a balanced use of funds considering liquidity position and safety of depositors' and stockholders' monies. To get the maximum income from these monies, considering the restrictive factors, requires careful control over the use of funds in the income producing categories. Current banking practices give rise to the increasingly important service income potential which must be controlled along with income resulting from use of funds. An equally important objective of a budgetary control system is the control of expenses necessary to produce required income.

[Heazy and Blakely, *An Application of Budgetary Control to Commercial Banks* (Madison, Wisconsin: University of Wisconsin, 1965), p. 12.]

TABLE 15

BANK DEFALCATIONS OF $10,000 AND MORE

Year	Number of Cases	Amount Involved	Cases in Excess of Blanket Bond	Excess Over Blanket Bond Amount	Number of Banks with $1MM Excess	Amount Insured under $1MM Excess	Number of Cases Under-Insured	Amount of Under-Insurance	FDIC Banks Failed	Non-FDIC Banks Failed
1958	90	$ 6,455,187	10	$ 1,628,070	1	$ 26,933	9	$1,601,137	3	2
1959	86	8,826,948	7	2,331,990	0	0	7	2,331,990	2	0
1960	111	10,109,698	10	2,951,602	4	2,421,422	6	530,180	1	0
1961	113	12,919,168	16	4,765,450	4	1,478,720	12	3,286,730	5	0
1962	120	8,877,444	7	1,734,449	3	814,854	4	919,595	0	2
1963	116	8,424,806	7	1,268,608	5	885,473	2	383,135	0	0
1964	118	11,205,502	9	4,502,660	5	2,033,794	5*	2,468,866	1	0
1965	138	13,351,081	8	1,681,786	5	1,204,792	3	476,944	4	0
1966	164	12,084,746	8	1,718,340	6	1,535,740	2	182,600	3	0
1967	132	13,727,042	9	2,830,334	9*	3,519,396	1*	310,938	2**	0
1968	146	11,174,466	6	1,586,793	6	1,586,793	0	0	1***	0
1969	189	16,909,519	11	1,607,128	10	1,538,768	1	68,360	2***	0
1970	245	32,736,018	17	11,208,162	12	1,830,353	5	9,377,809	2	0

*The loss in one bank exceeded both blanket bond and additional fidelity coverages.
**The dishonestry loss in one of these banks was reported in 1966.
***Banks were fully insured but closed because of questionable lending practices.

Source: Insurance and Protective Committee of the American Bankers Association. (Table based on reports from the Comptroller of the Currency, Federal Deposit Insurance Corporation, and the Federal Reserve board.)

dent who, ostensibly to finance a new industry in his community, permitted and engineered illegal overdrafts that exceeded $1 million and that bankrupted his institution.[3]

Although more fidelity losses (defalcations) are attributable to bank employees, the larger amounts, and the most serious cases, are the peculations of bank officers. In nearly every case, the person involved had been respected in his community and considered entirely trustworthy by his friends and associates. In many cases, he completely dominated the operations of his bank, a situation that is always fraught with danger.

Each fidelity loss, whatever its size, is a study in human nature. Unauthorized borrowing appears to occur when the individual is both under pressure and convinced that he can escape detection. Individual resistance to pressure varies widely, of course, and people without a strong sense of the difference between other people's money and their own should not be working in banks. It is virtually impossible, however, to predict who will succumb to a specific amount of pressure.

Losses through inefficiency are more difficult to measure, but they are unquestionably large. The differences in operating expenses between well-managed banks and average banks give some indication of the costs of inefficiency. Operating expenses as a percentage of gross revenue for commercial banks have climbed steadily during the last decade. Gross revenues have not risen enough to cover the costs of additional services that banks must offer to remain competitive. The resultant narrowing of profit margins highlights the need for efficient audit and control.

An example of what can be accomplished through vigorous attempts to control costs was furnished in 1955 by the Bank Relations Department of the Federal Reserve Bank of New York (Second District). This Federal Reserve Bank undertook a series of programs to call to the attention of its member banks the opportunities for cost saving through review and simplification of procedures. Representatives of the department, skilled in bank operations, reviewed individually the operating procedures of banks with assets ranging from $5 million to $20 million—banks that generally lacked the internal resources to review their own operations effectively.

From 1954 through 1959, the operating costs (excluding interest on time deposits) of all member banks in the United States increased by an average of about .45 percent of total assets. The increase in the Second District averaged only .31 percent, less than in any of the other eleven districts. Of even greater significance was the increase of only .19 percent among banks with assets of $5 million to $20 million in the Second District. The difference between this increase and the average increase

---

[3]*American Banker*, January 16, 1957.

in the entire Second District may seem small, but when applied to the total assets of the banks involved it represented a saving of over $2.7 million a year.

The problem for bank management is to prevent crime and waste to the greatest possible extent and to see that they are promptly detected when they occur. The audit and control function is the principal tool of management in this regard but not the only one. The first line of defense consists of basic personnel policies that are too often neglected.

PERSONNEL POLICIES IN RESTRAINT OF CRIME

It is almost self-evident that banks should be especially selective in their hiring policies. Frequently, however, under the pressure of needing hands to get a job done, banks have not thoroughly investigated prospective employees and have known too little of their background. References should be meticulously checked and all shadows of doubt eliminated.[4]

It should be equally clear that an adequate salary scale is an important factor in minimizing the pressures that may lead employees astray. On occasion, however, when a defaulting teller's salary has become a matter of public record, the courts have criticized the bank rather than the guilty employee. The excuse that banks cannot afford to pay salaries comparable with those for similar jobs in the community or commensurate with the responsibility of the position is little more than an admission of the inefficiency with which too many banks are operated. One of the principal aims of the kind of control and audit program advocated in this book, with its strong emphasis on efforts to increase operating effciency, is a bank staff of fewer but better-paid people.

Salary scales alone are not the sole answer to the problems of temptation. Most poorly paid bank clerks never steal. The character and integrity of the individual are the essential deterrents to crime.[5] This fact points up the vital need for bank management really to know something about the people who work in their bank. Bank directors and senior management often think they "know their people" without having made any systematic effort to do so. After a defalcation has come to light, they frequently wonder how they could have failed to recognize

---

[4]Examples of laxity in hiring are the cases of the individual who was dismissed for check kiting by one bank and hired as an auditor by another and the note teller who was fired for holding his own worthless checks as cash items and subsequently turned up as a bank examiner.

[5]Ben B. McNew, "Internal Audit and Fraud Control," *The Bankers' Handbook* (Homewood, Ill.: Dow Jones-Irwin, Inc., 1966), pp. 222–23.

situations that, after the fact, suddenly appear to have been so obvious.

Particularly in small banks in small towns, there is little excuse for the directors and senior management not to be familiar with the scale of living of their employees or of the problems with which they may be faced at home. In larger institutions, it is perhaps more difficult but no less necessary for management to keep reasonably close personal contact with the junior officers and employees. Periodic interviews with each individual during which his progress, aspirations, and problems are frankly discussed, will generally yield clues to the existence of a problem or pressure that might lead to wrongdoing.

Finally, banks should make abundantly clear, in practice as well as in theory, their willingness to assist their employees with financial problems. The provision of health insurance and especially major medical coverage would have removed the source of temptation in many known cases of fraud. In addition, sympathetic financial counseling and loans at favorable interest rates should be freely available. Legitimate borrowing should be made easy enough to counteract the temptation for "illegitimate borrowing." Employees who abuse these privileges are not likely to be good fidelity risks in any event, and severance pay will represent cheap insurance in the long run.

JUSTIFICATION OF AUDIT COST

Despite the most careful and progressive personnel policies, some fidelity losses are likely to occur. A bank may of course insure itself against the results of defalcation as well as against losses from burglary, forgery, misplacement, and the like. The Insurance and Protective Department of the American Bankers Association recommends specific minimum amounts of coverage for banks of different sizes. Bank examiners usually check to make sure that banks do hold at least this minimum coverage. In recent years, a form of additional fidelity coverage in the amount of $1 million has also become available, and supervisory authorities and others are strongly urging all banks (especially the smaller ones) to acquire it.[6]

The importance of fidelity insurance cannot be overemphasized, but it is not a substitute for adequate controls and effective audits. Often, bank directors, particularly those in smaller banks, rely on surety bonds and "knowledge of their people" and resist spending the bank's money for auditing because it is not productive. All authorities agree that this attitude is shortsighted and represents a failure of bank directors to live up to their responsibilities.

6"Money Well Spent—$1 Million Excess Fidelity Bonds that Save Banks," *American Banker* (New York), April 7, 1961.

Defalcations can be a source of extreme embarrassment to bank management, regardless of insurance protection. Screaming headlines always ask, in effect, how management could have been so incompetent as to permit such a thing to happen. The bank's good name is besmirched, even though its assets may be recouped.

The prevention of crime is even more important than its detection, and the avoidance of loss is better than its recovery. No one would deliberately leave oily rags and litter in the attic of his home merely because the house was insured against fire. The temptation to which all bank employees are subject increases as the chance of immediate discovery diminishes. Bank directors have a moral obligation to protect their employees as well as their depositors and stockholders by removing, as far as possible, the opportunities for wrongdoing and providing for the probability of swift detection of misbehavior.

A well-conceived and carefully executed control and audit program will "protect weak people from temptation, strong people from opportunity, and innocent people from suspicion."[7] If the audit program includes a regular and formal review of operating procedures as well as a check on the bank's assets, liabilities, and income, a competent auditor can more than earn his salary by suggesting or instituting cost-saving methods.

The cost of an adequate audit program should be considered as much a fixed cost of banking as the cost of depreciating the building and fixtures, and if the money is spent for a thoroughly competent person and the audit function enlarged as suggested below, the cost of audit can be a far more productive expenditure than many bank directors realize.

AUDIT AND CONTROL—DEFINITIONS

The words *audit* and *control* are usually referred to in that order, but controls, as a matter of necessity, come first. There can be no meaningful audit without established controls.

A control is a mechanical or procedural device introduced into a process or chain of events that will automatically require that something be done in a specified and predetermined manner. Thus, a lock on a door is a control requiring that the door may be opened by the insertion and turning of a specific key. Physical controls of this kind play an important role in banking operations. They range from the time lock on the vault door to the locked control in the savings posting machine. But of even greater importance are the procedural rules that are devised

---

[7]Marshall C. Corns, *Bank Auditing* (Cambridge, Mass.: Bankers Publishing Company, 1955).

and enforced to the end that banking transactions will follow certain specified channels that provide predetermined safeguards. The requirement, for example, that a bank's drafts, over a certain amount, must bear two official signatures, and the instructions to that effect given to the correspondent bank, constitute a control designed to make certain that at least two of the bank's officers will have knowledge of any transaction by which the bank's funds are expended.

Another common form of control is the proof. One can hardly think of banking transactions in any other terms than those of double-entry bookkeeping. Every debit must have its opposite credit, and at the end of the day or at intermediate intervals the sum of debits must be equal to the sum of credits. Proofs to demonstrate this equality are controls that assure accuracy and absence of error, vital conditions of a successful banking operation. It is for the purpose of making certain that he has committed no errors that the teller proves his work at the end of the day or that the bookkeeping department adds up all the checks paid and the deposits credited to ascertain that the net figure agrees with the changes in the controlling deposit ledgers. No operation in the bank should be without its control or proof.

The function of auditing, on the other hand, is to make certain that controls are maintained and that proofs are accurate. It is for this reason that the auditor makes an unexpected count of the teller's cash and reviews the proof or makes an additional audit run of the day's checks and deposits. It is for this purpose also that he reviews actual operating practices to make certain that the controls established by policy have not broken down in day-to-day operations. Too often, the control of a locked door to the vault, established to limit access to authorized persons, is vitiated by the key being readily accessible to anyone.

The initial responsibility for devising and establishing adequate controls rests with senior operating management. Every system and procedure in the bank should be set up with control in mind. Each suggested shortcut in operations and new piece of equipment needs to be evaluated in the light of control as well as efficiency.

In making decisions about controls, senior management can and should rely heavily on the auditor, because he will have the responsibility for maintaining and checking them. Bank directors, too, although not expected to be expert in operating procedures, should be aware of the need for control so that they may intelligently appraise audit reports and understand at least in general terms some of the operational complexities they are called upon to consider.

Many banks use an operating manual or manual of procedures as a kind of master control—a control of controls, as it were. Such a manual will contain a description of the approved procedure to be followed in every operation of the bank. The preparation of the manual entails a very valuable discipline; in the process, every one of the bank's controls and procedures must be reviewed and evaluated. Rarely will such a process fail to result in material improvements. A manual of operations provides an invaluable training guide as well as a compact reference for transactions that take place infrequently. Along with its advantages, however, a manual of procedure, once adopted, may increase the danger of inflexibility and resistance to change. It should always be in loose-leaf form.

PRINCIPLES OF CONTROL

There is not space here for a discussion of all the controls that have a part in banking operations. Nor does a person responsible for bank policy need to know all the details with which his operating people should be completely familiar. A few basic principles, however, should be well-known to anyone generally responsible for bank policy and supervision of operations.

The first principle, one that underlies most bank controls, is that wherever possible, the handling of funds should be separated from the posting of related records. A division of responsibility and a dual accountability are thus immediately established. Where this kind of inherent double-check cannot be conveniently built into the system, the responsibility for checking devolves immediately upon the audit function.[8]

A second basic principle of control is the requirement that money and securities, again where possible, be held under dual control. In this case, the two responsible parties act jointly, keeping watch over each other. Double locks on vault doors are examples of this form of control. Conversely, however, if dual control of valuables is not possible, as in a teller's cage, then the sole responsibility must be clearly isolated and enforced. Thus, each teller should have complete control over and sole access to his own cash while he is using it and should account for it *in toto* through his proof at the end of the day. Similarly, each bookkeeper is responsible for his own ledgers, lest, among other things, he be blamed for the errors of others.

A third general principle of bank control is the ideal requirement that no person shall work at a single job without interruption. Rotation of assignment between bookkeepers (exchanging ledgers) or between bookkeepers and mortgage clerks (exchanging jobs) will assure that control over any series of transactions or any set of records will not permanently rest with one individual.

Unfortunately, complete rotation of assignments is extremely rare in

---

[8]Bennie B. McNew and Charles L. Prather, *Fraud Control for Commercial Banks* (Homewood, Ill.: Richard D. Irwin, Inc., 1962), p. 12.

banks. It requires a good deal of extra training and runs into the resistance of bank employees (and officers) who are comfortable in well-accustomed routines. However, rotation will pay dividends in staff flexibility and efficiency as well as in improved control.

Enforced vacations of at least two weeks' continuous duration for all bank employees, including the senior officers, is another form of the same control principle. It is one on which bank directors should adamantly insist, no matter how great the pressure of business or how selfless may appear the chief executive officer's devotion to duty. Few of the major defalcations in small banks would have gone undetected for so many years had the officer-perpetrators been required to be away from the bank for at least two consecutive weeks each year.

Finally, an important set of controls over bank income and expense, too infrequently availed of by smaller banks, is the accrual system of accounting. Although the primary purpose of accrual accounting is to prorate revenues and expenses over time to provide a reasonable measure of the bank's earnings, its contribution to control alone is probably enough to justify its cost. If, for example, demand loan interest actually collected and credited to undivided profits does not at least roughly equal the amount of interest estimated by the accrual process, the auditor has some important questions to ask.

As has been indicated above, many controls can be effectively introduced into systems and procedures; others are physically built into bank equipment. A useful and inexpensive method of control that is often overlooked is the simple carbonized form. With no additional time or effort, it produces an extra copy of bank entries for the auditor. Costing little more than the paper it is written on, the "auditor's copy" provides the auditor with a means of checking most bank entries when he has the time to do so. The knowledge of its existence can be a powerful damper on temptation.

AUDIT PRACTICES

It is not the intention here to describe how banks should be audited. A number of excellent manuals are available for the professional auditor or the member of a directors' examining committee who wishes to familiarize himself with specific audit techniques.[9] Rather, this discussion will concern itself with those fundamental audit concepts with which every bank director should be familiar.

---

[9]For example, The Committee on Bank Accounting and Auditing of the American Institute of CPA's, *Audits of Banks* (New York: American Institute of CPA's, 1968).

Good auditing can be said to consist of substantial verification of the accuracy and completeness of a bank's records and of the safety and efficiency of its operations. The auditor of a large New York City bank has stated that the audit responsibility is:

1. to see that the assets of a bank are safeguarded
2. to see that all liabilities are properly recorded
3. to see that all income to which the bank is entitled is received and recorded in the proper income account.

Additionally, continuous appraisals of operating systems assure that internal controls are providing adequate protection and that waste and unnecessary expense are eliminated.[10]

The most direct form of auditing is simple rechecking, having a second person redo what someone else has already done. Obviously, such procedures would be intolerably time-consuming and wasteful. The first problem of good auditing is therefore to devise satisfactory methods of ascertaining that a series of transactions has been correctly performed without having to recheck each one. This, of course, is where control fits into auditing. Generally, where controls are effective, the auditor's task is mainly to see that they are maintained and to check totals. Where controls cannot be (or are not) built into the procedural system, auditing tends to require more direct rechecking.

Some direct spot-checking has an important place in the audit program even where controls are well developed. Although he may be generally satisfied that he has checked all the entries and withdrawals of securities in and out of the vault, the auditor will nevertheless occasionally wish to count them to make sure he has not missed anything. For similar reasons, he periodically counts the tellers' cash or makes a proof of the notes.

The principal problem in auditing is to determine how much checking is needed to accomplish the purposes listed above. No auditor would have time to check the proceeds of every note to the deposit ledgers, and he does not need to. Accuracy is generally assured by the system of proofs; to serve as a deterrent to wrongdoing, auditing needs merely to create a knowledge in the minds of bank employees that some number of every variety of transaction will be checked, that there is no way of knowing which transaction will be checked, and that any one transaction might be checked.

The two basic elements of sound auditing practice are surprise and variation. There should be no discernible routine to the auditor's work aside from his daily matching of controls to assure accounting accuracy.

---

[10]Morris A. Engelman, "Auditing under Automation," *Auditgram*, March 1961.

Both the timing and the scope of audit work should vary unpredictably. If these elements are carefully maintained, spot-auditing and sampling will provide effective audit control.

One specific audit procedure perhaps requires special comment. It is the procedure of verifying loans and deposits directly with the bank's customers. Many banks, particularly the smaller ones, have resisted this practice,[11] although it is urged by every authority as essential to a well-rounded audit program.[12] The fact is that the only matching records or controls for many of a bank's accounts are the records of its customers. No auditor or examiner can be absolutely certain of the accuracy of a bank's record of a savings account unless he sees the customer's passbook or be sure of the validity of a note unless the customer acknowledges his debt. Direct verification is most effective when the customers are asked to reply positively to confirm balances. Negative verification—a request to customers to check the information supplied by the bank with their own records and to notify the auditor only if there appears to be a difference—assumes that the account is correct if the customer does not reply. Both kinds of vertification usually involve a random sample of at least 20 percent of the accounts each year, including some accounts audited during the immediately preceding years.

No one, of course, can verify ledger records that have been abstracted or destroyed, as in occasional large defalcations, especially in small banks operated or dominated by one man.[13] It has been suggested that bank directors could at least partially close this loophole in communities where customers are used to the verification process, by advertising in the local press the fact that certain accounts of the bank are in the process of being verified by the bank's auditor. A request might be made, through this medium, that the auditor be notified immediately if any customer with an account of the kind being verified should fail to receive a request for confirmation.

---

[11]Stanley E. Shirk, "Special Problems of Bank Audits," *Journal of Accountancy*, April 1960, p. 39.

In bank auditing, confirmation procedures present a special problem as many bankers are reluctant to permit the use of the procedure. They are concerned both with the cost and the possible impact on depositors and borrowers. They feel that the customers will think that there is something wrong with the bank.

[12]The NABAC manual devotes an entire chapter to the techniques of this procedure.

[13]When a large defalcation that has been going on for a number of years is discovered, people always ask how the examiners failed to discover it. The examiners prove the books as they find them but cannot be aware of liabilities that are not shown in the records.

THE AUDIT PROGRAM

The audit program is a formal summary or schedule of audits to be performed. It stems from policy decisions about the scope and frequency of individual audits. How often and how completely shall the various operations and accounts be checked? What percentage of transactions and accounts shall be verified internally and directly with customers? The bank's directors should make these policy decisions, taking into consideration the recommendations of operating management and the auditor, their own common sense, and the suggestions contained in a recognized audit manual.

Many auditors set up programs on file cards. Each card covers a specific audit procedure, describes briefly the audit to be performed, indicates the scope and frequency approved by the directors, and provides space to record the work done. The cards can be filed to provide a "tickler" or time schedule for the program. Care should be taken to assure that the time schedule is not available to anyone but the auditor, and that the schedule does not become routine. Each month the auditor should report directly to the Board of Directors or its examining committee the progress made with the program and the full details of any unusual findings.

Operational Reviews

The most effective way for the auditor to review operating procedures is to prepare and periodically review a manual of procedures. Methods and procedures are not established by the auditor, of course, but rather by the operating officers of the bank or the heads of departments who are responsible for the work done. The auditor's interest in them is from the dual viewpoint of control and efficiency. He has the primary responsibility for control; but with respect to efficiency, he has only an advisory role, so his effectiveness will depend heavily on his competence and his ability to sell ideas.

If the bank is large enough to have an officers' Operating Committee —and even very small banks would benefit from some such formal attention to operating problems—its membership should include the auditor. In this capacity, he can take part in the development of new systems and procedures and make suggestions about the old ones. Whether the change under consideration be the introduction of a new carbonized form or a new electronic computer, the auditor's role is essentially the same. He must understand the new system and what it is intended to accomplish, and he must satisfy himself on behalf of the directors that the new procedure provides adequate controls and will contribute to the overall efficiency of the bank's operations.

As every bank clerk knows, proofs do not always prove, and looking for differences is one of the most time-consuming and wasteful efforts in daily bank operations. One of the auditor's principal responsibilities should be to review all the proof errors that occur and to try to analyze the reasons for them. It is easy to attribute most of the errors to employee carelessness or failure to follow directions, but perhaps the opportunities for carelessness might be reduced if the directions were made more explicit.

A New England banker,[14] who made something of a hobby of reducing errors and simplifying his bank's operations, found that the use of numbers keyed to the bank's records, the use of different-colored tickets and plus and minus signs for debits and credits, and explicit instructions printed on every entry ticket virtually eliminated proof errors in his bank. He also found that these same innovations greatly reduced the time needed to train new employees and substantially reduced the time previously spent by officers in answering the same questions over and over again. Work simplification is a veritable gold mine that few banks have adequately tapped. It poses a real challenge to an imaginative auditor.

Examinations

A distinction is sometimes made between internal and external audits as well as between audits of all kinds and examinations. The examinations made by the supervisory authorities are clearly stated not to be audits, although in most cases they include a verification of some of the assets and liabilities and a proof of the general ledger controls.[15] Examinations made by directors or by accountants engaged by the directors may include a considerable amount of auditing, including proof of income and expense and direct verification of assets and liabilities.

Functionally, an examination is primarily an evaluation of assets, procedures, policies, and the effectiveness of management. Supervisory authorities are also directly concerned with a bank's compliance with

---

[14]Charles N. Bachelder, former president, Hanover National Bank, Hanover, N.H.

[15]T.P. Kane, for many years Deputy Comptroller of the Currency, stated:

Bank examiners are not auditors. Unfortunately, the distinction between an examination and an audit is seldom recognized in the criticisms of examiners when banks suffer losses through dishonesty or other causes which have remained concealed for some time, undiscovered by the examiner through several successive examinations.

the law.[16] In the same functional sense, auditing is the process of verifying the existence of assets and the accuracy of accounts, whether it be done as a continuing process internally or periodically by outside accountants or directors. Unquestionably, there is a good deal of overlap. When the auditor counts the teller's cash, he is doing the same thing an examiner does and for the same reason—namely, to make sure it is all there. To the extent that internal auditing is effective, however—and it is the examiner's duty to determine if it is—the examiner may withdraw from the audit field; this has been the recent historical trend. For a number of years, some supervisory authorities have conducted only balance-sheet examinations of very large banks. Such an examination assumes the correctness of the bank's statement, relying on elaborate and complete internal audit procedures that are carefully reviewed in the course of the examination.

National banking regulations and the laws of most states require that, in addition to the supervisory examination, the directors themselves make examinations of the bank. But few bank directors have the necessary competence to make an adequate examination.[17] Many of the very large banks in the country and an increasing number of large- and medium-sized ones engage the services of public accountants to assist them. The state of New Jersey now requires that the directors' examination be conducted by public accountants and that it include a direct verification of at least 20 percent of the loans and deposits.

In spite of the progress, a report made for the Subcommittee on Domestic Finance of the Committee on Banking and Currency of the House of Representatives stated that about 90 percent of the commercial banks do not use independent public accountants for unqualified independent audits—that is, audits unrestricted as to scope and time.[18] There are three principal reasons for the failure of more banks to use outside accountants to conduct comprehensive audits or directors' examinations: (a) banks that do not have well-developed internal audit programs are generally those that have less than $10 million in assets and that are

---

[16]Russell G. Rankin, *Safeguarding the Bank's Assets* (New York: New York State Bankers Association, 1953), p. 5.

> The prime objective of examination by Federal and state examiners is to evaluate the financial condition of the bank on a given date and to ascertain whether or not the management of the bank is conforming to the requirements of the applicable banking statutes and regulations. It is not to detect fraud.

[17]Stanley E. Shirk, "Are Your Directors' Examinations a Sham?", *Auditgram*, September 1960, pp. 20ff.

[18]Lester Pratt, "Tighter Fraud Control with Outside Audits," *The Bankers Magazine*, Summer 1966, p. 68.

managed by persons who mistakenly believe the cost of an outside audit to be too large; (b) directors tend to place too much reliance on the examinations of the supervisory authorities despite the protests of the supervisors that they do not audit; and (c) only relatively few of the thousands of smaller accounting firms working regularly in communities where small banks are located have sufficiently familiarized themselves with bank audit problems and procedures. A well-known bank accountant has said, "In a sense, banking is one of the last frontiers of the public accounting profession."[19] It is to be hoped this frontier will become more settled and populous, because the outside accountant can effectively complement and support the internal audit program and in small banks substitute for it. The certified public accountant in effect provides the answer to the not entirely facetious question, "Who audits the auditor?"

THE CONTROLLER-AUDITOR

It should be emphasized that the institution of controls and the review of systems and procedures are part of the function of preventing both crime and waste, and inefficiency is probably a more important thief of bank profits, day in and day out, than the bank officer or employee who makes the headlines for a defalcation.

The control and audit functions go hand in hand. The importance of auditing is not diminished by the recognition that in all probability the control portion of the dual function is in the long-run the more important. It requires more skill and talent and calls for more initiative and imagination to establish effective controls and efficient systems and procedures than it does simply to check to see that they are properly executed.

In large banks, as a matter of organization, the two related functions are often separated and placed under the direction of two people, the controller and the auditor. The controller is nearly always the more important, and incidentally the more highly paid, individual. He is usually a member of the senior management group responsible for financial planning, cost-accounting, budgeting, systems control, and methods analysis. The auditor frequently works under the direction of the controller, even though he should report his audit findings directly to the Board of Directors.

In medium-sized banks, the auditor and controller are likely to be

---

19Shirk, "Special Problems of Bank Audits," *op. cit.*, p. 42.

one person. He directs the work of the audit staff, reports their findings to the Board, and at the same time participates actively in the planning and accounting functions of the bank. In still smaller banks, the control function tends to be assigned to or assumed by the chief operating officer, who is probably designated as cashier or treasurer, and the auditor, if there is one, is a more or less dignified clerk with little more than audit duties to perform. In very small banks (assets under $5 million), auditing, if performed at all, is a part-time job. One of the officers or senior employees should be formally · designated "control officer" by the Board of Directors and made responsible for the audit program. Ideally, he can assign purely audit duties to an outside accountant who assists the directors with their annual examination and spends one or two days a month performing audit duties in the interim. The officers and employees of such smaller banks cannot readily be separated from their operational duties.

Over the years, there has been a good deal of debate on how large a bank should be for the appointment of a full-time auditor-controller to be justified. Supervisors consider the dividing line to lie somewhere between $15 million and $20 million in assets. In banks above this size, there is no question that a capable person can profitably spend full time supervising the audit work and reviewing and strengthening procedures. To the extent that the duties and responsibilities of the auditor-controller can be enlarged, the position can be justified in even smaller banks.

Cost accounting and budgeting, which are seldom applied in smaller banks, fit naturally into the area of the control officer's responsibility. In fact, almost any job that does not involve making original book entries or receiving and disbursing funds can be assigned to the individual who is responsible for audit and control. The maintenance of credit files, so often neglected in small banks, the review of outstanding loans, or the supervision of a program of rotational training are ideal tasks for such a person. The latter, particularly, can be worked in with the audit program, which in itself can be an effective training medium. Other possible duties for the control officer in a small bank could include watching the reserve position, preparing reports to directors and supervisory authorities, and conducting at least rudimentary market research studies of the community served by the bank.

Many of the duties suggested for the controller-auditor are far closer to the real problems of bank management than the ordinary platform work or operational responsibilities to which junior officers are usually assigned. This fact suggests that the position of auditor-controller is an ideal training ground for management succession, particularly in moderate-sized banks. The more duties that can be assigned to this position, the more a bank is justified in filling it with a person of more than average potential. Auditing duties, in themselves, require a more able person[20] than is frequently assigned to them. Often, in small- and medium-sized banks, management has reluctantly established the auditor's position under pressure from the supervisory authorities and has assigned to the task the least capable and effective person in the organization, for example, a long-service employee who does not meet the public well and who has little prospect for future promotion. This is a shortsighted policy. The position of controller-auditor is not a necessary evil; it is one of the most challenging opportunities in banking today.

---

[20]Walter Kennedy, *Bank Management* (Boston, Mass.: Bankers Publishing Company, 1958), p. 154.

An efficient bank auditor must be a versatile person. While he must be necessarily thoroughly versed in banking operations he must remain objective and refrain from engaging in activities which he will be called upon to check or evaluate. His close contact and association with all departments necessitates that he be a person of tact and skill in his human relations. The fact that the auditor's duties frequently require him to correct or criticize makes it important for him to maintain a constructive attitude and not become a chronic fault-finder. The auditor must be articulate and able to express himself both orally and in writing in a clear and concise manner.

15

PERSONNEL POLICIES

Many of the preceding chapters have emphasized the management of bank assets and liabilities through the formulation and implementation of constructive policies. The present chapter invades a field outside the usual concepts of banking theory but nonetheless vital to successful bank operations. It is trite but true that people are the most important asset of any organization—as well as the most difficult to manage. Perhaps the reason is that the managers themselves are subject to all the vagaries and instabilities of human nature.

What follows is far from a complete treatise on personnel management, which is a field in its own right with its own extensive literature. Indeed, no more will be attempted here than a brief summary of the authors' observations on personnel policy at work in commercial banks, with special emphasis on the problems most frequently found in actual banking situations.

Like other policies, personnel policies should be directed toward well-defined objectives and guided by clearly understood principles. Those responsible for policy should at least know of the various tools and organizational arrangements available for the implementation of policy. Bank directors and top management need not be personnel experts, but they should be acutely aware of the fact that the human relationships that in the aggregate produce a high level of morale seldom simply take care of themselves. Human relationships require direction, encouragement, and understanding. To see that these are provided is the role of the policy maker.

MANAGEMENT OBJECTIVES

The primary objective of personnel policy is to get jobs done effectively, economically, and with as little friction as possible. The job of commercial banks is, broadly speaking, to render banking services to the community and to manage the bank's assets in the best interests of the stockholders. To accomplish these objectives, a number of people, at different levels of skill and talent, must work together under effective leadership. People are the instruments, not the objects, of policy. Desired results—the long-range objectives of policy—are produced through people, not upon them. In other words, the aim of personnel policy is not to make people happy but to get the job accomplished by having people do what you want, the way you want, because they want to do it. Job satisfaction is fine for the individual, but from management's viewpoint it is only a means to an end—the most effective performance of the bank as a whole.

A second and closely related objective is to devise better ways to perform banking operations and new and better services to render to the community. For the accomplishment of this aim, the inventiveness and imagination of people must be stimulated. Personnel policies should therefore encourage rather than stifle initiative.

A third major objective is to train and develop successor management, a task that many small banks have woefully neglected and that even large banks find difficult to accomplish.

To bring these broad and generally recognized aims to fruition requires an awareness of some fundamental principles of personnel management, an organization to apply them effectively, and a knowledge of some of the tools or instruments that will help attain the desired goals.

MANAGEMENT PRINCIPLES

A few basic concepts underlie effective personnel administration. The leader in banking, as elsewhere, follows them almost intuitively. It will be useful, nevertheless, to make them explicit—to understand how and why they are effective.

The first of these principles is clear definition of duties and responsibilities throughout the organization. Such definition in effect constitutes the organizational structure of the bank itself. Each officer's responsibilities should be clearly defined. Even the lowest clerk is entitled to know as exactly as possible what is expected of him. Job descriptions and job evaluations are the tools that put this principle into operation.

Somewhat more elusive is the principle of good communications. The willingness, the ability, in fact the determination to maintain mutual understanding throughout the organization is a basic prerequisite of success. Management's failure to communicate adequately and to issue clear, concise instructions defining objectives in ways that all can understand probably leads to more wasted effort and individual frustration than any other factor in bank operations. The lack of adequate channels of communication upward can stifle initiative, keep new ideas long buried, and produce pressures of discontent that are completely destructive to morale.

A third general principle involves the quality of leadership itself. In the judgment and selection of people for promotion, the man himself is more important than his knowledge or skill. The ability to inspire others to do their best is the essential talent of management at all levels. It is a function of the true leader's whole personality, often characterized by an objective awareness of his own limitations coupled with a compassionate knowledge of the strengths and weaknesses of others.

The need to find this talent in top management underlies the modern emphasis on a broad training for executives. Many succesful bankers have been men with a broad grasp of history, an acute awareness of their community responsibilities, and diversified interests in the fields of art, politics, or community planning—men who have had a philosophy of banking as well as the necessary technical knowledge. Some have been men who came into banking from other fields to outperform men who had spent all their lives in banks. By bringing imagination and a broad approach to banking problems, the outsider can sometimes strip away the moss of routine and custom to uncover new and vital possibilities.

PERSONNEL ORGANIZATION

The organizational structure needed to put these principles into effective operation starts with the Board of Directors. It is customary in banks of all sizes for the directors to appoint or approve the appointment of officers and to establish levels of compensation for both officers and employees. Directors also authorize pension plans, bonuses, and other fringe benefits. Too often, regrettably, directors are not interested in most other aspects of personnel administration. They make little formal effort to satisfy themselves that sound and effective personnel programs are being carried out—if, indeed, they are even aware that such programs exist. For this reason it may be helpful, particularly in smaller banks, if the directors designate a Directors' Personnel Committee. At least a few specially interested directors should be aware of the ways in which the bank's policies are being implemented and of the progress being made in the development of future officer potential. Directors should state the broad aims of personnel policy and raise serious questions if sound policies are not being followed and progressive programs are not being utilized to full advantage.

The responsibility for the execution of policy rests with the bank's top management. Top management should keep the board informed and interested on the one hand and set the example of effective leadership on the other. The "boss" sets the pattern, good or bad. No matter how great his talents for analyzing credit or attracting new business, the bank's operations will suffer if a high-level executive officer cannot provide effective, sympathetic, and dynamic leadership to his entire staff.

In larger banks, the top executive officers will have the assistance of a personnel officer and his staff. Many of the day-to-day responsibilities of policy execution and record-keeping can be readily delegated to staff officers. But true leadership can never be delegated. It can be inspired in others and thereby passed down through the ranks of the largest organization, but it is always personal. It is a matter of spirit rather than program or policy and, as such, permeates every echelon of a well-run organization.

Effective leadership will of course seek the widest practical participation of others in the formulation and carrying out of constructive policies and practices. Delegation of authority, the effective use of committees, and the assignment of responsibility for directing and evaluating the work of others will be parts of an effective personnel administration.

THE TOOLS OF PERSONNEL MANAGEMENT

The professional personnel officer will find little that is new in this discussion. The ideas expressed here are used currently in progressive banks and other industries, have been discussed in hundreds of articles in personnel journals, and are stressed in all the various banking schools. Nevertheless, they are still too seldom found in actual use, particularly in the small- and medium-sized banks that have not developed a professional approach to personnel problems.

The junior officer goes to school, but the policy maker needs to know at least enough to encourage, if not insist upon, the application of the new knowledge. Those who lecture to bank officers are told repeatedly, "All that you say is true, but you should tell it to my boss."

Putting most of the proven tools of sound personnel administration into effect does not require a professional personnel officer. It does require policy makers to recognize that people are a vital ingredient of a smoothly functioning organization. That viewpoint provides focus for the remainder of this chapter, which considers some of the basic instruments of personnel administration.

Recruiting

The standards set when a bank first selects its employees will largely determine the caliber of the staff in the future. Bankers have too frequently said, "We cannot afford to compete for the best people in the community." If banks are to be successful, they cannot afford to do less.

Recently, the president of a sizable bank related his difficulty in bringing potential officers into the bank. He had urged the recruitment of several young MBA's at competitive salaries. The most influential director, a substantial stockholder and owner of a local manufacturing business, adamantly stated, "We can hire plenty of good young boys in our business for a substantially lower salary."

This director, like many others, was unaware of the first rule of good recruiting, to know what one is hiring the person for. There is obviously no point in hiring MBA's to be tellers and bookkeepers when one is simply looking for reasonably intelligent and personable people who will be content to work, for a while at least, in routine positions. On the other hand, if there is a known need for officer replacements in five or ten years, it behooves management to look for prospective employees who are believed at the outset to have officer potential because of their education, aptitude, interest, or previous experience. It is important to take the time to select the best prospects available for every level, bookkeeper to officer candidate. A poor selection is always a waste of time and money.

The best people rarely come to the bank of their own accord. Successful banks seek out the more talented prospective employees. For clerical personnel, they maintain close relationships with guidance directorss of local high schools and junior colleges; they encourage employees to bring in their friends; they see to it that school children have opportunities to visit the bank and hear about some of the advantages of working there.

In recruiting for more responsible posts, many larger banks recruit at the outstanding colleges in their area or throughout the country,[1] have summer employment programs to allow college students to see the chal-

---

[1] In the early postwar years, banks obtained the reputation of offering low-paying and nonchallenging jobs. Bankers should stress at every opportunity that most banks are now offering competitive pay, challenging jobs, and great opportunities for advancement.

lenges of banking careers, and are always alert for able and interested people employed at other banks or in other fields. Although smaller banks obviously cannot recruit extensively, they must not ignore recruiting for responsible positions. Study after study has stressed that the greatest problem in smaller banks is management succession.[2] Enlightened smaller banks often recruit for responsible positions by carefully judging people who visit them (such as the bank examiners), closely following the college careers of local young people who may be interested in finance, and developing one or two meaningful summer positions for such interested students. Good recruiting requires a policy of actively seeking the people with the specific qualities that the bank needs without counting the cost too closely. It is difficult to pay too much for quality personnel.

Training

The newly hired employee generally starts as a clean slate on which nothing has yet been written. His attitudes toward the bank and the job will be shaped by his first few weeks of experience. How quickly will he be made to feel a part of the organization? In the process of learning the first few simple tasks, will he grasp the relationship between what he is doing and the work of the department or the bank as a whole? New employees have a fundamental need for a broad idea of their jobs— in short, for orientation.

Many bankers complain that the young people they hire do not seem interested in learning about banking. These young people probably will not be interested unless an opportunity to learn is provided for them and unless someone in the bank is willing to instruct them. A few will insist on learning, but most need patient teaching. Too frequently, the person selected to train new employees is someone whom the bank plans or expects to replace, perhaps a girl who is leaving to get married and is no longer interested in the bank. Similarly, a junior clerk who is not very sure about his own job may be asked to provide the orientation for newcomers. Good training is an art, if not a science, and should be entrusted only to those within an organization who have an aptitude for it or who have received special training in the instruction of others.

Nor should training cease just because a person has learned a job well. Whether for a clerical position or an assignment of considerable responsibility, training should be a continuing process. The most valuable

---

[2]Examples include Eliott L. Atamian, "Strategies for Success in the Seventies for Small Commercial Banks," *Business Topics*, Vol. 18, No. 2, Winter 1970, pp. 49–55, and Donald P. Jacobs, *Evaluation of the Management Succession Problem in the Commercial Banking Industry*, Committee on Banking and Currency, HR 88th Congress (Washington, D. C.: Government Printing Office, 1964).

people in banks are those who can take over any one of a number of tasks or responsibilities and do them well.

Unfortunately, in some banks the better a person knows and does one job, the less likely he is to have an opportunity to learn another. After a time, he reduces the job to a routine and either becomes incapable of change or leaves to seek change and new knowledge elsewhere. Training in new areas of work is a challenge to the individual and provides a flexibility of staff that is an essential ingredient of an efficient organization. Belief in this principle, which can be readily demonstrated in practice, calls for job rotation and continued training. At one bank with which the authors are acquainted, all clerks are taught most functional jobs in the bank within the first eighteen months of their employment, and all are regularly rotated so that they each spend a few weeks in every assignment. Knowledge and usefulness are thus enhanced, boredom is reduced, and the result is a job done better by fewer people at substantially lower cost in the long run.

Good training also requires that a reasonable level of responsibility be assigned to the employee in the first few weeks of his new assignment. Prolonged training without any responsibility often results in boredom and poor response to training. The responsibilities should be in line with the employee's training and previous experience. For a recent graduate from high school, the responsibility for achieving a daily balance may be a sufficient challenge. On the other hand, at least one very large bank allows MBA's to make loans up to two hundred thousand dollars without prior approval after only a couple of months of employment. The major emphasis in both cases is to challenge the employees so that they will continue to be interested in banking and will realize the need for continued training as their responsibilities become greater.

Job Description and Evaluation

Job descriptions and job evaluations are standard tools of personnel administration. They are widely used by large banks and can be adapted to even the smallest.[3] A written description of each job details what is expected of any person in that particular capacity. The evaluation of that position in relation to other jobs in the bank helps assure each individual of fair and comparable treatment. Job descriptions and evaluations are most likely to be accepted and effective if formulated with the help of those who hold the jobs in question. A job evaluation committee on which responsible employees serve in rotation will not only enhance

---

[3]See *How to Set Up a Salary Program in the Smaller Banks* (Washington: American Bankers Association).

acceptance of the program but provide valuable management training to the participants as well. A constant review of position descriptions and evaluations will allow prompt adjustment to changing circumstances. Care should be taken that a job description and evaluation program does not result in unnecessary rigidities. A program that is too strict may reinforce the hierarchy system that is already too prevalent in banking.

Performance Review

The primary value of the job description and evaluation program is to serve as the basis for a review of the individual's performance in the job. Each employee must understand what is expected of him if an appraisal of his performance is to have any validity. Working in a bank or any other organization and not having one's progress periodically evaluated and made a matter of record is like playing a game without keeping score. This obvious fact, attested to by all who have worked intelligently in the field of personnel administration, is nevertheless frequently ignored in daily banking practice because other things seem more important at the moment, because no one really likes to point out other people's shortcomings—in brief, because it is not made a matter of definite policy. Too few bank officers even take the time to mention the good points of their assistants' performance! Yet nothing will do more to strengthen an organization or to improve the performance of the people in it than a periodic, full, and frank discussion of objectives and the accomplishments of each individual in each and every job.

To be effective, performance review must start at the top, the chief executive officer setting the example by periodically reviewing with them the performance of the other officers. Only then can top management expect the junior officers to do the same with the department heads and the department heads to conscientiously review the performance of the employees working under their direction.

Adequate credit should be given for the ability of an individual to perform more than one task when called upon to do so. Each new job learned under a rotational training program should improve the individual's performance rating. The performance review program needs to be fairly formal. The individual should be appraised in accord with mutually accepted standards, and appraisals should be written on standard forms or along standardized patterns. Off-the-cuff evaluations are generally carelessly phrased and frequently evoke emotional responses that tend to defeat the purposes of a careful and objective appraisal. Both the appraisal and discussion of it with the individual should be made a matter of record, and each employee who is not satisfied with his appraisal should have easy and regular access to a higher authority for further review. The objective in all such procedures is to help the individual employee help himself.

Salary Administration

The principal criteria for a well-considered salary policy are, first, the relationship of the bank's salary scale to salaries paid for comparable jobs in the community and the industry and, second, the relationship of the salary paid to one person to that paid to others for jobs of comparable difficulty within the bank. Both elements are affected by the fact (often lost sight of) that salaries, in the long run, are set in a competitive market for talent.

Compensation, of course, encompasses more than salary. Working conditions, job security, prestige, and opportunity for advancement all enter into the competitive package. Despite opportunities to earn higher wages elsewhere, many fine employees stay in banks because of shorter hours or better working conditions or simply because their jobs are interesting. However, banks cannot rely too blindly or heavily on these or other fringe benefits. The only sure test of the adequacy of a bank's scale of compensation is the caliber of officers and employees it keeps. The objective of salary policy is to insure that, at whatever cost, the bank maintains a competent and enthusiastic staff.

It has been repeatedly demonstrated by those who pursue such a policy that competent people at almost any price are less costly in the long run than the incompetent (or even the mediocre), because they produce more. In short, the ancient maxim that one gets pretty much what one pays for applies aptly to the policy decisions regarding a bank's salary scale. The converse applies just as aptly to salary decisions within the bank. One should pay for what he has! This means simply that a bank should pay well for merit, withhold increases in the case of mediocrity, and promptly dispose of those who do not measure up to standard. Even within the framework of a job evaluation plan, salary should be related to performance, not solely to length of service or to what someone else may earn.

Logical and simple as these assertions may sound, salary administration too seldom follows them. Some sort of paralysis seems to grip management at the thought of giving an unusually large increase to a truly outstanding employee, and a comparable fear makes management reluctant to pass by the well-meaning but inept. The result is likely to be a program of regular increments that makes too little distinction between the star performer and the weaker employee. Carried on long enough, such a policy results in a preponderance of weaker employees and higher aggregate costs for salaries of too many low-paid and inefficient people. The star performer, meanwhile, will have attained his proper level by finding a job in another bank or business. The same results are likely if one sticks to a rigid salary schedule in hiring new employees. A bank that continually refuses to pay the competitive market rate for the level of skill and training it desires will end up with employees and officers of lower caliber.

In general, banks provide fringe benefits comparable to or better than those offered in other industries. Pension plans, hospitalization, and group life insurance are the rule except in the smallest banks. In addition, some banks pay cash bonuses of a flat percentage of salary. Bonuses are appropriate in many situations; however, they are inappropriate if the directors persuade themselves that by this means they can compensate their officers and employees more adequately without increasing salaries. In theory, the bonus can be discontinued if the bank's earnings decline. In practice, the employee measures his total compensation, including bonus and fringe benefits, against what he might earn elsewhere. The discontinuation of a bonus has an effect no less depressing than that of a general cut in salaries.

A more effective incentive is a well-designed profit-sharing plan with benefits that vary from year to year in direct proportion to the financial success of the bank's operations. As long as clerical salaries are adequate, profit-sharing is probably most effective when participation is limited to those persons who have sufficient responsibility to make a true management contribution to the bank's success.

Stock options have from time to time been used by some banks. They are particularly advantageous for the higher-salaried officers because of their tax advantage (profits from sale are treated as capital gains), but these advantages were materially reduced by the Tax Reform Act of 1969. Most banks that have issued options in the past have become somewhat disillusioned and are searching for other ways, such as deferred salary arrangements, to provide tax benefits to their highest-salaried officer.

Communications

A good deal of verbal interchange takes place in every bank each day, but not all of it is necessarily effective communication. Orders are given and requests made that are not clearly understood because the person giving them does not take time to find out whether he has made himself clear or whether the person to whom a task has been assigned understands the objectives. Misunderstanding resulting from faulty communication is without doubt one of the major sources of wasted time and effort in banks.

Communication is a two-way street. The competent officer discusses rather than directs; he listens as well as instructs. The importance of this basic concept can perhaps best be illustrated by the true story of a bank president who had been listening to a discussion of communications. He suddenly got the point and exclaimed, "You know, I've been in this business for thirty years, and I have just realized that every time I call my cashier into my office I say, 'Joe, do this,' 'Joe, this is what I want,' and then I wonder why the stupid dolt doesn't have any initiative."

It cannot be stressed too often that teamwork—the essential ingredient of success in business—depends on mutual understandings, on letting people know what the bank's objectives are, and on seeking and listening to their suggestions. Good communication starts with the written policies adopted by the directors or senior management and should run all the way down the line in the form of clear and understandable instructions related to known and agreed upon objectives.

The major portion of the communication necessary for the day-to-day operations of a bank consists of simple person-to-person conversations. More complex ideas, however, gain clarity if they are put in writing. The ability to write clearly is an invaluable management talent that needs constant practice and development.

One of the most effective of all communications media is the staff meeting. Essentially, it is an extension of the conversational or discussion technique but embraces a larger segment of the organization. Such meetings are regular features of efficiently operated banks and take a wide variety of forms, ranging from daily or weekly officers' meetings to annual weekend conferences. The size of the bank and the number of people involved of course tend to shape the specific program. In very small banks, the entire day's operations are virtually a continuous staff meeting. The need to maintain the same kind of group effort makes a more formal program essential for larger organizations.

Many large banks have employees' handbooks and publish employee newspapers that aim to keep employees informed of the bank's (and fellow employees') activities. These are only a few of the wide variety of communications media available.

Executive Training and Development

The shortage of successor management, particularly in the smaller banks, has already been pointed out. The need is not just for more people to replace present bank officers and to staff a growing banking system but also for improvement in the quality of all bank officers. Banking itself is becoming increasingly complex. New forms of lending, the changing banking structure, electronic data-processing, national and international problems unknown to the banker of yesterday, all require a higher degree of talent and knowledge than the simple common sense that largely sufficed in the past. At least a dozen banking schools throughout the country are attempting to remedy the situation through banker education, but the problem still exists.[4]

In the light of these banking schools and all the available literature on this vital subject, it can only be suggested here that perhaps too much emphasis has been placed on training and too little on development. Training may increase the knowledge and skills of an individual, but it seldom turns him into a true executive—a person with high qualities of leadership, constructive imagination, and a desire to assume responsibility. An executive makes effective decisions and gets tasks accomplished through the organized efforts of others. Training can improve management techniques; it can help people make better decisions; but training alone will seldom result in a person *wanting* to make decisions.

Development, on the other hand, has a different connotation; it is the growth of the inner man and his motivation. Some understanding of the nature of this growth and a conscientious effort to foster it in each individual are necessary if the tremendous amount of training to which well-meaning bank directors and top management have subjected their junior officers is to be productive. The bank director interested in this problem and especially the senior officers seeking to develop their successors need to know something of psychology as well as the techniques of banking.

The following statement by an industrial psychologist presents the essential concepts:

> First we believe that we must have a basic philosophy of personal improvements, a philosophy which says, by developing the people who comprise our organization we develop our organization. Secondly, we believe that all development is *man* development. That is, each man submits a separate and unique development problem. Three, we believe that development or growth must come from within each individual, that he must want to change and, of course, change or develop purposefully. Four, we believe that each man's boss creates a climate which either fosters or hampers personal development. Finally, we believe that action is the thing, not specifically placement charts, not lists of promising young men, not detailed psychological procedures. By action, we mean developmental action and planning with each individual concerned.[5]

---

[4] The American Bankers Association in Washington, D.C., has published several manuals and pamphlets describing the various banking schools throughout the country.

[5] Joseph Trickett, *Journal of American Society of Training Directors*. Vol. 12, No. 8, August 1958.

Bank directors and senior officers seeking to develop successor management cannot rely on banking schools and other training devices alone. At the best, such training can only provide opportunity and encouragement to the individual—opportunity to use and develop his talents and encouragement to assume responsibility for himself. Often the most effective form of counseling between senior and junior management is essentially a parental-type relationship in which the senior manager takes personal pride in the accomplishments of his subordinate.

The directors and senior management in a bank should see to it that the climate of the bank is favorable for the growth and development of potential executives. They can insist, for example, that junior officers occasionally attend top-level meetings or make reports to the directors and senior management. They can insist on being apprised regularly of the progress of the bank's executive development programs. In smaller banks, they can personally explore the minds and talents of the junior officers and lend encouragement to their assumption of responsibility. At the very least, they can assure themselves that a few managers are not abrogating all decision-making to themselves and thus effectively stifling the exercise of initiative.[6]

RECENT INNOVATIONS IN PERSONNEL ADMINISTRATION

Management by objectives is one of many recent developments in personnel administration. This system, which has been used successfully in industrial firms and banks, calls for the superior and subordinate manager of an organization to jointly identify its common goals, define each individual's major areas of responsibility in terms of the results expected of him, and use these measures as guides in operating the unit and assessing the contribution of each of its members. The assessments are generally made separately by each manager and his superior; then the two sit down together to compare notes.[7] Most firms using the system of management by objectives have found that it generally results in higher goals, better motivation, and more critical appraisals of performance.

Job design for motivation is another personnel approach that has been increasingly emphasized in recent years. Job content, methods, and

---

[6]For more detailed discussions of executive development, see Ralph C. Davis, "Development of a Bank Management Philosophy," *The Bankers Magazine*, Winter 1967, pp. 56–66, and Samuel S. Dubin, "Bridging the Educational Gap in Banking," *The Bankers Magazine*, Winter 1969, pp. 102–5.

[7]For a thorough description, see George Odiorne, *Management by Objectives* (New York: Pitman Publishing Co., 1965).

relationships are structured not only to satisfy technological and organizational requirements but also to accommodate human needs for meaningful and self-fulfilling work. Job design for motivation is rooted in the behavioral sciences. Jobs are being designed to fit the people who hold them in the hope that greater employee motivation (which is essential to higher productivity) will result. The methods of job design for motivation include job enlargement—assigning several related tasks to an employee who previously performed a single one; work simplification—analyzing the job by steps to eliminate unnecessary duplication and to combine logical sequences; job enrichment—increasing the difficulty of the basic task to demand more of the employee's capabilities; plan-do-control—adding planning and control to the employee's actual performance of the job; and job rotation (discussed earlier).[8] Banks and other firms using job design for motivation report that it has stimulated widespread and growing interest among managers and appears to lead to increased productivity.[9]

Sensitivity training and/or organizational development programs have been used to aid in the broad development of top executive talent and teamwork. The primary aim of sensitivity training is to enable the individual to understand and evaluate himself so that he will work better with others. Organizational development or organizational renewal programs tend to be more problem centered and aim to enhance the ability of managers to work together to achieve a common goal.

Also deserving mention because of recent emphasis is the so-called affirmative action program for commercial banks, a name applied to various means that are designed to eliminate the various forms of employment discrimination.[10] Many banks that were leaders in providing equal employment opportunities have gone beyond the requirements of the law and have begun positive actions, such as assistance in the establishment of training institutions for minorities.

Finally, several banks have recently moved to the four-day work week. Although there is some variation in four-day plans, they typically allocate the total hours of a normal work week over four days instead of five. The primary reason cited for the four-day week is that it offers employees more leisure time, which in turn leads to improved morale

---

8For a thorough description, see Harold M. F. Rush, *Job Design for Motivation* (New York: The Conference Board, 1971).

9*Ibid*, pp. 32–78.

10The affirmative action program had its origin in the following: Equal Pay Act of 1963, Civil Rights Act of 1964, Presidential Executive Orders Numbers 1141, 11246, and 11375, and Age Discrimination in Employment Act, 1967. The American Bankers Association in Washington, D.C. has brochures describing several possible programs designed to lead to equal employment opportunities in banking.

and reduced absenteeism. The results appear to have been positive so far. Banks going to the four-day week believe that it makes bank work more interesting and attractive, because each employee has a broader variety of responsibilities. Employees who were reluctant to share their responsibilities with others have had to do so in order to be off three days a week. The opportunity to replace one another and the training that makes it possible have made the duties of most employees less routine. These advantages, accompanied by the attraction of three days off a week, have tended to reduce employee turnover.[11] Because it will probably be difficult for a bank to change its movement to a four-day work week, a bank should carefully evaluate the results of such plans in other banks in light of its own situation before making the shift.

---

[11]"Bank Holding Firm Tries Four-Day Week," *St. Louis Post-Dispatch*, Sunday, August 1, 1971, p. 5.

16

MARKETING
AND COMMUNITY RELATIONS

Although seldom viewed in this manner, marketing and community relations programs are appropriate and in fact essential means by which a bank may pursue its purpose of supplying needed financial services to its community at a profit to itself. This chapter sketches the basic marketing concept and activities in banking and then presents a constructive approach to fostering good community relations—an activity that enables a bank's marketing policies to take root and grow.

THE MARKETING CONCEPT IN BANKING

During the 1950s, a substantial portion of American business began to pay homage to the "marketing concept," a philosophy that advocates consumer-oriented organizations and views consumers as the lifeblood of a business. General acceptance of this concept advanced the status of marketing in many types of enterprises. During this same period, banks, while still the largest financial intermediary, were declining in relation to most other financial institutions.

These two movements influenced many bank directors and managers to get out and sell their products (financial services). The more foresighted bankers realized that a broader approach was needed. For example, banks needed to find what product consumers wanted. Although in some banks marketing remained only a new name for business development or public relations, for others marketing and the so-called marketing concept represented a fresh and essential viewpoint.

Marketing can be defined as the creation and delivery of consumer-satisfying products (goods or services) at a profit to the bank. The three elements of this formal definition deserve separate comment. First, the creation of new products is as important an aspect of bank marketing as the delivery of existing services. Second, bank marketing must be consumer oriented. It is critical that consumer needs and wants be fulfilled by the product the bank offers. For example, a bank should not be selling the idea of saving for a new car if most customers want the satisfaction of immediate ownership and are willing to pay for it through time payment plans (at banks or other financial intermediaries). Third, the bank's equity capital is supplied by owners whose return is measured primarily by the profits that the bank earns. This is not to say that banks should ignore serious community problems because they are not immediately profitable to the bank. The bank is a member of its community, and at least part of the bank's long-run success will depend on the growth and vibrance of that community.

The starting point for bank marketing is the realization that marketing is not just an activity, although it encompasses many activities; it is also a point of view that should permeate all banking activities. Bank directors and management should recognize that most decisions in the operation of the bank must be made in the light of customer needs and preferences. Once this concept is accepted throughout the bank, the activities necessary to accomplish this objective seem to develop normally. Management must then blend these activities, especially in the areas of:

1. Identification of consumer wants and needs through marketing research
2. Development and management of products fulfilling the identified consumer wants and needs
3. Promotion of the products developed for customers
4. Establishment and maintenance of meaningful relationships with the community and other special groups
5. Coordination of marketing as an integral part of most banking activities

MARKETING RESEARCH

Marketing policies and decisions should be made not in a vacuum but with an awareness of competition, of economic conditions, and—above all—of bank customers. *Marketing research* has been defined as "the gathering, recording, and analyzing of all facts about problems relating to the transfer and sale of goods and services from producer to consumer."[1] Marketing research should not replace the element of experience and judgment in decision making, but it can add a new dimension by providing facts to supplement experience and judgment. That a bank should know its customers, their needs, and their prospects seems obvious, but some banks, which systematically attempted in recent years to find out something about the people they serve, have learned how little they previously knew.

Bank officers and directors have always known a great deal about their customers, of course. If the directors are representative business and professional people, they will be in close touch with the community's economic, political, and social life. Daily contacts with the bank's customers can yield a fruitful harvest of knowledge if those relationships are sympathetic and designed to serve the customer. Nevertheless, a more formal and systematic program of marketing research will develop facts about present customers and potential opportunities of which many banks are only partially aware.[2]

There are two basic types of formal marketing research: secondary and survey research. Secondary research is the analysis of previously available data, either published externally or obtainable from internal records. Such research is usually relatively inexpensive. Published secondary data can generally be gathered rather rapidly, but internal data may take a long time to be assembled in a usable form.[3] On the other hand, it is often difficult to find secondary data appropriate for the specific need or problem. Survey research includes not only analysis but also the generation of data. This type of research tends to be slower and more expensive but can be fitted to meet a specific problem or need.

The American Bankers Association has prepared a series of booklets on the technical aspects of marketing research. The first of these sets forth the following objectives of a marketing research program:

> This first phase (customer analysis) involving the analysis of internal records, will place management in a position to take succeeding steps toward the full utilization of market research.

---

[1]Luther H. Hodges, Jr., and Rollie Tillman, Jr., *Bank Marketing: Text and Cases* (Reading, Mass.: Addison-Wesley Publ. Co., 1968), p. 231.

[2]For further discussion of this point, see Elisha Slayberg, "Why Won't Bank Management Exploit Marketing Research?" *Banking*, 61, March 1969, pp. 69–71.

[3]Internal secondary data have usually been developed for or generated out of operational needs. However, if marketing specialists are given a voice at the time that internal systems and reports are being set up, then the data are usually in a usable form, and market research is enhanced.

When an internal research program is coupled with an economic analysis of the trade area, management can chart the future of the bank, thus avoiding the nonproductive effort which often results when operations are on a day-to-day basis.

To supplement the facts gathered from internal records and trade area analysis, the bank can study the attitudes of its customers and then plan the most effective advertising, customer and community relations program.[4]

Although there is not space here for a discussion of the specific techniques of marketing research, the kind of information a progressive bank needs may be indicated by some of the questions marketing research can answer.

1. Who uses the bank's various services? What are their age, sex, and economic status?
2. To what extent do large or small accounts dominate the bank's business?
3. From which geographic, ethnic, or occupational segments of the bank's trade area do its customers come? Are any sections or groups not presently using the bank's facilities?
4. What are the community's land resources? How are they zoned? Are there prospects for greater utilization?
5. What are the volume and composition of the labor force? To what extent is it fully employed?
6. Who supplies competing financial services? How has the bank been faring in competition with them?
7. How do the bank's customers evaluate its services? What are their reasons for using them?

Relatively few banks could supply accurate or definitive answers, although questions of this sort might be asked by any intelligent new director or senior manager. The value of being able to answer such questions seems self-evident; only this kind of knowledge can provide an effective guide to a productive marketing program.

Marketing research can be used just as effectively by small banks as by larger ones. In some respects, the smaller the trade area served, the more easily the bank can know it well.[5] Banks of all sizes should consider the use of outside professional services. Many banks lack the

---

[4]American Bankers Association, Country Bank Operations Committee and Research Committee, *Customer Analysis,* ABA Market Research Series Number 1 (Washington: The American Bankers Association, 1961).

[5]Five suggested projects that demonstrate that profitable marketing research is usually well within the reach and resources of small banks are discussed in Jeffrey L. Pope, "Five Market Research Projects for the Small Banker," *Banking,* 62, January 1970, pp. 65–67.

"in house" talent to handle this unfamiliar area. Even if such talent is available within the bank, a skilled outsider may bring a fresh viewpoint and a professional objectivity to marketing research. The cost will often be lower than for doing the same job internally, because a good outsider should know how to survey needs, where to obtain relevant data, what analytical techniques to apply, and how to make projects run more smoothly.[6]

PRODUCT DEVELOPMENT AND MANAGEMENT

Once its customer's wants and needs are identified (often through marketing research), a bank should develop and manage its products to fulfill these desires. Although there are some limitations on the product line of every bank—imposed by size, location, regulations, managerial capabilities, and so on—a too narrow conception of what products they can provide has been the major shortcoming of most banks. Many banks have said in effect that their products are making loans and accepting deposits. In the authors' opinion, banking products should be viewed as customer satisfactions, and the products of banking should include rendering (at a profit to the bank) all the financial services the customer can use. Any banker who is unaware of the danger of defining the bank's product too narrowly should read Levitt's classic article, "Marketing Myopia."[7]

Emphasis on broad product orientation in bank marketing has been rewarding for the banks willing to move in this direction. For example, Carroll states:

> Experience to date would suggest that bank marketing organizations that have achieved only a low level of success, or that have failed outright, have frequently been departments that have been content to offer the traditional services of marketing. They have viewed their role as one of assuring that the bank had a competent advertising program, that its public relations endeavors were suitably noncontroversial, and that its inventory of published marketing data was complete and in a form that made it usable in speeches and quarterly reports. As exaggerated as that simplistic image may sound, there are still a large number of marketing organizations that would have to admit that the description fits uncomfortably but well.
>
> By way of contrast, the more successful bank marketing depart-

---

[6]L. A. Capaldini, "Management Consultants in Bank Marketing," *Bankers Magazine,* 153, Winter 1970, pp. 50–56.

[7]Theodore Levitt, "Marketing Myopia," *Harvard Business Review,* 38, July-August 1960, pp. 45–56.

ments have resisted this narrow definition of their role and have embarked upon rather energetic new product programs. These marketing organizations were expected to look at the product line and decide what changes were necessary and appropriate. Undoubtedly, this forthrightness had its unpleasantness in the beginning; after all, bank management had always decided what services would be offered and under what conditions. Those marketers without adequate conviction doubtless subsided at this juncture or at least after one further confrontation with bank management. Those that are today considered the successes of bank marketing persisted and ultimately had their way. They were permitted initially to suggest changes in banking services (products) and then, with some record of success, to pass upon any and all changes, even those which came from such supposedly esoteric places as trust and investment.[8]

Product development and management strategies may be divided into two groups. First, there are those that relate to each individual product—its means of identification, product quality and features, price, and so on. Second, for its whole line of products, the bank must form strategies covering the assortment of products, the essential supporting services, hours of business, and bank location and layout. Some of the basic policy aspects of bank product development and management for both groups are briefly described in the following paragraphs.[9]

Specific Product Strategies

Strategies that have proved useful for nonbanking firms include market segmentation and product differentiation. Market segmentation is the isolation of certain sectors of the total market and the creation of new products so uniquely designed for this sector that no immediate competition exists. This strategy may prove profitable for all banks in competition with other financial institutions. One problem with such a strategy for an individual bank is the speed with which other banks can copy most new banking products. Market segmentation also tends to limit a bank's potential market; therefore, the bank must make sure that the market segment is large enough to be worthy of exploitation.

The problems associated with market segmentation have encouraged many banks to develop a marketing strategy of product differentiation—in other words, to create a competitive image or psychological difference for their products. Often the purpose is to appeal to different segments

---

[8]Daniel T. Carroll, "Ten Commandments for Bank Marketing," *Bankers Magazine*, 153, Autumn 1970, pp. 74–80.

[9]These basic aspects were adopted from Hodges and Tillman, *Bank Marketing: Text and Cases, op. cit.*, pp. 1–301, and are discussed in greater detail there.

of the market with an essentially standardized product. Clearly, such product differentiation is a difficult task, and heavier-than-usual advertising and promotional expenditures are often required for the effective establishment of an aura or sense of difference.

Many banks have adopted a combination of these strategies for product development and management. They strive to develop new products to fill customers' wants in some segment of the market, to match their competition's new product when it appears desirable to do so, and to differentiate their products in the eyes of their customers.

New Products

Commercial banks must develop new financial services in order to compete successfully with other financial institutions. Ideas for new banking products may just happen, but they will happen more often if careful study of customers and sensitivity to potential needs are cultivated among all bank employees. Product ideas can come from customers, directors, employees, competing banks, other financial institutions, or trade magazines. Once the ideas are obtained, the development and selection process must start. As many as fifty to one hundred new product ideas may yield only one banking product that will ultimately be marketed successfully.

Seven stages that can lead from the initial idea to an acceptable product were suggested by the information systems expert at a bank marketing conference. In condensed form these stages were:

1. Screening—selecting pertinent and feasible ideas
2. Collecting sample evidence—initial marketing research on potential demands, competition, and so on
3. Devising sample systems—developing technical processes for delivering the product (financial service) to the customers
4. Analyzing benefits and costs—costing-out the proposed new products at various levels, with pricing estimates to show expected income and profits
5. Evaluating the market place—surveying customer reactions to the proposed product
6. Compiling results—reviewing and studying all information regarding the new product.
7. Bringing the new product to the market (if it passes the tests of market trial and profit analysis) [10]

---

[10]Adopted from Arthur S. Krangley, "Introduction of New Services for Profit," *Proceedings of the Bank Marketing Workshop* (Chicago: Bank Public Relations and Marketing Association, 1966).

Product Identification

Even if a bank is able to bring new banking products into the market or successfully copy the products of a competitor, it will be likely to face competition from similar products within a relatively short time. Creative pressures will create a need for product identification (which often requires at least some differentiation). The brand name, trademark, trade character, slogan, and other identification devices common to manufactured goods all have potential application to bank marketing. They may be employed for individual products or for the entire bank.

The image of a bank is related to these identification devices. A bank's image is a complex collection of attitudes and awareness on the part of customers and potential customers. All trademarks, all brand names, all contacts with bank facilities and bank personnel must combine to create a favorable image in the customer's mind. When a large part of the product is an intangible feeling of confidence, security, and trust, as it is in the case of many bank services, a favorable image is essential.

Broad Product Decisions

Good marketing should deliver the right products to the right customers, at the right price, at the right time, and at the right place. The assortment of products that the bank offers is often an enticement to bank customers. More and more banks have become full service banks in order to offer their customers a more convenient, one-stop assortment of financial services. Price, which is also a part of a bank's broad product decisions, has been discussed in prior chapters. Even with an acceptable assortment of financial services at competitive prices, however, bank management must not ignore the hours during which the bank provides the various services it offers and the bank's location and layout. General policy suggestions relating to these aspects of broad product decisions are not presented in this book because specific conditions affecting such policies vary widely, for example, differences in competition and allowable banking structure.

PROMOTIONAL ACTIVITIES

To promote its products and enlarge its market share, the individual bank should plan and carry out specific programs based on the sound and basic precepts of marketing research and product development discussed above. A bank's promotional activities will encompass most areas of direct competition with other institutions. In the competitive world, it is not enough to be a good fellow; one must aggressively seek business.

Promotional activities include, among other things, the bank's advertising, its program of customer calls, and its training of employees in the customer relations aspects of their jobs. In all of these activities, bank management should remember the importance of cross-selling to its existing customers, who are often the bank's best potential customers for new financial services.

Advertising

Although the trend of advertising expenditures for all commercial banks, shown in Chart 18, is upward, commercial banks still spend proportionately less on advertising than savings and loan associations, their main

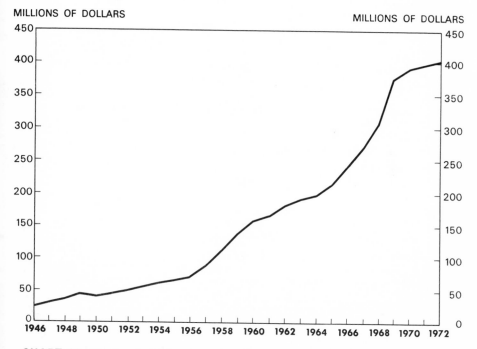

CHART 18 The Trend of Advertising Expenditures, All Commercial Banks, 1946–71 (Source: William Knobler and Lawrence J. Newman, "Banks Spent $376,000,000 in 1969, Up 25% from 1968," *Banking*, 63, October 1970, p. 57. 1970 and 1971 actual expenditures and 1972 planned expenditures are from the 1972 Bank Marketing Advertising survey conducted by the American Bankers Association and the Bank Marketing Association published in *Banking*, 65, August 1972, pp. 22–26.)

competitors for "deposits."[11] It seems strange that mutual institutions not spurred by the profit motive should outspend commercial banks in this major area of promotional activity. Perhaps commercial bank directors have been penny wise and pound foolish in their approach to advertising, falsely feeling themselves secure in a comparative monopoly and being unmindful of the mutuals' aggressive challenge.

The amount of money spent is less important, however, than the effectiveness of the advertising purchased.[12] Bank directors and senior management should give at least as much consideration to the impact of a bank's advertising on the public as to its impact on the budget. Even for the smaller bank, which may not be able to afford professional assistance, a good deal of sound guidance is readily available. There is ample literature on productive advertising techniques, and various bankers' associations have prepared effective material in the form of advertising "kits" for banks.[13] Despite this, too much bank advertising is still purely institutional or lacks imaginative or motivational content.

TABLE 15

ADVERTISING EXPENDITURES BY BANKS IN
VARIOUS SIZE GROUPS

Deposit Size (millions of dollars)	Average Expenditures per Bank, 1972	1971 Expenditures as Percentage of 1971 Expense
Under 5.0	$ 2,700	1.3
5.0 to 9.9	6,500	1.8
10.0 to 24.9	14,800	1.8
25.0 to 49.9	33,600	1.7
50.0 to 99.9	66,100	1.7
100.0 to 499.9	172,100	1.5
500.0 to 999.9	510,000	1.3
1,000 and over	1,571,000	9

Source: Advertising data obtained from 1972 survey conducted jointly by the American Bankers Association and the Bank Marketing Association (Published in *Banking*, 65, August 1972, pp. 22–26). Bank expenses obtained from *Annual Report of the Federal Deposit Insurance Corporation, 1971* (Washington, D.C.: Federal Deposit Insurance Corp., 1972).

11In 1969, banks spent 1.46 percent and savings and loan associations spent 1.83 percent of their respective gross incomes on advertising (John E. Meyers, "Advertising: Banks Are Spending $331,000,000 in 1969," *Banking*, 61, August 1969, pp. 57–62).

12For an excellent discussion of this topic, see Gabriel M. Gelb, "Creative Budgeting for Better Bank Advertising," *Banking*, 62, February 1970, pp .61–64.

13One of the most effective publications is *Advertising and Promotion— Practices of Full Service Banks* (Washington: American Bankers Association, 1970).

Some general information may prove useful to bank directors and senior management. The advertising expenditures by banks of various sizes are presented in Table 15. Table 16 ranks bank advertising objectives. The types of services advertised appear in Table 17, and the major media utilized in bank advertising are summarized in Table 18. Annual tabulations of this type of information are available from American Bankers Association.

Although such summaries may provide broad guidelines, bank directors and senior management are not likely to be advertising experts and should not hesitate to call in the best professional talent available. Bank directors and managers should, however, be able to judge the effectiveness of the bank's major advertising efforts by simply putting themselves in the place of the prospective audience and considering the impact of

TABLE 16

RANKING OF MOST IMPORTANT OBJECTIVES FOR BANK ADVERTISING
(FOR 1969)

Advertising Objectives	Ranking in Importance (percentage of all banks)		
	First	*Second*	*Third*
Increase deposits	16.6	7.7	3.0
Attract new customers	15.4	8.6	5.9
Promote bank services	13.3	15.1	12.1
Promote bank's image	11.6	12.5	17.3
Keep bank's name before public	9.7	4.7	5.4
Increase profits	5.6	3.6	5.7
Promote full service banking	5.4	3.9	4.3
Increase demand deposits	4.7	4.0	2.1
Increase loans	3.4	12.2	11.5
Increase savings deposits	3.2	7.1	4.8
Improve public relations	2.5	5.4	5.2
Promote community good will	1.9	3.3	7.2
Educate the public	1.7	3.2	4.3
Promote credit cards	1.4	1.7	2.9
Increase specific type of loan	1.3	1.8	1.9
Promote a specific service	0.9	2.1	2.0
Promote new services	0.7	1.3	1.3
Meet competition	0.7	1.7	2.1
Miscellaneous	0.2	0.2	1.1

Source: John E. Meyer, "Advertising: Banks are Spending $331,000,000 in 1969," *Banking*, 61, August 1969, pp. 57–62. © 1969 by the American Bankers Association.

TABLE 17

BANK SERVICES OFFERED AND ADVERTISED
(PERCENTAGE OF ALL BANKS IN 1969)

Services	Offering	Advertising	Most Emphasis in Advertising
Checking accounts, personal	92.5	79.3	13.8
Auto loans, direct	93.6	75.5	26.4
Savings accounts, regular	86.5	70.9	6.1
Bank by mail	91.5	67.3	0.9
Full service banking	77.9	66.0	11.9
Safe deposit	89.3	64.5	0.1
Personal loans	87.3	62.7	2.4
Checking accounts, commercial	88.2	61.3	6.6
Home improvement loans	74.7	52.0	0.6
Commercial loans	86.3	51.4	1.1
Savings and time deposits, other	69.0	50.9	9.6
Christmas and other thrift clubs	58.6	49.1	0.3
Night depository	72.6	48.6	0.0
Savings certificates, consumer	61.9	48.3	5.1
Drive-in banking	57.4	47.9	0.4
Home appliance loans	72.8	42.0	0.1
Mortgage loans	69.7	35.9	0.8
Farm loans other than real estate	61.2	33.8	3.1
Credit cards	40.5	33.2	6.8
Free parking	54.9	31.2	0.2
Farm real estate loans	56.1	25.2	0.4
Financial counseling	45.1	22.4	0.3
Trust services	28.2	21.2	0.3
Auto loans, indirect	50.2	15.9	1.1
Educational information	31.9	15.2	0.4
Life insurance premium loans	43.9	11.7	0.1
Overdraft loan plans	9.5	6.5	1.1
Check guarantee plans	6.7	5.3	0.3
Correspondent banking	16.1	4.3	0.1

Source: John E. Meyer, "Advertising: Banks are Spending $331,000,000 in 1969," *Banking*, 61, August 1969, pp. 57–62. © 1969 by the American Bankers Association.

the bank's advertising efforts on themselves. If they did so, thousands of dollars now spent on such nonproductive aims as reminding the public that the First National Bank was established in 1898 and that is accepts deposits would be put to more effective use.

The most effective advertising copy, whatever its form, will be that which clearly relates a potential customer's needs or desires to specific services that a bank is able and anxious to provide. Backed up by the bank's marketing research and product development, productive advertising will stress the bank's sincere desire to fill legitimate banking needs.[14]

It is important, therefore, for policy makers not only to determine how much the bank will spend for advertising but also to continually evaluate the contribution of the bank's advertising program to its overall marketing objective.

Direct Customer Solicitation

Advertising is aimed at a widespread and largely unseen audience. By contrast, conversations with actual and potential customers that can be focused directly on specific objectives and for certain goals can be far more effective. Consider the experience of a relatively small bank with two-dozen unrented safe deposit boxes. A fairly prominent advertisement in the local weekly newspaper for four successive weeks resulted in the renting of two boxes. The bank's cashier then urged the entire staff (fifteen people) to try to sell safe deposit boxes to their friends and neighbors. The remaining boxes were rented in a week!

This experience does not prove that advertising is relatively useless; it demonstrates, rather, that for specific purposes, direct personal contacts produce more spectacular results. In truth, the two go hand in hand.

TABLE 18

MAJOR MEDIA USAGE BY BANKS THAT ADVERTISE

Media	Percentage of Banks Using in 1971	Percentage of 1969 Budget Allocated
Newspapers	97	20
Radio	84	10
Television	35	13
Outdoor (billboards, signs, etc.)	61	6
Magazines	53	7
Premiums and specialties	82	6
Direct mail	50	3
Booklets, literature, etc.	60	5

Source: Data obtained from 1972 survey conducted by the American Bankers Association and the Bank Marketing Association (published in *Banking*, 65, August 1972, pp. 22–26).

[14]For example, the advertising of a large New York City bank stresses that, whatever your banking problem, "You have a friend at Chase Manhattan."

Effective advertising, over a period of time, will create the receptivity to banking services and to a particular bank that effective direct solicitation requires. Imaginative advertising causes the fruit of potential customer relationships to grow and ripen; some may fall to the ground of their own accord, but the best fruit requires individual picking.

Also implicit in this illustration is that calls on current or prospective customers are most useful if made for a specific purpose. Purely social calls may build a certain amount of good will; on the other hand, they may backfire if the customer finds them to be a waste of *his* as well as the bank representative's time.[15] The most effective call is related to a specific offer of service; this principle cannot be overemphasized.

Calling on the bank's larger commercial customers (whether they are currently borrowing or not) should be a regular part of the lending officers' duties. The rendering of effective credit service requires first-hand knowledge of the customers' operations and financial problems. Many banks expect their officers to make a certain number of such calls each month and to submit brief reports of these visits. Such calls provide the bank with essential information not only about the borrowers' present and future credit needs but also about the probable ebb and flow of their deposit balances. The calling officer will also have the opportunity to discuss some of the bank's other services, such as time deposit facilities, trust services, in-plant banking, and so on. In calls on potential customers (most of whom are already banking elsewhere), the bank's representative may offer some new and valuable service as an incentive for changing banks.

Where industrial and commercial activity is expanding, the opportunity to visit first with the management of new enterprises is obviously a competitive advantage that alert bank managers avidly seek. They look to their correspondent banks for leads and to their directors for inside knowledge and make every effort to offer their services as soon as possible. Some banks also seek contacts with new residents of the community.[16] They may either join with other businesses to use the services of professional solicitors[17] or use their own personnel to represent the bank. The offer of a free book of checks, for example, to a new

---

[15]Country bankers themselves have often complained about the purely "social" visits of some of the representatives of city correspondents. The solicitation of an account is never as effective as the offer of a service.

[16]A comprehensive strategy for reaching new business and consumer residents (this group is large in our mobile society) is presented in Harvey D. Hirsch, "New Approaches in Bank Marketing," *Banking*, 62, October 1969, pp. 45–46.

[17]"The Welcome Wagon," whose representatives offer gifts and introductory free services to new residents on behalf of a number of local merchants providing a wide variety of services, is an example.

resident is both a good reason for making the call and a potent induce-
ment for the newcomer to open a "convenience" checking account. A
modest prize or premium, similarly offered, will often result in the transfer of savings balances from the customer's previous place of residence.

An elaboration on the customer calling program is the new-business
contest, which has become increasingly popular. In such contests, points
are assigned for various types of new accounts and valuable prizes
offered to the employees who obtain the most points within a stated
time period. Such campaigns have been outstandingly successful not
only in increasing business but in building employee enthusiasm and
morale as well. Even without formal contests, it is important that all
officers and employees of a bank be encouraged at all times to obtain
new business and be rewarded for their success. In fact, such solicitation
should start with the directors themselves. Some banks divide the directorate into teams to which points are awarded for new business obtained.
Competition, thus engendered, not only brings in new accounts but also
supplies a lively source of conversation and interest at directors' meetings.
The losing team, of course, buys the dinner.

In short, if the bank's advertising has imaginatively portrayed the
value of the products it is prepared to render, the groundwork will have
been laid for an effective program of personal business soliciation. Such
a program should use all the talents of everyone in the bank, from the
directors themselves to the newest bookkeeper.

Direct Customer Contacts

The keystone to bank marketing is the customer's impression when he
enters the bank. Is it really the warm and friendly place described in
the advertisements? Having actively advertised for mortgage loans, what
does the bank do with mortgage applications?[18] In the long run, bank
marketing will stand or fall across the tellers' windows and the loan
officers' desks.

Banks have spent sizable sums in recent years to improve their
facilities and to make them more attractive. This is certainly the first
step in making the actual and potential customer feel welcome. Drive-in
facilities and adequate parking for his convenience; off-hour and evening
banking hours to suit his needs; the substitution of low, accessible
counters for the forbidding cages of yesteryear; carpeted lobbies, attrac-
tively decorated—all are part of a good bank marketing mix. They represent a substantial change from the picture of towering and formidable

---

[18]One large bank hired professional "shoppers" to find the answer to this and
similar questions. What they learned led to an intensive educational program and to
the decision to "shop" its offices on a continuous basis.

strength, which banks sought to create in the past, to the modern banking image of friendliness and community participation.

Even more than physical facilities, however, the human equation plays the vital role at the point of direct contact between a bank and its public. This key fact makes a continuing program of marketing education imperative for bank officers and employees. Bank management cannot take for granted that its admonitions of politeness and patience will be uniformly followed. It must be ever alert to customer reactions; in this regard, attitude surveys (a part of marketing research previously discussed) can play a valuable part. Without repeatedly checking on this vital phase of bank marketing, the directors and senior management will never know how much business the bank may have lost because of the manner in which a bank guard approached a stranger in the lobby, because of a teller's impatience or inattention, or because of a bank officer's unconscious but erroneous assumption that a shabbily-dressed or odd-appearing person could not possibly be a good potential customer. Customers most frequently switch from one bank to another not because the other bank offers better service but because they feel in some way slighted or neglected. It is such a slight, real or imagined, that usually brings to fruition the competitor's solicitation.

A special facet of direct customer relations is the art of loan declination. Competent lending officers who are acutely aware of the importance of bank marketing will spend twice as much time turning down a loan as granting one. If a loan cannot be made, the lending officer should attempt to suggest alternatives or patiently explain the reasons for the bank's decisions while trying to demonstrate that an unsound extension of credit often harms the borrower as much as the lender. In addition to being sound customer relations, such explanations represent an important phase of the bank's educational effort, instruction in sound credit principles. A surprisingly large number of customers thus treated will in time come to appreciate the bank's counseling.

COMMUNITY RELATIONS

The relationship between a bank and the community it serves is a vital and dynamic one. A bank is an integral part of the community's economic life, and in this respect it may function either poorly or well. The object of a bank's community relations, therefore, is not directly sales and promotion but the effective functioning of the bank as a vital organ in the community's economic life and growth. In this conception, community relations is not specifically a program, although a bank may need a program to make its community relations meaningful. Banks offer the means of satisfying human wants and business needs within the limits of constructive credit and banking safety.

The key to a bank's community relations, therefore, lies in its financial leadership, the extent to which it fulfills its responsibilities as the holder of the community's liquid resources and the supplier of its essential credit needs. In this sense, all that has gone before—liquidity, capital adequacy, and sound lending and investing policies—are the first requisites of a community relations program. And, in truth, no amount of high-pressure advertising or promotion will long disguise a bank's failure to make the loans or to supply the other banking services its community requires. Dissatisfied customers will simply go elsewhere, if they have the choice.

This is not the whole story, however. Unprogressive banks can actually retard the growth of their communities just as a weak heart will curtail the activities of the human body. Progressive banks, on the other hand, can stimulate growth and simultaneously spur their own progress and augment their long-range profits. The overall objective of a bank's community relations program should be the growth of the community itself. A bank's fundamental contribution to such growth is productive credit. Beyond this lies the advancement of community welfare through a wider range of activities, including economic education and direct participation in community affairs. All these together constitute a full-scale community relations program.

Educational Aspects of Community Relations

An important part of a bank's community relations is educational. The community looks to the bank for financial guidance of all kinds, and it is the bank's responsibility to make certain that the community understands the role of money and banking in the economy. Bankers can contribute to the nation's battle against inflation and its striving for sound economic growth through a continuing educational campaign. Banks have a vested interest in sound money and a growing and prosperous economy. Inflation steals away the value of their customers' savings, and the sharp decline of inflated values has been a principal cause of bank losses and bank failures in the past.

Once a bank consciously assumes financial and economic leadership in its community, many avenues of activity immediately open up. First, the bank must assure that its own officers are well informed. Does the bank subscribe to a variety of banking periodicals, economic analyses, important market letters—and are they read? Here, perhaps, is grist for the staff meeting. Herein lies justification for a rather wide attendance at bankers' schools, meetings, and conventions followed by reports to the board or the staff on what was learned or discussed. Education, like charity, begins at home.

Much of a bank's educational effort will take place naturally across the officers' desks or in the midst of social or business contacts away from the bank. At cocktail parties, for example, bankers are invariably a target for quizzes about current financial headlines. And the banker who takes his community relations seriously will be prepared to answer such questions intelligently.

More formal educational programs range from tours of the bank for schoolchildren to adult business forums where selected customers are invited to listen to experts in various fields of business, investment, or finance. A number of banks have established "speakers' bureaus," consisting of their own officers and senior personnel who are willing to discuss the banking activities with which they are most familiar at service clubs and meetings of other interested groups. The community's demand for this kind of educational endeavor is virtually insatiable, and in meeting this need, banks often discover unsuspected talents in their own officers and employees.

The range of possibilities for educational activities is restricted only by the imagination of the bank's officers and directors. What is essential is that a bank recognize clearly its opportunities in this field.

Participation in Community Activities

Another phase of a bank's community relations is the participation of its officers and directors in community activities. The encouragement of such participation should be an explicit policy. In general, banks have a good record in this regard. Progressive banks not only pay their officers' membership dues in service clubs and the chamber of commerce but also provide the time for active participation in charitable drives and other civic efforts. It goes almost without saying that a person who works in a bank will be asked to serve as treasurer in whatever organization he has actively joined. The bank should at least inventory and give formal recognition and encouragement to this important kind of community service. An annual report of all such participation to the Board of Directors and the circulation of the report to officers and employees is a simple means of accomplishing such recognition.

Outstanding bankers are frequently active in the more significant community efforts. Many have taken leading parts in community redevelopment, urban renewal, campaigns for better farm management—whatever activity will lead to the fullest possible use of the community's resources. Directorships in important local industries and civic organiza-

Relations with Less Privileged Groups and Regions

It is essential for commercial banks to establish useful relationships with less privileged groups and regions within their market area. The disadvantaged status of ethnic and racial minority groups and ghetto areas in larger cities receive the most publicity, but bankers in smaller towns can often find equally serious problems in their communities. If commercial banks are to contribute fully to community welfare, they must go beyond just "good, sound banking" in their lending and employment policies and practices and in excercising their influence as community policies take shape.

The importance of action above and beyond the call of normal banking duty is illustrated in this statement by John Morsell:

> Nothing is easier than to propose sweeping reforms and new departures for someone else's institution. Making sure that the proposals are relevant and that they have a chance of being implemented is something else again. Yet there are times when the need for change is so commanding that boldness, rather than routine prudence, becomes essential. After all, the reputations of the greatest generals have most often been based upon the risky decisions they took—and less frequently upon the diligence with which they weighed alternatives.
>
> The United States finds itself today in a crisis which calls, not, indeed, for the abandonment of prudence, but supremely for readiness to experiment and to dare. For many segments of the community this means that generations of complacency and security may have to be paid for by a generation of danger.
>
> The choice of a road containing major risks may be made easier for some if it is pointed out that, in all trust, to choose "safely" in no way diminishes the risks. It simply means that other and probably worse dangers are ahead.[20]

There are a number of reasons, beyond community responsibility, for which progressive bankers should look to minority groups and ghetto areas. First, minority groups represent a relatively untapped, growing market comprising almost 17 percent of the population nationwide and a majority of the population in some major cities. Second, the number of people in this segment of the market and the amount of their disposable income are growing faster than the national average. Third, the improved educational and economic outlook for minority groups is reflected in their desire to save more, to be meaningfully employed, and to own or manage business entities. Fourth, an expanded outlook has

---

20John A. Morsell, "Banking's Role in the Racial Crisis," *Banking*, 61, July 1968, p. 40.

tions offer opportunities for putting the banker's specialized fina knowledge to work for the healthy growth of the community. Hund of examples of such civic leadership could be cited. Unfortunately, t are still too many banks—particularly the smaller ones—to which s a concept would be foreign.

Directors as well as officers can play an important role in this pha of community relations; in small banks theirs will be the major role. I fact, in the selection of new directors, the community mindedness c prospective candidates should be a key factor.

When space has been available, banks have often provided meeting rooms for civic and social groups. This, too, is a form of community participation. In the same general category is the provision of space in the bank's lobby for displays of local products or the wares of merchants. Exhibiting the work of local artists or the collections of hobbyists can be both educational and community activity. The specific community relations programs that may be developed are varied indeed. They will be sound if their guiding principle is meaningful participation in the economic and educational life of the community.

RELATIONS WITH SPECIAL GROUPS

So far, the discussion has dealt with bank customers mainly in the aggregate. Actually, of course, a bank's market is not homogeneous but is made up of a number of overlapping segments and special groups toward which specific marketing activities should be directed. The approach to potential customers of the trust department will differ widely from a campaign to increase the bank's outstanding consumer credit. Specialized programs can be developed, for example, for schools, ethnic groups, the savings market, the farm community, or other groupings that market research has identified within the bank's trade area. The larger the bank and the more extensive the markets it serves, the more numerous will be such groupings.[19]

A few of these groups merit special comment because, in spite of current awareness of the community relations obligations of banking, these groups have often received less attention than they deserve. Among them are less privileged groups and regions in the bank's market area, the bank's own stockholders, the legislative representatives of the bank's trade area, and the examiners and supervisors of the bank.

---

[19]Educational and promotional programs may be devised even for rather narrow groupings: automobile dealers, accountants, teachers, association executives, and so on.

created certain socioeconomic attitudes and expectations that tend to bring changes in existing conditions—changes that are a creative force if properly developed.[21]

In spite of these positive reasons, bankers should not expect any of the three principal areas in which action is required to be immediately profitable.[22] In the lending area, many minority and ghetto area loans pose problems common to other small business loans—undercapitalization, lack of working capital, and shortage in management talent and experience. A bank cannot stretch its lending policy to accept every applicant, nor can it expect every loan to be profitable. Often the bank must take a greater risk and spend more time giving advice, with the hope that the minority business will finally develop and grow until it serves a basic community need and is profitable for the bank as well. Several government agencies—the Office of Minority Business Enterprises, the Small Business Administration, and the Minority Enterprise Small Business Investment Company—are trying to provide Federal assistance in this area. The area of employment presents many dilemmas to even progressive banks. Most bankers believe that they should not employ a member of a minority group at the expense of a more qualified nonminority person, yet they realize that the opportunities for education and experience have been severely limited for many members of minority groups. One approach has been special training programs for members of minority groups. Finally, there will be costs of time and possibly some shortsighted customer indignation in banks that advocate programs and actions that will contribute to progress for minority groups and depressed regions.

Relations with Stockholders

Stockholders have a direct financial interest in the success and growth of the commercial bank in which they own shares. Wide distribution of a bank's stock is a foundation stone of good community relations. Banks that pride themselves on being truly community institutions will be constantly seeking ways to increase the number of their shareholders.

Despite their vital role as the suppliers of capital and their potential value as representatives of the bank in the community, the stockholders are often neglected. Annual reports to shareholders have improved noticeably in recent years, but even in many large banks, as well as in

---

[21]Maurice H. Stans, "The Untapped Market for Banking," *Banking*, 63, december 1970, pp. 51–52.

[22]For an analysis of some of the difficulties faced when banks try to alleviate urgent urban problems, see E. Sherman Adams, "Banks and the Urban Crisis," *Banking*, June 1968, pp. 42–49.

the vast majority of small ones, stockholders are still left in the dark about many aspects of the bank's operations.

It is difficult to see why bank shareholders are not entitled to such information, yet many bankers still oppose the required publication of detailed information on bank earnings. It has been repeatedly demonstrated that informed shareholders can do much to strengthen a bank's community relations. Those banks that publish their earnings in detail and have done so for many years do not seem to have suffered any ill consequences. On the contrary, they have found increased acceptance for their stock in the market at higher price levels and greater community support from a wider circle of informed shareholders.

Aside from adequate reporting, the most important contact with the stockholder is the annual meeting. Seldom, however, is the small stockholder directly encouraged to attend such meetings. Too often, management faces the annual meeting with trepidation lest some unexpected stockholder show up to ask embarrassing questions. The few banks that have made a definite effort to broaden stockholder participation have been delighted with the results. But something more than a dry reading of the minutes and the election of directors is needed: a buffet lunch, a tour of the bank, a review of local economic conditions, a frank discussion of the bank's plans and prospects are examples. The possibilities of attracting stockholders to the annual meeting are legion and should be energetically explored. Interim reports to the shareholders and personal letters suggesting that they call the bank's services to the attention of their friends and business associates are also productive. No other group in the community is as interested in hearing about and promoting the bank's business as those who collectively own it.

Relations with Legislators

Bankers generally have long considered themselves the forgotten man of politics. Their attitude may be one of "holier than thou" or simply abject defeatism. Over and over again, bankers talk to each other about needed legislation or importune the bank supervisor to seek constructive changes in the law, but at the first suggestion that they approach their representatives in the legislature directly (or even write them a letter) they shy away as if the idea were somehow immoral. If banks are to play their rightful role as financial leaders in the community, they have a duty to be at least on speaking terms with the political leaders of that same community. It is not that they should seek favored legislation, although at times bankers have received less than equal treatment from the lawmakers. It is, rather, that sound legislation that in the long run will benefit both the community and the bank is most likely to be enacted by legislators who have been adequately informed about the economic consequences of legislative proposals. Members of Congress and of state legislatures have often stated that they seldom hear from bankers and would welcome closer contacts.

A bank's obligation to provide financial and economic education to its community has already been highlighted. It can hardly direct its educational efforts better than by making its views and its sound supporting arguments known to those who pass the laws that will shape the directions and conditions of the community's economic growth. And it can best do so through personal acquaintanceship and face-to-face discussion.

Relations with Examiners and Supervisory Agencies

The bank examiner, originally something of a policeman and still responsible for enforcing an elaborate set of banking laws, has become in recent years more like a family doctor. His primary concern is the healthy functioning of his bank "patients." His annual physical examination of bank assets and management policies is directed to helping banks function more effectively as well as safely in their respective communities.

Bank managements have become increasingly aware of the potential helpfulness of supervisory examinations. Many bank officers have learned to welcome the examiner and willingly subject themselves and their thinking to the challenge of his objective review and occasional criticism. They have gradually realized that the examiner has no other interest than the soundness of the bank and its ability to serve the community needs safely and constructively. They look to him for that cross-fertilization of ideas that stimulates growth and innovation; however, they seldom introduce him to their directors.

When difficulties develop in a particular bank, the examiner calls a meeting of the directors. Such meetings are apt to be awkward and painful at best. The directors are generally on the defensive. Criticism by the examiner, though warranted, is seldom conducive to good understanding and good feeling. On the other hand, if the directors were to invite the examiner to meet with them so that they might learn from him all they can about sound banking practices and the trends that may be developing in the banking field, the atmosphere would be quite different. In a free and voluntary exchange of questions and answers, the examiner may be able to shed a good deal of light on the very problems of policy with which the directors have been struggling. For such meetings to be most effective, the initiative must come from the directors themselves or from management, rather than from the examiner.

In the absence of a formal meeting, the bank director who takes his position seriously should at least stop in and visit with the examiners when they are in his bank. It is a rare opportunity for the directors to ask searching questions about banking policies and practices, to get the "feel" of what other banks are doing, and to obtain an objective view of the adequacy of his own bank's practices.

The value of closer relations with bank examiners and supervisory agencies will depend, of course, on the competence of the examiners and the supervisory organizations that they represent. Banks have a great deal to gain from effective and enlightened supervision. Bankers themselves should therefore insist, as a matter of public policy, that bank examining and supervisory staffs continue to be composed of highly competent people.

MAKING THE MARKETING CONCEPT WORK

Many commercial banks have rushed headlong into some or all of the marketing and community relations programs described above without being fully aware of certain necessary prerequisites: (1) acceptance of the marketing concept at the top and throughout the entire banking organization; (2) integration and coordination of all aspects of marketing —goals should be set and long-range plans made so that the elements of marketing reinforce one another; and (3) adequate budgetary support for the utilization of skillful professionals and executives and the implementation of reasonable marketing and community relations programs. It is often primarily bank directors' responsibility to make sure that these and other underlying conditions prevail.

Role of the Bank Director

The bank directors' development of policies to guide their bank's marketing and community relations effort is one of the most vital aspects of their job. In a sense, the directors represent the community as well as the stockholders. In the long run, the interests of the stockholders and those of the community are identical because a bank will prosper only if its community thrives. In establishing policies in the area of bank marketing, the directors are in effect setting the long-range objectives of the bank, determining what kind of a bank they want it to be and how full a part it should play in community life.

As in other banking activities, the broad objectives of the bank's marketing programs should be stated by the board, and the execution of policy should be left to the active management. A special committee of the Board may well be charged with seeing that the established policy is carried out. The day-to-day decisions, however—the decisions about specific programs and the nature of advertising copy—should be left to duly designated and competent officers. In large banks, the marketing programs are generally the responsibility of specially designated officers versed in the best and latest techniques. In smaller banks, where marketing is not a full-time job, the responsibility for marketing and community relations might be combined with that for personnel management, because employee training and employee attitudes toward customers are such a vital part of bank marketing.

The directors personally represent the bank in the community. They can and should seek business for the bank. Their participation in the life of the community, as well as the effectiveness of their overall leadership, will determine the esteem in which the bank is held. A final aspect of the director's role is alertness to community opinion concerning the bank, its services, and the attitudes of its employees. Directors should always try to get to the root of legitimate community complaints.

A bank directorship is a challenge as well as a unique opportunity to serve the welfare of the community. No other duty of bank directors is more important than that of insisting that their banks know and serve customers' wants and needs to the fullest possible extent.

17

MANAGING
THE BANK'S
CAPITAL STRUCTURE

In the discussion of capital adequacy in Chapter 5, bank capital was treated as a single, homogeneous item. Earlier in this century, such treatment would have been reasonably accurate, but it no longer is. There are now several different types of bank capital and even different ways of raising a given type of bank capital. In addition, such conditions as the growth in the number of bank holding companies and shortages of funds for long-term financing needs will probably encourage banks to devise new forms of bank capital in coming years. Directors and senior management of commercial banks must therefore develop policies that establish not only how much capital is adequate in relation to assets and deposits but also what proportion of total capital should be raised in each of the various forms of capital.

MAJOR METHODS OF RAISING
BANK CAPITAL

Table 19 shows the dollar balances in the major categories of bank capital at the end of each year from 1960 to 1971. Each of these forms and the reasons underlying the trends in their usage are briefly described in the following paragraphs.

TABLE 19

CAPITAL ACCOUNTS OF INSURED COMMERCIAL BANKS
(IN MILLIONS OF DOLLARS)

As of Year End	Total Capital	Capital Notes and Debentures	Preferred Stock	Common Stock	Surplus	Undivided Profits	Equity Reserves
1960	20,658.6	23.2	14.6	6,170.1	9,916.2	4,020.9	513.6
1961	22,123.0	22.1	14.7	6,584.7	10,798.4	4,156.8	546.3
1962	23,752.3	20.5	34.8	6,882.0	11,458.4	4,789.7	566.9
1963	25,322.7	130.0	37.8	7,283.0	12,163.5	5,113.4	595.0
1964	27,438.1	810.7	41.7	7,886.4	12,893.2	5,113.0	693.1
1965	29,905.0	1,652.7	39.9	8,507.8	13,464.8	5,437.6	802.2
1966	31,693.2	1,729.9	61.6	8,856.8	13,998.7	6,166.5	879.7
1967	34,005.9	1,984.4	87.1	9,253.6	14,983.4	6,610.7	1,086.7
1968	36,628.0	2,110.1	90.7	9,772.6	16,173.9	7,419.7	1,061.0
1969	39,576.2	1,998.3	103.4	10,529.3	17,460.8	8,426.8	1,057.6
1970	42,266.4	2,091.9	107.3	11,137.8	19,172.6	11,145.8	1,011.0
1971	46,905.0	2,956.2	91.9	11,811.1	19,895.8	11,135.1	1,014.9

Source: *Annual Reports of the Federal Deposit Insurance Corporation, 1960–71* (Washington: Federal Deposit Insurance Corporation, 1961–72).

Capital Notes and Debentures

Capital notes and debentures are interest-bearing obligations to repay a fixed amount of money at some future time. They have a fixed claim on earnings and assets, ahead of preferred and common stock; however, they cannot be secured by specific assets, and their claim for payment is subordinated to that of depositors and other customers. Beyond these characteristics, there is a considerable amount of variation in specific terms and issuing procedures. Some capital notes of relatively small denominations have been sold directly to bank customers. Other notes and debentures have been sold to the issuing bank's major correspondent banks. Large debenture issues with medium-term (seven- to ten-year) and long-term (twenty- to twenty-five-year) maturities have been sold through investment bankers to the public (financial institutions such as life insurance companies and pension funds have been heavy purchasers). About one-third of the amount of debentures sold have been convertible into the banks' common stock at some predetermined price.

The first widespread use of capital notes and debentures (in all their various forms) occurred during the early 1930s. Because this was a period of banking crisis, bank supervisory authorities and bank customers tended to associate such bank indebtedness with bank weakness. Consequently, most bankers tried to eliminate the indebtedness from the capital structure of their banks as quickly as possible. From a peak of approximately $950 million in 1934, the value of capital notes and debentures outstanding declined to less than $21 million in 1962.[1]

In spite of the negative public attitude toward capital notes and debentures, the Commission on Money and Credit recommended in 1961 that banks seek authorization to issue indebtedness subordinated to the claims of depositors. Shortly afterwards, the Advisory Commission on Banking to the Comptroller of the Currency recommended that national banks be permitted to issue capital notes and stated, "There is no sound reason why national banks should be deprived of any legitimate capital-raising method that is available to corporations generally."[2] In late 1962, new published rulings stated, "It is the policy of the Comptroller of the Currency to permit the issuance of convertible or nonconvertible capital debentures by national banking associations in accordance

---

[1]In mid–1933, senior capital (debt and preferred stock) totaled about $1.125 billion, or almost one-sixth of total bank capital. Source: Charles M. Williams, "Senior Securities—Boon for Banks?" *Harvard Business Review*, July-August 1963, pp. 82–94. In late 1961, senior capital totaled approximately $37 million, or less than .16 percent of total bank capital. Source: Table 19.

[2]Cited by Alfred C. West, "Senior Capital Financing by Commercial Banks," *Bankers Monthly*, Vol. 81, No. 5, May 15, 1964, p. 38.

with normal business considerations."[3] Nearly all states have subsequently given authorization to their state banks to issue capital notes and debentures.

The rapid increase in the amount of these debt instruments outstanding during the mid–1960s is documented in Table 19. This growth tended to slow in the late 1960s because of rising interest rates and a relatively lower need for additional bank capital. These and other factors affecting the amount of debt an individual bank should issue are discussed later in this chapter.

Preferred Stock

Stocks given preferential claims on assets and/or earnings above common stock are called preferred stocks. The dividend and asset claims of preferred stockholders are fixed in amount and are subordinated to the claims of depositors and to all indebtedness of the commercial bank. Preferred stocks do not mature; however, most preferred stocks may be called at a fixed price at the option of the issuing bank. A commercial bank may issue either straight (nonconvertible) preferred stock or preferred stock that is convertible into common stock at a predetermined price at the option of the preferred stockholder.

The historical usage pattern of preferred stock closely parallels that of capital notes and debentures. Preferred stocks were first used widely during the banking crisis of the early 1930s. After the crisis subsided, bankers gradually retired their preferred stock (through call or open-market purchase), because bank supervisory authorities and customers tended to view bank preferred stock, like bank indebtedness, as a sign of weakness. Finally, the recommendation of the Commission on Money and Credits in 1961 and the rulings of the Comptroller of the Currency in 1962 reversed the supervisory viewpoint, and preferred stock became an acceptable form of capital. As Table 19 shows, however, preferred stock still contributes a relatively insignificant amount of total bank capital.

Common Stock, Surplus, Undivided Profits, and Equity Reserves

The common stock account consists primarily of the par or stated value of all outstanding shares of common stock. The surplus account comes from two sources: the accumulated premiums over par or stated value at which common stock was sold to the public (with some minor exceptions—see below) and whatever proportion of accumulated, undivided profits has been shifted to the surplus account. The primary reason for such a bookkeeping shift is that in the past the legal loan limit for all

---

[3]Code of Federal Regulation, Title 12, Section 14.5a.

national banks and most state banks was a percentage of the combined total of the common stock and surplus accounts. The Comptroller now recognizes undivided profits and equity reserves as well as senior capital as part of the lending base; however, many state banks are still subject to the older legal loan limit.[4]

The undivided profits account is the accumulated retained earnings (earnings after interest and taxes less dividends and equity reserves) less any amounts that have been shifted to the surplus account. It is illegal for banks to pay dividends in excess of their undivided profits. Most newly chartered banks, in order to be certain to cover organizational costs and initial losses, will label a small amount of their original stock offering as undivided profits.

Equity reserves consist of retained earnings that have been set apart for some contingency or expected event. Examples include a reserve for the expected retirement of preferred stock or for an expected court settlement. The reserve for loan losses (see Chapter 11) and the reserve for security losses (see Chapter 13) are technically asset valuation reserves rather than equity reserves. They are considered to be expenses (even though the reserve for security losses is not deductible for tax purposes) in the determination of earnings. The Comptroller and some states do include part or all of these reserves as part of a bank's lending base.[5]

The sum of the common stock, surplus, undivided profits, and equity reserve accounts represents the book value of the common stockholder's investment in the business. The same figure can be reached by subtraction of the deposits, other liabilities, and senior capital from total assets. Even in the early 1970s (when debt instruments and preferred stock have general respectability), Table 19 shows that common stockholders have contributed approximately 95 percent of the total capital of commercial banks.

BASIS FOR POLICIES REGARDING THE USE OF SENIOR CAPITAL

Common equity capital will probably continue to be the dominant part of total capital, because retained earnings will probably continue to be the most practical source of capital for nearly all banks. However,

---

[4]Interpretative Ruling 7.1100, "Comptroller's Manual for National Banks" (Washington, D. C.: U.S. Comptroller of the Currency).

[5]For example, in establishing lending limits, the Comptroller allows an adjusted reserve for loan losses on bad debts—that is, the reserve less the amount of tax that would become payable if the tax-free portion of the reserve were transferred from the reserve—and the valuation reserve for securities to be included as part of the unimpaired surplus (Interpretative Ruling 7.1100, *op. cit.*).

senior capital—debt instruments and preferred stocks—has grown rapidly in recent years, and no rapidly growing bank in need of additional capital should overlook this avenue for raising it.

Advantages of Senior Capital

The two major advantages of senior capital over common stock as a source of capital are illustrated in Table 20. First, the issuance of senior capital results in a less marked immediate dilution of earnings per common share unless the financing cost exceeds the amount the bank is earning on shareholders' equity. Second, in the longer run, senior capital

TABLE 20

EARNINGS RESULTS UNDER ALTERNATIVE METHODS OF RAISING CAPITAL

	Present Capital	Additional Capital Financed with Common Stock ($50)	Additional Capital Financed with 8% Preferred Stock	Additional Capital Financed with 8% Subordinated Debentures
A. Earnings on Existing Assets				
Earnings on assets (1.3%)	$1,300,000	$1,313,000	$1,313,000	$1,313,000
Less interest	—	—	—	80,000
Net income before taxes	$1,300,000	$1,313,000	$1,313,000	$1,233,000
Taxes (at 30% rate)	390,000	393,900	393,900	369,900
Net income after taxes	$ 910,000	$ 919,100	$ 919,100	$ 863,100
Preferred dividends	—	—	80,000	—
Net for common stock	$ 910,000	$ 919,100	$ 839,100	$ 863,100
Number of shares	200,000	220,000	200,000	200,000
Earnings per share	$4.55	$4.18	$4.20	$4.31
B. Earnings on Increased Assets*				
Earnings on assets (1.3%)	$1,430,000	$1,443,000	$1,443,000	$1,443,000
Less interest	—	—	—	80,000
Net income before taxes	$1,430,000	$1,443,000	$1,443,000	$1,363,000
Taxes (at 30% rate)	429,000	432,900	432,900	408,900
Net income after taxes	$1,001,000	$1,011,100	$1,011,100	$ 954,100
Perferred dividends	—	—	80,000	—
Net for common stock	$1,001,000	$1,011,100	$ 931,100	$ 954,100
Number of shares	200,000	220,000	200,000	200,000
Earnings per share	$5.01	$4.60	$4.66	$4.78

*Assuming existing assets increased $10 million

usually increases the earnings per share on common stock, because the senior capital usually introduces favorable financial leverage.[6]

In reference to the top part of Table 20, assume that the bank earns 1.3 percent before taxes on total assets and has an effective tax rate of 30 percent (roughly the average for insured commercial banks in the early 1970s). Having grown rapidly, the bank now has $100 million in assets but only $8 million in capital funds. The bank examiners strongly suggest that it raise $1 million in additional capital. The present capitalization consists of two hundred thousand shares of $10 par-value stock and $6 million in surplus, undivided profits, and reserves. Assume further that the bank has three alternative methods of raising the additional capital: (1) selling twenty thousand shares of common stock at $50 a share (approximately eleven times earnings); (2) selling preferred stock with an 8 percent dividend rate; and (3) selling subordinated debentures with an 8 percent coupon. Immediately after any of the financing alternatives, the bank will have assets of $101 million and capital of $9 million.

The top part of Table 20 illustrates the immediate dilution of earnings per share under the various alternatives. Senior capital (particularly debt, in this example) causes less dilution, even when its cost is relatively high. For this bank, the sale of additional common stock decreases earnings per share by 8.1 percent, but the sale of debt adversely affects earnings per share by only 5.3 percent.

The lower part of Table 20 illustrates what would happen if the bank's assets increased by $10 million over time. For example, earnings per common share would be $4.60 if the additional capital had been raised by the issuance of common stock and $4.78 if the additional capital had been raised by the issuance of 8 percent debentures. This example portrays favorable financial leverage. The highest earnings per share, of course, would result if no additional capital were raised, but the bank is assumed to be seeking a more adequate capital position.

The conclusions that can be derived from Table 20 rest primarily on four important variables: (1) the amount the bank can earn on its total capital (or assets with a given proportion of capital) before income taxes; (2) the fixed cost of the senior capital; (3) the effective income tax rate; and (4) the proportion of total capital that is senior capital. Table 21 shows the effect on the earnings per common share from Table 20 when any one of these variables is changed after the additional capital has been raised and assets have increased by $10 million. Numerous generalizations can be made from Table 21. For example, a bank that earns

---

[6]Financial leverage is the use of funds with fixed costs and is said to be favorable if the returns earned on these funds exceed their fixed cost.

TABLE 21

EFFECT OF CHANGING AN IMPORTANT VARIABLE
ON EARNINGS PER COMMON SHARE

Variable Changes From Table 2 Sample Bank[a]	Additional Capital Financed with Common Stock	Additional Capital Financed with Preferred Stock	Additional Capital Financed with Subordinated Debentures
No change	$4.60	$4.66	$4.78
Earnings on assets rise to 2.0% before taxes	7.06	7.37	7.49
Earnings on assets fall to .5% before taxes	1.77	1.55	1.66
Cost of senior capital falls to 6%	4.60	4.75	4.85
Cost of senior capital rises to 10%	4.60	4.55	4.71
Tax rate is 50%	3.28	3.21	3.41
Tax rate is 0%	6.56	6.82	6.82
Senior capital (when used) was $2 million rather than $1 million[b]	4.60	4.86	5.13

[a]*The specific variable mentioned is the only one allowed to change. All other variables were left the same as in Table 20 (assuming additional capital was raised by one of the three methods and that assets have increased by $10 million).*
[b]*When senior capital was used, the equity account was reduced from $8 million to $7 million (175,000 shares). All other variables were left the same as in Table 20.*

considerably more on its capital before taxes than its interest cost and pays a high rate of income taxes will find subordinated debentures an attractive source of capital. The basic message of Table 21, however, is that each bank must consider the important variables as they apply to its particular circumstances.

Bank debt instruments, even if not currently required for capital, may also have several advantages over long-term deposits as a source of funds. First, if they meet certain requirements, debt instruments are not subject to Regulation Q rate ceilings or reserve requirements.[7] Second, because these instruments have fixed maturities, there is not as great a need for liquidity reserves, and most of the proceeds can be invested in longer-term, higher-yield assets. Third, the handling and

---

[7]In June 1970, the Board of Governors of the Federal Reserve extended the coverage of Regulations D and Q to include subordinated debentures of less than seven years' original maturity or in amounts of less than five hundred dollars.

placing costs associated with debt instruments may be lower than the costs of acquiring additional time deposits. Finally, the funds acquired through debt instruments are not subject to the deposit insurance costs of the Federal Deposit Insurance Corporation.

Limitations and Disadvantages of Senior Capital

For many small banks, senior capital is not a realistic alternative. Handling and placing costs for an impersonal issue are relatively fixed and would be very high for small issues. In addition, most impersonal investors would not purchase the securities of banks with assets of less than $5 million, and a significant secondary market is not available for banks with assets of less than $25 million. A few small banks have sold senior securities (usually capital notes) to large correspondent banks and to the bank's friends, customers, and stockholders often at prices below general market rates. Banks considering the sale of senior securities should be aware, however, that issuing and redemption expenses may be very high and that the buyer of such securities may become disenchanted if interest rates increase or if they discover no secondary market for the bonds. The sale of senior securities to a large correspondent can be a good arrangement for all concerned if it is carefully evaluated in the light of all correspondent relationships between the banks.[8]

Supervisory limitations on the use of senior capital affect banks of all sizes and vary among regulatory authorities. Most supervisors apparently try to limit debt capital to somewhere between one-quarter and one-third of total capital funds.

The disadvantages of senior capital are extremely difficult to quantify. The bank's use of debt or preferred stock may tend to lower the price-earnings multiple of its common stock by increasing the variability of earnings per share, changing the shareholders' expectations about earn-

---

[8]The limited use of senior capital by small banks is shown in the following statistics for December 31, 1971, from the *Annual Report of the Federal Deposit Insurance Corporation, 1971* (Washington: Federal Deposit Insurance Corp., 1972), p. 207.

Insured Commercial Banks with Deposits of	*Capital Notes and Debentures as a Percentage of Total Assets*
Less than $5 million	.0
$5 to $25 million	.1
$25 to $50 million	.2
$50 to $100 million	.3
$100 to $500 million	.4
$500 to $1,000 million	.5
More than $1,000 million	.7

ings per share, and increasing their "risk of ruin." Reduced management flexibility is another disadvantage. A bank with a strong common equity base can compete favorably for capital (in any form if it is a larger bank) in the marketplace. Strongly capitalized banks of any size are less likely to encounter criticism of their plans and operations and can gain approval more readily for their new undertakings. They can take greater operating risks and need be less concerned with lead time before innovations return a profit. On the other hand, banks that borrow all they can may have a harder time raising capital (particularly in the debt form) when it is needed, may be forced to pay excessive financing costs, and in extreme cases may have to curtail some of their activities.

A Balanced Approach

Balancing these advantages and disadvantages to determine the appropriate amount of senior capital is a difficult task. The final balance will depend on each individual bank's circumstances and managerial practices. Some broad generalizations may nevertheless prove helpful for the development of policy in this area of bank management.

Small- to moderate-sized banks need some financial flexibility, and are therefore generally advised to meet all their capital needs with equity and to issue senior capital only when their capital needs exceed expectations or when the market for their stock is unusually poor. (In the latter case, they should consider convertible capital, discussed below.) The primary source, when small- or medium-sized banks do decide to issue senior capital, should be principal correspondent banks.

Most larger banks should seriously consider the use of senior capital to meet part of their capital needs. The majority of larger commercial banks are subject to more than minimal income taxes and should use subordinated debentures as their source of senior capital.[9] The amount to be used will depend partially on the current and expected cost of such debentures in relation to the bank's pretax return on its entire capital base. A bank should use debt within reasonable limits as long as its earnings on total capital exceed the current cost of debt by approximately

---

[9]Because preferred dividends must be paid from net earnings after taxes, and interest on debt capital is normally deductible from earnings before taxes, preferred stock will only be attractive to banks that have a low effective income tax rate or that pay no income taxes. The earnings-per-share figures in Table 21 show that preferred stock produces the same after-tax earnings as similar-cost debt in the no-tax situation. Preferred stock might be attractive in such a situation because of its lower priority and generally smaller charges (because repayment or sinking funds are not usually required). And in low-tax situations, interest payments on debt capital may not be deductible from earnings before taxes if the Internal Revenue Service can associate tax-exempt income with the proceeds of the debt issue.

50 percent or more. Bank managers should limit indebtedness to between one-half and two-thirds of the maximum amount acceptable to regulatory authorities in order to assure themselves of some financial flexibility. The limit should be broad and flexible because of the economies of issuing debt in large blocks.

Convertible Senior Capital: A Special Case

The reasons for issuing senior capital that is convertible into common stock are quite different. In essence, the sale of such convertible capital usually represents a deferred sale of common stock, typically at a price between ten and twenty-five percent above current market value. The dilution effect of convertible capital is less immediate and smaller than that of a new issue of common stock.

Convertible debentures have been used much more often than convertible preferred stock.[10] Such debentures usually have lower interest costs than those of straight debentures because of the potential value of the conversion privilege. This lower cost further reduces the immediate dilution in earnings per share (see Table 21 for examples). In addition, when converted into equity these debentures will tend to restore a bank's borrowing reserve. On the other hand, convertible debentures usually carry higher underwriting fees to protect the underwriters against possible fluctuations in the market price of the bank's common stock prior to the issuance of the debentures. Another possible disadvantage of convertible denbentures is that if the bank does poorly it will still have to pay the interest charges, because the holders (who have the option of deciding when and whether to exercise the conversion privilege) probably will continue to hold the debentures in the debt form.

Because of these considerations, bank policy should encourage the issuance of convertible debentures, particularly when management believes the common stock to be underpriced and when it wants the additional capital to be permanent rather than temporary.

BASIS FOR POLICIES REGARDING THE USE OF COMMON EQUITY

As we previously stressed, retained earnings are and will probably continue to be the principal source of equity capital for nearly all banks. The amount of a bank's retained earnings may affect both the need for external common-stock financing and the market price at which the common stock can be sold.

---

[10]Convertible preferred stock is appropriate primarily in unusual situations, such as when the bank has a very low tax rate or when it is financing acquisitions.

Dividends and Retained Earnings

A low dividend pay-out (cash dividends as a percentage of earnings) means that retained earnings will provide a larger proportion of total common equity financing. Because their stock is not widely owned or traded, many smaller banks may find that retained earnings are the only reasonable source of common equity. Even if an external issue of stock is a realistic possibility, retained earnings have advantages; stockholders do not have to pay personal income taxes on earnings left in the bank, and there is no issuing cost. On the other hand, although a high dividend pay-out lowers the amount of retained earnings, it may allow additional common equity to be sold to the public at a more favorable price.[11] For banks with a significant number of publicly held common shares, the important factors affecting dividend pay-out policy usually are the expected rate of profitable future growth, future needs for additional capital, and the distribution of ownership.

An adequately capitalized bank in a stable or economically declining community can typically retain enough earnings to finance its limited equity needs and still pay an adequate or liberal dividend. Many banks find themselves in this condition, and yet the directors continue to hoard capital. The reason is usually found in a small list of stockholders who are more interested in capital gains than in income; however, such hoarding may be futile because of the limited growth potential for profits.

In dynamic communities where the banks themselves are expanding and can see the need for additional equity capital in the future, the choice lies between high retention of earnings and a dividend policy that will maintain the market price of the bank's stock and its desirability as an investment so that additional capital, when needed, can be readily

---

[11]Nearly every study on the subject concludes that cash dividends paid by publicly held banks tend to have a positive effect on their common stock price. For example, E. Sherman Adams (in "Are Bank Dividend Policies Too Conservative," *Banking*, 60, November 1967, p. 116) compiled the following statistics for a group of large banks:

Range of Pay-out Ratios	Average Price-Earnings Ratios
Over 55%	15.0
50%–55%	12.2
35%–49%	11.7
Under 35%	11.3

Other studies supporting this idea include Gilbert R. Whitaker, Jr., *The Market for Bank Stocks,* Subcommittee on Domestic Finance, Committee on Banking and Currency, House of Representatives, 88th Congress, 2d Session, 1964; and James Van Horne and Raymond C. Helwig, "Patterns in Bank Dividend Policy," *Bankers Magazine,* 150, Spring 1967, pp. 61–65. Although we cannot question the overall results of these empirical studies, we do believe that there are exceptions. For example, the stocks of rapidly growing, larger banks may actually be more appealing to institutional buyers if the dividend pay-out is low.

obtained in the marketplace. The choice should depend on the estimated marginal income tax rate of the bank's stockholders (higher tax rates make retention more favorable), the estimated impact of dividends on the bank's market price, and the directors' interest in encouraging wider distribution of the bank's common stock. At the present time, a majority of the banks facing this choice appear to believe that high retention of earnings—that is, low dividend pay-out—is the preferable policy.

Very rapidly growing commercial banks with capital needs that clearly exceed the amount of earnings that can be retained face a complex policy decision. If bank management believes that dividends will not significantly affect the market price of the bank's stock (the authors believe this to be the case for many rapidly growing banks, particularly larger banks whose stock is often acquired by growth-oriented institutions), the preferable policy is to pay a modest cash dividend and use low-cost retained earnings to finance as much of the expansion as possible. On the other hand, if bank management believes that dividends will have an appreciable positive effect on the bank's stock price, the bank may gain from paying higher dividends and raising much of its needed capital by selling higher-priced common stock.[12]

Several other suggestions can be made pertaining to dividend policy regardless of the pay-out level chosen as appropriate. Banks should consistently apply whatever dividend policy they select. One broad group of investors (such as performance-oriented mutual funds) seems to prefer stocks with lower pay-outs and (hopefully) higher appreciation, although another broad group seems to prefer the greater certainty of higher cash returns. Vacillation between the two groups will probably not appeal to either group and may hurt the bank's market performance. Investors also seem to prefer relatively stable dividends, even at low levels, to widely fluctuating dividends. Finally, even banks that pay a

---

[12]A similar approach was suggested by Roland I. Robinson and Richard H. Pettway in *Policies for Optimum Bank Capital* (Chicago: Association of Research City Bankers, 1967):

> The most important part of an individual bank's capital planning is its dividend policy. The evidence seems clear and unmistakable that bank share prices are influenced by dividend pay-out. If a bank retains earnings to increase its rate of capital growth, it increases its cost of external equity capital. Except for banks in areas of exceptionally fast growth, bank stocks have been considerably less than star price performers in postwar equity markets. It is not clear that different dividend policies would have improved the performance, but a general reexamination of dividend policy seems indicated. Rather than follow a median dividend policy, an individual bank may have to go to one or the other extreme: retain a larger part of earnings with consequent damage to its stock prices; or pay out rather generous dividends with the hope that such pay outs will be more than returned in higher share prices when external equity financing is undertaken.

substantial percentage of their earnings as dividends should select a pay-out level low enough to assure the maintenance of dividends when earnings drop.

New External Issues of Common Stock

Most capital strategies should include only minimum issuance of new common shares. The potential of advantageously selling senior capital or using lower-cost retained earnings should be carefully explored before new shares of common stock are issued. Nevertheless, under certain conditions it is appropriate for a bank to sell additional common shares. When such conditions arise, the bank should try to sell the shares in a way that is fair to both existing and prospective owners.

When a new bank is organized, its capital stock is usually sold to a small group of interested investors. Additional stock may later be offered to this group and their friends; however, if the bank grows rapidly and needs larger amounts of additional common stock, it may have to offer its stock to the public.[13] The pricing of a bank's initial public offering is extremely difficult. Generally, the bank's book value, earning power, and dividends are compared with actively traded stocks of similar-sized banks for the determination of a reasonable stock price. It is not generally advisable for the issuing bank to try to squeeze the last dollar out of such an offering. The presence of a group of pleased initial shareholders who are satisfied because of appreciation in the market price of their stock will encourage higher common stock prices in future years. It is also generally advisable for the initial public offering to be priced in the popular range for new issues. A stock split may be used to adjust the price of previously issued shares if their value is not between ten and thirty dollars per share.

Once the stock is reasonably actively traded, the offering price of new issues will be determined primarily by the market price of outstanding shares. In addition to improving operating efficiency, bank directors and senior management may take several steps to improve their bank's market price. First, they should foster an effective dividend policy (discussed above). Second, they should try to publicize their bank and its activities as much as possible (for example, in the news media and to financial analysts' meetings). It is imperative that the senior management and directors always be honest and realistic in presenting information about the bank. The investment community is very slow in forgetting unjustifiably optimistic predictions. The directors and senior manage-

---

13Common shareholders usually benefit from public ownership and trading that tend to facilitate transfers, add the dimension of marketability, and help establish tax costs for estate planning.

ment should also use stock splits,[14] to keep the market price of the stock in an attractive price range. Most financial analysts seem to favor between $20 and $60.

Finally, bankers should consider various alternative procedures—such as preemption (offering new shares to existing shareholders on a *pro rata* basis), public offerings, and private placements—for external issues of common stock. Most banks are not forced to make preemptive offerings; national banks and most state banks are no longer subject to laws requiring preemptive rights, and corporate articles requiring preemption can be amended. Flexible bank directors and senior management should evaluate the probable costs and benefits of all available alternative procedures.[15]

ALTERNATIVE METHODS OF RAISING BANK CAPITAL

There are several alternatives to the major methods of raising bank capital discussed above. The two alternatives briefly described here—holding company indebtedness and the sale-leaseback—are only desirable under certain circumstances. Additional innovative methods of raising capital seem likely to appear in future years.

Bank holding companies can issue their own term loans or sell bonds and then use the proceeds to purchase common stock in a subsidiary bank. The subsidiary's balance sheet shows the additional equity capital, but the (hopefully favorable) leverage effect of debt capital will appear on the consolidated accounting reports. The degree to which a major bank holding company can use debt to achieve leverage will depend heavily on the acceptability of its debt securities in the investment market. Some people expect bank holding companies' debt to grow to as high as 50 percent of total capital in the years ahead.

The sale and leaseback of a bank's buildings or other fixed assets

---

14Stock dividends can also be used for this purpose. Stock dividends tend to be smaller than splits, and they force the bank to capitalize a portion of its undivided profits. Smaller stock dividends provide shareholders with a lower-cost opportunity to sell a small portion of their holdings but are more expensive to effect than stock splits.

15In an article on preemptive rights in banking, Paul Jessup ("Why Preemptive Rights in Banking?", *Bankers Magazine,* 153, Summer 1970, pp. 85–90) concludes, "In the innovative and competitive environment of modern banking, use of preemption—as one possible financing procedure—is not rejected. What must be rejected are traditional provisions requiring preemption, and unexamined decisions to use preemption, without analysis of alternative financing procedures that may better serve the interests of a bank and its shareholders."

is advantageous under certain circumstances. Under the typical sale-leaseback, a lessor buys some or all of the bank's fixed assets, borrowing the money to pay for them from insurance companies or other available mortgage buyers, and leases the assets back to the bank. The bank has reduced its capital requirements by replacing its most illiquid assets with cash, which will generally be used to purchase fairly liquid assets.[16] Sale-leaseback is often the most practical way for a smaller bank to raise fixed cost capital. The major drawback to sale-leaseback arrangements is that, if the bank continues to need outside capital in the future, it may discover that its capacity to meet other fixed financial payments has been sharply limited by the leasing payments it must make.[17]

---

[16]Banks used to be able to execute a tax-free sale to a subsidiary of depreciated fixed assets at their appraised value and add the untaxed profits to the bank's unearned surplus. At the present time, banks are required to consolidate such subsidiaries, so sale-leaseback to a subsidiary has lost its charm.

[17]For an excellent comparison of leasing equipment and borrowing money to purchase equipment, see Charles D. Pearce, "The Corporate Purchase-Borrow or Lease Decision," *Bankers Magazine*, 153, Autumn 1970, pp. 95–102.

INDEX